Where No Black Woman Has Gone Before

Where No Black Woman Has Gone Before

Subversive Portrayals in Speculative Film and TV

DIANA ADESOLA MAFE

University of Texas Press ◆ *Austin*

Requests for permission to reproduce material from this work should be sent to:
Permissions
University of Texas Press
PO Box 7819
Austin, TX 78713-7819
utpress.utexas.edu/rp-form

♾ The paper used in this book meets the minimum requirements of
ANSI/NISO Z39.48-1992 (R1997) (Permanence of Paper).

Library of Congress Cataloging Data
Names: Mafe, Diana Adesola, author.
Title: Where no Black woman has gone before : subversive portrayals in speculative
   film and TV / Diana Adesola Mafe.
Description: First edition. | Austin : University of Texas Press, 2018. | Includes
   bibliographical references and index.
Identifiers: LCCN 2017021809| ISBN 978-1-4773-1522-4 (cloth : alk. paper) |
   ISBN 978-1-4773-1523-1 (pbk. : alk. paper) | ISBN 978-1-4773-1524-8 (library
   e-book) | ISBN 978-1-4773-1525-5 (nonlibrary e-book)
Subjects: LCSH: Women, Black, in motion pictures. | Women on television. | Blacks
   on television. | Sex role in motion pictures. | Sex role on television. | Science
   fiction films—History and criticism. | Fantasy films—History and criticism. |
   Horror films—History and criticism. | Science fiction television programs—
   History and criticism. | Horror television programs—History and criticism. |
   Fantasy television programs—History and criticism. | Motion pictures—
   History—21st century. | Television programs—History—21st century.
Classification: LCC PN1995.9.N4 M25 2018 | DDC 791.43/652996073—dc23
LC record available at https://lccn.loc.gov/2017021809

doi:10.7560/315224

for colored girls, invisible women, hidden figures, and blerds everywhere

Contents

Acknowledgments

I want to thank everyone who supported the researching, writing, and publishing of this book. Denison University provided invaluable support by way of a sabbatical and an R. C. Good Faculty Fellowship. The Denison English Department has been a wonderful source of enthusiasm and encouragement, as have so many colleagues and friends. Thanks to those who shared links, articles, and suggestions, among them Lauren Araiza, Marlaine Browning, Rebecca Kennedy, and Anna Nekola. To Jespal Panesar, who has listened, debated, affirmed, and been a lifelong friend, I say thank you. Jim Burr, my sponsoring editor at the University of Texas Press, has generously and thoughtfully shepherded this project from its earliest proposal form to this published version. I am incredibly grateful to the rest of the editorial and copyediting team, including Sarah McGavick and Cynthia Buck. My thanks to all the external readers of this project, including Kwakiutl Dreher, who contributed so much time and energy. Thanks to Vineyard Columbus for keeping me grounded in my Christian faith. Thanks to my siblings David and Miranda Mafe for being my oldest allies in all things science fiction. And thank you to my parents, Tunde and Trudy Mafe, who cultivated my love of popular culture, bought my first video game console, made sure I was never short of books, and taught me from an early age that the stars were always within my reach.

To Boldly Go

The heart of a woman goes forth with the dawn,
As a lone bird, soft winging, so restlessly on,
Afar o'er life's turrets and vales does it roam
In the wake of those echoes the heart calls home.
GEORGIA DOUGLAS JOHNSON, "THE HEART OF A WOMAN" (1918)

According to Geoffrey Mandel's apocryphal *U.S.S. Enterprise Officer's Manual*, she was born on Stardate 1281.2 or, by the Gregorian calendar, January 19, 2233. But her other birthday (shared with her crewmates) is Tuesday, September 6, 1966, when she appeared for the first time on television sets across Canada on the network CTV (followed two days later by her American premiere on NBC).[1] Hers was the first and sometimes only name people mentioned when they learned I was writing this book. And she is rightly considered an icon of the twentieth-century small screen. As an officer on a prime-time show about space exploration, she immediately symbolized change and possibility for black people, especially in the midst of the civil rights movement. Her ability to go where no black woman had gone before—outer space and, more literally, an empowered role on network television—made her a cinematic pioneer. Known only by her surname, at least in the original series, Lieutenant Uhura (Nichelle Nichols) was the solitary black female crew member of the starship *Enterprise* on the American cult classic *Star Trek* (1966–1969). And fifty years after her debut, she remains the symbolic face of black women in science fiction (SF) and a touchstone for fans and critics across cultures and generations.

In 1971, two years after the cancellation of *Star Trek*, Rosalind Cash starred as Lisa in Boris Sagal's horror film *The Omega Man*. A savior and love interest for the white male protagonist, Robert Neville (Charlton

Figure 0.1. Uhura (Nichelle Nichols) at her communications station in *Star Trek* (1966–1969).

Heston), Lisa embodies the Black Power aesthetics and politics of the day. After briefly appearing to Robert in a department store, she later materializes in a black turtleneck, red leather jacket, matching pants, and Afro to calmly point a gun at him and state, "All right, you son of a bitch, you just hold tight." Despite appearing to abduct Robert, Lisa in fact rescues him from the mutated antagonists of the film. The two characters sustain witty banter for much of the narrative and quickly become friends and then lovers. Their interracial kiss is often cited as a groundbreaking moment in film, much as the 1968 kiss between Uhura and Captain Kirk (William Shatner) is hailed as a groundbreaking moment in television. The fact that both of these moments take place in the speculative genre says something about the potential of this genre to show viewers something new.

The shortcomings of *Star Trek* and *The Omega Man* aside—most notably the reinforcement of white male authority at the expense of Otherness and a predictable eroticization of black womanhood—these examples put black women squarely on the speculative fiction map. Late-twentieth-century American speculative cinema subsequently produced a number of other memorable black female characters—Grace Jones as Zula in *Conan the Destroyer* (1984), Tina Turner as Aunty Entity in *Mad Max Beyond Thunderdome* (1985), Whoopi Goldberg as Guinan in *Star Trek: The Next Generation* (1987–1994), Angela Bassett as Mace in *Strange Days* (1995), and Alfre Woodard as Lily Sloane in *Star Trek: First Contact* (1996). This book is precisely about representations of black female characters in contemporary American and British speculative cinema and television. But my goal is to extend analysis of black women in this genre beyond iconic but isolated twentieth-century examples. Now that we have entered the new millennium (the same millennium in which futuristic narratives like *Star Trek* take place), are we seeing "new" representations of black femininity on the big and small screens?

By definition, speculative fiction implies limitless potential where raced and gendered imaginaries are concerned. The *Oxford English Dictionary* cites a 1953 remark by the American SF writer Robert Heinlein as a definition: "The term 'speculative fiction' may be defined negatively as being fiction about things that have not happened." From a critical race and feminist perspective, imagining "things that have not happened" is not necessarily "negative" in a pejorative sense—it can be a very powerful and subversive act. Speculative fiction remains a contested label that is sometimes used as an umbrella term for the fantastical, the supernatural, and SF. It speaks to both utopian and dystopian possibilities and captures fiction on both the page and the screen. And while this genre has certainly been complicit in sustaining and even promoting social prejudices against Others, it has also been a remarkable site of possibility when it comes to interrogating and reinventing social constructs such as race, gender, and class. I use the term "speculative fiction" broadly and suggest that all of the case studies presented here constitute speculative fiction. Some lean more obviously toward SF in that they incorporate space travel, aliens, time machines, and so on. Others are gothic or fantastical but not necessarily SF. My approach is to treat SF as a subgenre of speculative fiction and to read all of my case studies as fictions that stretch the limits of imagination and plausibility.[2]

This book examines four films, *28 Days Later* (2002), *AVP: Alien vs. Predator* (2004), *Children of Men* (2006), and *Beasts of the Southern Wild* (2012), and two television series, *Firefly* (2002) and *Doctor Who: Series 3* (2007). With the exception of *AVP*, which has been categorically dismissed by critics as a formulaic film with the sole purpose of generating new revenue from two celebrated franchises, all of these films and shows have received critical acclaim, whether as award winners, cult classics, or indie cinema. Three of my case studies are British (*28 Days Later*, *Children of Men*, and

Doctor Who), and three are American (*AVP*, *Beasts of the Southern Wild*, and *Firefly*). As such, they speak to questions of race, gender, class, nation, empire, and so on, in very different ways. Some of these works have generated a significant amount of academic interest. *Children of Men*, for example, has been hailed as "the first global blockbuster marketed as a teaching text" (Amago 212). The 2007 DVD edition includes commentary by a range of cultural critics, including Slavoj Žižek and Naomi Klein. A number of book-length studies and journal articles are dedicated to *Firefly* and the *Doctor Who* franchise, the latter being "the longest-running science fiction television series in the world" (Orthia 208). But *28 Days Later* has received only sporadic scholarly attention despite its popularity, and *Beasts of the Southern Wild* has yet to generate any significant scholarship despite its polarizing reception as a "best" and "worst" film of 2012. Similarly, *AVP* has not triggered much academic discourse.

These case studies have never been read together or primarily through their representations of black femininity, but each one includes a black female character in its main cast. More importantly, the character in question—Selena (Naomie Harris) in *28 Days Later*, Alexa "Lex" Woods (Sanaa Lathan) in *AVP*, Kee (Clare-Hope Ashitey) in *Children of Men*, Hushpuppy (Quvenzhané Wallis) in *Beasts of the Southern Wild*, Zoë Washburne (Gina Torres) in *Firefly*, and Martha Jones (Freema Agyeman) in *Doctor Who*— is arguably subversive. So this book is not intended to be a comprehensive survey of black women in Western SF cinema. Rather, I have tried to pinpoint the most compelling and critically complex examples of black female characters in new millennial British and American speculative film and television. This selection process is subjective, but these particular examples are crucial to a project like this one, or at least an excellent place to start.

I do not address seemingly obvious blockbuster franchises such as *The Matrix* trilogy (1999 and 2003), the *X-Men* films (launched in 2000), and the rebooted *Star Trek* films (2009, 2013, and 2016) precisely because the black female characters are neither central nor especially nuanced.[3] My strategic decision to explore only two television series also means that a number of speculative shows are not addressed, for example, *Dark Angel* (2000–2002), the rebooted *Battlestar Galactica* (2003–2009), *The Walking Dead* (2010–), *Black Mirror* (2011–), *Once Upon a Time* (2011–), *American Horror Story: Coven* (2013–2014), *Sleepy Hollow* (2013–), *Z Nation* (2014–), *Sense8* (2015–), *The Expanse* (2015–), and *Westworld* (2016–). Most of these shows have memorable, even pivotal, black female characters, but addressing all of them is simply beyond the scope of this book.[4] So I hope that other scholars with an interest in cinematic representations of black femininity will explore these titles and sustain this research.

Of course the new *Star Trek* franchise introduces Uhura, now played by Zoe Saldana, to a whole new generation of fans. And I will return to the new Uhura in my conclusion, not least because Saldana is the black actress in Hollywood currently associated with SF cinema and a successor of sorts to Halle Berry. But ironically, neither Berry nor Saldana has ever played a speculative role that is primary *and* radical. Berry's speculative work tends to fluctuate between critical failures like *Gothika* (2003), *Catwoman* (2004), and *Extant* (2014–2015) and epic productions like the *X-Men* franchise and *Cloud Atlas* (2012), where she is a secondary player in a very large ensemble cast. Similarly, Saldana's best-known speculative roles to date are Neytiri in *Avatar* (2009), Gamora in *Guardians of the Galaxy* (2014), and Uhura in the *Star Trek* franchise, all films in which she plays a supporting part.[5] And Saldana's reprisal of Nichols's famous role aside, part of my purpose here is to look beyond Uhura (to borrow the title of Nichols's autobiography) and to focus on other significant, if less popular, black female characters. At the same time, I try to spotlight the underrated actresses who bring these characters to life.[6]

I am ultimately interested in identifying patterns of representation and answering the following questions: How do these characters replicate dated stereotypes of black femininity? How do they subvert stereotypes? What are the implications of imagining these characters through speculative fiction? Do these new millennial examples bring something "new" to their representations of black femininity?

The chapters are chronological—I proceed in the order in which the films were released and do the same for the two television shows. Each chapter can technically stand on its own as a careful study of a specific black female character in a specific film (or a pair of characters when it comes to the final chapter on television). But a chronological approach also builds a useful trajectory and allows me to highlight remarkable thematic resonances between these otherwise very different cinematic texts.

Black Women on Screen

The black female body is a notoriously vexed cultural signifier, as critics such as Sander Gilman and bell hooks emphasize in their studies of nineteenth- and twentieth-century Western art and popular cultures. In the white Western imaginary, the black female has historically been a pa-

limpsest upon which fantasies of Otherness, particularly sexual Otherness, are inscribed. The exhibition of the Khoisan woman Sarah Baart-
man, the so-called Hottentot Venus, in the early 1800s epitomizes the
Western pseudoscientific fascination with the black female body. And this
centuries-old blueprint of dehumanizing spectacle continues to shape representations of black femininity in Western cinema today. To put it another way, Hollywood betrays a powerful inertia when it comes to images
of blackness.

The dominant screen versions of black womanhood in the first half of
the twentieth century were the tragic mulatto and the mammy. The former trope, epitomized by films such as *Pinky* (1949), connoted an exotic
but tainted desirability, while the latter, immortalized in *Gone with the
Wind* (1939), connoted an aggressive but *un*desirable maternity.[7] Indeed,
Pinky showcases both stereotypes by casting the tragic mulatto protagonist as the granddaughter of the mammy figure. The rise of television as
a popular medium in the 1950s did little to mitigate the static iconography of black women, who continued to play limited and stereotypical roles
on the small screen. Ethel Waters, Hattie McDaniel, and Louise Beavers
starred as various incarnations of the eponymous mammy on the ABC
show *Beulah* (1950–1952). The contemporaneous CBS show *Amos 'n' Andy*
(1951–1953) cast Ernestine Wade in the now-infamous role of Sapphire
Stevens. And while late-1960s characters such as Uhura on *Star Trek* and
Julia Baker (Diahann Carroll) on the NBC sitcom *Julia* (1968–1971) were
groundbreaking, they were also out of touch with the civil unrest sweep-
ing the nation. The blaxploitation films of the 1970s produced the more
militant "supermama," and sitcoms such as *Good Times* (1974–1979) and
The Jeffersons (1975–1985) simply repackaged the mammy figure for a new
generation of television audiences.

The final decades of the twentieth century largely preserved extant
stereotypes of black women. Citing the seemingly irreproachable Claire
Huxtable (Phylicia Rashad) on NBC's *The Cosby Show* (1984–1992), Beretta
Smith-Shomade argues that "most roles for African-American women
(and men) on television remained outside of drama and within situation comedy—making people laugh and perpetuating the image of Black
women as sidekicks to leading men" (*Shaded* 22). And black women on the
big screen remained exoticized and sexualized Others, as evinced by characters such as Zula in *Conan the Destroyer* and Aunty Entity in *Mad Max
Beyond Thunderdome*. Although the 1980s and 1990s produced controversial "triumphs" in *The Color Purple* (1985), *The Bodyguard* (1992), and *Waiting to Exhale* (1995), these isolated mainstream successes had little bearing
on the general lack of quality film and television roles for black women.

The iconography of black women in British cinema has been similarly static. Stephen Bourne's *Black in the British Frame: The Black Experience in British Film and Television* (2001) spotlights British examples. His chapter on black actresses—informatively titled "Invisible Women"—provides a narrative that clearly resonates with the American context: "The story of black actresses in British cinema is one of invisibility and yet those who have made an impression, such as Elisabeth Welch, Nina Mae McKinney, Cleo Laine, Shirley Bassey, Cassie McFarlane, Cathy Tyson and Marianne Jean-Baptiste, are constantly 'written out' by film historians" (142). Bourne covers the very few black women who had high-profile careers from the 1930s to the 1990s and cites a familiar preponderance of stereotypical roles, including "sexy slave girls," "an occasional vampire," and "an occasional exotic superstar" (148). He laments that "[b]y the end of the 1990s the only black female movie star we could offer the world was Scary Spice in *Spice World*" (150). These respective histories of American and British film and television reveal a pervasive and persistent devaluation of the black female body over the course of the twentieth century.

The black female body in speculative cinema risks even greater fetishization and exoticism because the genre (perhaps more so than others) has been ubiquitously white and male in both authorship and audience. If mainstream Western cinema traditionally presumes a white and male gaze, then that presumption is all the more definitive in speculative genres such as horror and SF. The Western tradition of white men studying black women in the name of so-called science cannot be disassociated from the Western tradition of white men imagining black women in the name of science fiction. H. G. Wells and Jules Verne are literary forefathers of speculative fiction, but a range of other canonical names can be added to the list—Isaac Asimov, Arthur C. Clarke, Robert Heinlein, Ray Bradbury, Frank Herbert, Philip K. Dick, and so on. Women as producers of speculative fiction are certainly present, and their important contributions go at least as far back as Mary Shelley's *Frankenstein; or, The Modern Prometheus* (1818). But they have historically been the minority, and women of color as writers of the genre are all the more rare. Octavia Butler is invariably cited as the most famous black female SF writer in much the same way that Uhura is cited as the most famous black female character in SF television.

When it comes to the production of speculative cinema, these historical trends of white male authorship persist. Whether one thinks back to the Verne-inspired creations of the French filmmaker Georges Méliès, who directed the iconic films *A Trip to the Moon* (1902) and *The Impossible Voyage* (1904), the expressionist horror film *The Cabinet of Dr. Caligari*

(1920) by the German director Robert Wiene, or the SF classic *Metropolis* (1927) by the Austrian German director Fritz Lang, the genre implicitly "belongs" to white male auteurs. All my film case studies and the majority of the episodes in my two television case studies were directed, written, and produced by white men. The visions and gazes of auteurs such as Danny Boyle and Joss Whedon are inextricable from the versions of black femininity that appear on the screen. Black women are so rarely behind the camera in *any* cinematic genre that white and/or male filmmakers usually direct their roles.[8]

Most of my case studies also have a dominant or at least focal white male protagonist, thus replicating yet another traditional model for speculative fiction; the notable exceptions are *AVP* and *Beasts of the Southern Wild*. And where white and/or male protagonists are present, black female characters quickly become absent, reliant, or marginal. At the outset, these examples may seem less than conducive to subversive or empowering readings of black femininity. Instead, they imply a familiar Eurocentrism and phallocentrism that belies anything new for black women in new millennial speculative film and television. But I argue that these cinematic texts do complicate the historical precedents of black womanhood through the speculative genre. I am enough of a postmodernist to argue that the writer or director does not determine the interpretation of the text. And I submit that each of the black female characters (and the actresses behind the roles) perform the social constructs of race, gender, and class in ways that challenge audiences to rethink entrenched expectations regarding black femininity.

To varying extents, all of these films and shows are apocalyptic. Films such as *28 Days Later* and *Children of Men* imagine the literal end of the world. *Beasts of the Southern Wild* presents a more localized apocalypse— not the end of the world but the end of the protagonist's world through a natural disaster. *Doctor Who* uses time travel to show the births and deaths of planets and galaxies. In each case, the viewer must suspend "reality" and enter the realm of the speculative. And it is under those imaginative conditions that the black female character becomes indispensable and empowered. In her collection *Alien Zones II: The Spaces of Science Fiction Cinema* (1999), Annette Kuhn tries to put her finger on what sets SF cinema apart from other genres or even other SF media: "Is there, then, anything peculiarly distinctive about science-fiction in *cinema* as against science fiction in other media? Sobchack has suggested that the science-fiction film provides 'concrete narrative shape and visible form to our changing historical imagination of social progress and disaster': in other words, the

genre's fictions of progress—as well, *pace* Susan Sontag, of disaster—
are precisely rendered *visible* in science-fiction films" (4). These fantastical worlds, where progress and disaster are intertwined, are made as concrete as possible, short of the viewer experiencing the "real" thing. What
this particular grouping of new millennial speculative films and television
series makes visible to mainstream audiences is a rarely acknowledged
fact—that black female characters can be symbols of social progress, vital
players in the face of disaster, and complex cinematic agents.

Approach

My approach to these case studies is grounded in close reading and textual analysis. So I pay special attention to the narrative content and I consider dialogue, screen time, and screen presence important to the "stories"
of these black female characters. Black feminist critics have long argued
against the erasure of black women not only in film but also in film criticism. In her 1993 essay "Race, Gender and Psychoanalysis in Forties Film:
Lost Boundaries, Home of the Brave and The Quiet One," Michele Wallace
acknowledges the "impressive outpouring of academic feminist film criticism in the US" (258), which is indebted to Laura Mulvey's pioneering work
on the gaze and gendered spectatorship. But Wallace points out that this
feminist criticism excludes black women entirely and promotes "the cultural phenomenon of 'invisibility,' both racial and gendered, in the case
of the Black woman" (259). In the essay "The Oppositional Gaze: Black Female Spectators," originally published in *Black Looks: Race and Representation* (1992), bell hooks similarly advocates a theoretical approach and
gaze that frames black women as both active screen subjects and active
spectators.

Although Wallace's and hooks's essays are now well over twenty years
old, their arguments remain incredibly pertinent, even in the new millennium, and afford a theoretical framework for my own analysis. The primary goal for each chapter and for this book as a whole is to place the
black female characters at the literal and symbolic center of the analyses,
and always with an eye to the subversive and to readings of agency. This
approach requires a very specific kind of spectatorship because the majority of these characters are *not* intended to be at the center of these films
and shows. Wallace recalls growing up with reruns of 1940s and 1950s
films that featured white female movie stars such as Lana Turner, as well
as troubling minor appearances by black female movie stars such as Hattie

McDaniel (the quintessential mammy). Wallace explains how black female viewers still enjoyed and claimed these films: "Even as the 'Law of the Father' may impose its premature closure on the filmic 'gaze' in the coordination of suture and classic narrative, disparate factions in the audience, not all equally well indoctrinated in the dominant discourse, may have their way, now and then, with interpretation" (264). Here Wallace identifies a form of spectatorship that both challenges and refocuses the traditionally white, male, and heterosexual lens of Hollywood cinema in order to yield alternative subject positions and interpretations from those of "classic" psychoanalytic theories. In the same spirit, hooks writes, "Identifying with neither the phallocentric gaze nor the construction of White womanhood as lack, critical Black female spectators construct a theory of looking relations where cinematic visual delight is the pleasure of interrogation" (*Black Looks* 126). I channel this subversive spectatorship, this oppositional gaze, in my examination of these four films and two television shows.

If psychoanalysis has been integral to the broader evolution of film theory, then it has been especially fruitful for critics engaging with speculative cinema. Horror, SF, and fantasy films, which so often imagine dreamscapes, alien invasions, and Other possibilities, lend themselves to a psychoanalytic approach. Monsters, doppelgängers, nightmares, birth, death, terror, and, of course, pleasure speak to Freudian and neo-Freudian notions of the unconscious, the uncanny, and the repressed. Representations of the maternal and the paternal, whether by way of a mother ship or a mad scientist, also evoke the oedipal family drama and the negotiation of human sexualities and subjectivities. My psychoanalytic approach is informed by this rich tradition of scholarship but necessarily grounded in the critical interventions of black feminist scholars such as Wallace and hooks.

Admittedly, psychoanalysis has been less prominent in television studies, in part because concepts such as the gaze, the screen, spectatorship, voyeurism, and viewing pleasure operate differently. Television critics are still interested in these things but have primarily tackled the medium from a sociological perspective rather than a psychoanalytic or textual one. Psychoanalytic film theory in the 1970s was originally premised on the experience of watching a film in the darkness of a movie theater, a quasi-dream state. While one can still experience the cinematic apparatus in this way, the evolution of technology has resulted in new and virtually infinite ways of seeing and consuming cinema. Now movies can be watched on anything from an IMAX screen to a cell phone, and movies can be streamed, recorded, paused, rewound, and screen-grabbed. Similarly, television is no longer easily restricted to a specific cable channel or network, and shows are no longer accessible only at specific broadcast times. Internet sites, DVD box sets, streaming services, and digital platforms make television shows more accessible and viewing experiences more controllable than ever before. But for critics, like myself, who prioritize textual analysis in their approaches to film and television, psychoanalytic theories remain pertinent and have evolved along with the media itself to present fresh possibilities.

For all of my case studies—none of which I have ever watched in a theater, viewing them instead via a range of formats (Blu-ray, DVD, cable television) on either a flat-screen television or a laptop computer—I engage with questions of text, context, and spectatorship. My methodology also draws on various postmodern feminist theories, as well as theories of cultural and postcolonial studies, all of which have been shaped by semiotics, structuralism, and poststructuralism.[9] I try to be sensitive to the sociohistorical moment in which each film or show was released. Speculative fiction is often strategically read as an allegorical mirror for the social and political agendas and anxieties of the day—communism, civil rights, viral pandemics, climate change, terrorism, and so on. These case studies are "texts" that reflect and inform the cultures and systems in which they were produced. But this book does not take such a broad discursive view that historical and cultural contexts overshadow close reading of the black female characters themselves. Lastly, along with content, I address questions of form—mise-en-scène, cinematography, and marketing—because these elements factor into how and where these black female characters get to *be* in these case studies.

Mind the Gap

Put simply, there are no book-length studies that explore representations of black femininity in speculative film and television, new millennial or otherwise. This gap is itself heavy with meaning—once again, it speaks to the erasure of black women not only in the speculative genre but also in scholarship about the genre. Certainly, more black female writers are publishing SF than ever before. Along with the work of Octavia Butler, one can now read speculative fiction by Nalo Hopkinson, Nnedi Okorafor, Nisi Shawl, N. K. Jemisin, and Andrea Hairston. These writers, in turn, have sparked new millennial scholarship on their work—for example, Marleen Barr's edited collection *Afro-Future Females: Black Writers Chart Science Fiction's Newest New-Wave Trajectory* (2008).[10] Yet black actresses and their speculative roles remain largely outside this cultural shift and the discourse it has generated.

Where there is academic interest in the cinematic roles of black women, studies tend to track the broader evolution of those roles over the last century. Donald Bogle's *Brown Sugar: Over One Hundred Years of America's Black Female Superstars* (2007), Mia Mask's *Divas on Screen: Black Women in American Film* (2009), and Charlene Regester's *African American Actresses: The Struggle for Visibility, 1900–1960* (2010) are all valuable works in this vein.[11] Film studies of black women also tend to prioritize those few and telling genres in which black women have traditionally been "allowed" to play leading roles—blaxploitation cinema, biopics, "race films" with an all-black cast, and those dramas and comedies built around the star power of singular actresses, ranging from Dorothy Dandridge in the 1950s to Whoopi Goldberg, Angela Bassett, and Halle Berry in the 1990s.[12] In the context of television, media, and communication studies, a number of monographs and edited volumes focus broadly on blackness.[13] But Smith-Shomade's *Shaded Lives: African-American Women and Television* (2002) is the only one to foreground black women, specifically in 1990s comedies, music videos, national news stories, and talk shows. So speculative cinema is a genre yet to be explored with black female characters—or black female viewers, for that matter—clearly in mind.

Within the framework of SF studies, Adilifu Nama's *Black Space: Imagining Race in Science Fiction Film* (2008) remains the primary study on blackness in contemporary SF film.[14] Nama describes the scope of his book as follows: "The present work examines the symbolic discourse and ideological messages encoded into black representation, including its structured absence, across a multitude of SF films as a symbolic dialogue with the multiple racial discourses and ideas surrounding black racial formation, past and present, that are circulating in American culture" (4). *Black Space* covers an impressive array of films—roughly one hundred titles are listed in the index—and provides a thoughtful discussion of how these films imagine blackness. But the book takes such a broad sociohistorical approach and touches on so many titles that textual analysis of the films themselves is limited. None of my case studies is addressed beyond a cursory citation, with the exception of *28 Days Later*, to which Nama dedicates a couple of pages. However, he focuses exclusively on the symbolism of a minor black male character and completely, albeit tellingly, ignores the implications of the primary black female character.[15]

There are few works that explicitly tackle both race and gender in speculative cinema.[16] Christine Cornea's *Science Fiction Cinema: Between Fantasy and Reality* (2007) is one such example, although it too models a familiar erasure of black women. Her chapter on gender in SF opens with a full-scale black-and-white photograph of Linda Hamilton as Sarah Connor in *Terminator 2: Judgment Day* (1991), an image that foreshadows the analysis. The chapter discusses only white women, particularly iconic characters such as Ellen Ripley (Sigourney Weaver) of the *Alien* franchise (1979, 1986, 1992, and 1997), Sarah Connor in *The Terminator* (1984) and *Terminator 2*, and Rachael (Sean Young) in *Blade Runner* (1982). Similarly, the chapter on race and SF opens with a full-scale black-and-white photograph of a mud-covered Arnold Schwarzenegger as Dutch in *Predator* (1987) and the caption "[t]aking on the black mask." Although Cornea covers a number of films and characters in this chapter, she includes only one black woman—Mace in *Strange Days*—and a white man remains the literal face of the chapter.

Ultimately, none of the aforementioned studies zoom in, as it were, on black women in the context of twenty-first-century British and American speculative film and television. From the analysis to the symbolic choice of illustrations, SF criticism (and related criticism on horror and fantasy) regularly omits or expunges black female characters, a trend that replicates their erasure on-screen. In her 1995 book *Killing Rage: Ending Racism*, hooks makes the following statement: "Devaluation of black womanhood is central to the maintenance of white supremacist capitalist patriarchy" (78). In other words, the sustained and calculated exclusion of black women across discourses has everything to do with the formation of a genre like speculative fiction and the scholarship it generates. *Where No Black Woman Has Gone Before* seeks to address this gap and to also look beyond pioneering but increasingly dated examples of speculative black female characters from the twentieth century.

Layout

Chapter 1, "Seeking a Friend for the End of the World: *28 Days Later*," focuses on Danny Boyle's critically and commercially successful British horror film *28 Days Later*. This zombie film with an interracial cast is indebted to George Romero's oeuvre, particularly *Night of the Living Dead* (1968). *28 Days Later* is also a direct descendant of *The Omega Man* and deals with the popular postapocalyptic theme of a last man. Familiarly, a "tough" black female character, Selena (Harris), rescues a white male protagonist, Jim (Cillian Murphy). Selena's agency, much like Lisa's in *The Omega Man*, seems to diminish as the narrative progresses. However, when viewed through an oppositional gaze, Selena is a compelling figure through whom to explore black femininity as a site of feminist empowerment.[17]

In a film rife with abjection—blood, vomit, corpses, and viral infection—Selena (the only adult female) embodies an abject femaleness, a role exacerbated by the historical dehumanization of black women. Critics such as Robin Wood, Steve Neale, and Barbara Creed convincingly demonstrate the ways in which female sexuality and reproduction are rendered monstrous in horror films, and *28 Days Later* is easily read along these lines. Selena also signals the generic cinematic threat of women as inducers of castration anxiety—she butchers enemies with her sizable machete, but the threat is "diffused" through her feminization and fetishization. Nevertheless, her very performance of these multiple, sometimes conflicting, roles challenges and complicates archetypes of the horror heroine—passive victim, "monstrous-feminine" (to use Creed's term), and what Carol Clover calls the "Final Girl," a heroine who "is a physical female and a characterological androgyne" ("Her Body" 108). Clover concludes that even the Final Girl is a male projection that does little to challenge phallocentric spectatorship. Yet Selena—named for the goddess of the moon—is not quite a Final Girl either. Hers is a model of black female subjectivity and heroism in horror cinema that arguably disrupts the power of a clichéd white and male cinematic gaze *and* the white patriarchies represented within the narrative.

Chapter 2, "Last One Standing: *Alien vs. Predator*," addresses Paul W. S. Anderson's American SF horror film *AVP: Alien vs. Predator*. The gimmick of the film is implicit in its title, which promises a face-off between the titular monsters from the two respective franchises. If, as Wood argues, the "basic formula for the horror film [is that] normality is threatened by the Monster" (71), *AVP* gives us two monsters. Set in the present day, the narrative follows a team of explorers to Antarctica, where they accidentally reignite a millennia-old war between the Aliens and the Predators. Nothing about the film's marketing or publicity suggests that it has a black female protagonist, let alone that she will be the sole survivor of this epic battle. Yet the heroine, Lex (Lathan), is quite literally the last one standing among monsters and humans by the end of the film. Building on the iconic role of Weaver as Ripley in the *Alien* universe and, to a lesser extent, the performances of Schwarzenegger as Dutch in *Predator* and Danny Glover as Mike Harrigan in *Predator 2* (1990), the film imagines a black woman as the hero of its crossover universe. Indeed, Lex is *the* protagonist of the film in a way that Selena, her heroism notwithstanding, cannot claim.

In *Femmes Fatales: Feminism, Film Theory, Psychoanalysis* (1991), Mary Ann Doane frames a useful reminder: "[T]he category of women is usually used to refer to white women, while the category of blacks often really means 'black men.' What is lost in the process is the situation of the black woman. Her position becomes quite peculiar and oppressively unique: in terms of oppression, she is both black and a woman; in terms of theory, she is neither" (231). An unambiguous black female hero is "quite peculiar" precisely because black womanhood signifies an ultimate Otherness. In a genre that traditionally markets itself to a white male audience and pits a version of the societal self against a repressed Other, Lex's battle with the Aliens and the Predators models "difference" in a way that complicates notions of the Ripley-esque heroine. Ironically for a formulaic spin-off, *AVP* deconstructs some of the most predictable tenets of a horror film, including racist and patriarchal paradigms regarding monstrosity, Otherness, who is allowed to look, and who gets punished for looking.

Chapter 3, "The Black Madonna: *Children of Men*," focuses on Alfonso Cuarón's British film *Children of Men*. This postapocalyptic narrative imagines a dystopian future in which the entire human population is infertile with the exception of a heavily pregnant young African woman named Kee (Ashitey), a refugee living in the last so-called bastion of civilization, Britain. I open with the premise that Kee is a hyperbolic signifier that connotes a range of stereotypes. Zahid Chaudhary rightly argues that "her body signifies too much: Eve, Madonna, Earth Mother, figure of subjection, animal-like black woman, humanity's last and only hope, excessively fertile black woman, damsel in distress" (96). The camera also repeatedly displays and fetishizes her body in an uncomfortable reenactment of racist nineteenth-century discourses. More than any of my case studies, *Children of Men* projects and invites what E. Ann Kaplan calls an "imperial gaze," namely, a white, European, and imperialist perspective.

Yet there are critical moments of agency for Kee, particularly in the film's conclusion. I argue that Kee, whose name suggests a literal "key," constitutes a metaphor for "Africa" and that her very excess as a signifier serves to deconstruct the Eurocentric models of power that seemingly sustain her character and her journey. This reading, informed by the work of postcolonial feminists such as Kaplan and Anne McClintock, allows for fresh interpretations of Kee's character as not only "dark continent" and "white man's burden" but also postcolonial nation state and feminist dissident. Similarly, her hyperbolic role as fetish leaves room to at least interrogate the phallocentric logic of fetishism itself. I conclude my analysis by highlighting those specific moments when Kee resists her fetishization in order to articulate and frame a *self*-motivated and independent future.

There is virtually no critical scholarship on Benh Zeitlin's American fantasy film *Beasts of the Southern Wild*, which makes it an exciting case study and an opportunity to generate new scholarship. While models of adult black women are rare but at least identifiable in speculative cinema, models of young black girls are almost nonexistent. Chapter 4, "Thank Heaven for Little Girls: *Beasts of the Southern Wild*," looks at the character Hushpuppy (Wallis), a vulnerable and yet fiercely independent child protagonist. Despite hooks's scathing online review of the film, "No Love in the Wild," which argues that Hushpuppy is marginalized and stereotyped, I propose that she is a unique and constructive character because she is the unprecedented heart and soul of an acclaimed Hollywood film. At face value, Hushpuppy is a stand-in for the disenfranchised—a black female child living in a poverty-stricken Louisiana bayou. But I argue that the film promotes an active and very literal confrontation of oppressive forces by way of its young protagonist.

To make this case, I return to Kaplan's feminist film criticism, as well as Fatimah Tobing Rony's scholarship on the "returned gaze" of the Other. As a white male director's documentary-style portrait of a destitute but indomitable black female spirit, *Beasts of the Southern Wild* hints at ethnographic spectacle. However, Hushpuppy's perspective matches and regularly displaces the camera itself, even as she challenges the monitoring patriarchal gaze of her father. The film also functions as the symbolic quest narrative of a black daughter seeking to reclaim and re-member her black mother despite the pervasive Law of the Father. In multiple ways, then, the film complicates notions of a default white and/or male spectatorship and a default black female marginalization—Hushpuppy could not be more *present* in this film. Appropriately for my analysis, Hushpuppy herself practices an oppositional gaze, deconstructing what hooks describes as "dominant ways of knowing and looking" (*Black Looks* 128) and emerging with a powerful black female subjectivity.

Both of the television series discussed in Chapter 5, "Intergalactic Companions: *Firefly* and *Doctor Who*," are SF cult classics set primarily in outer space and both include a primary black female character. Zoë (Torres) is a former military officer turned smuggler in Joss Whedon's space western *Firefly*. And Martha (Agyeman) is a medical student who gets sucked into the space adventures of the Doctor in the third series of the new *Doc-*

tor Who, produced by Russell T. Davies. Admittedly, these characters are never protagonists but rather intergalactic traveling companions. Their roles, even more so than the black female characters in the films, hinge on white male leads. However, each character breaks away from her identity as sidekick and forges a new and independent role by the end of the series. While openly acknowledging the limitations on these black women in SF television, I frame them as subversive figures, not only on a narrative level but also on a symbolic one.

Both *Firefly* and the new *Doctor Who*, like their generic predecessor *Star Trek*, are postmodern space operas.[18] Even as they channel the swashbuckling and melodramatic adventure of space opera, these narratives inject a measure of ambiguity regarding human dominance, exploration, and conquest. Yet these shows also rely on what M. Keith Booker calls "certain assumptions (especially regarding the superiority of the masculine and of a worldview drawn from the Enlightenment)" (206). A diverse crew may come along for the ride, but these series prioritize white male captaincy, enterprise, and individualism. It thus falls to the black female characters in *Firefly* and *Doctor Who* to frame a critical and indeed postmodern intervention in what is otherwise a grand narrative of white male mastery and control. There is a certain irony at work here because the respective captains, Malcolm "Mal" Reynolds (Nathan Fillion) and the Doctor (David Tennant), are pitched as heroic rebels locked in oedipal conflicts with oppressive incarnations of the Law. Yet they themselves represent patriarchy and leave little room for alternatives. Zoë and Martha embody and articulate the interests of Others even when their characterization affords little leeway to do so. Especially because they are compelling doubles for the heroes in question—Zoë is a Browncoat like Mal, and Martha is a medical student and thus an approximation of the Doctor—these characters constitute important countermodels. Their moments of resistance are easily overlooked, and one must again invoke an oppositional gaze in order to even see them. But such moments factor into the popularity of these shows and the messages that they disseminate.

The coda, "Final Frontiers," is an opportunity to review my case studies of black female characters in cinematic speculative fiction spanning roughly the first decade of the new millennium. My hope is that the "results" will be encouraging in terms of modeling new and exciting directions for the representation of black femininities through this genre. I also use this final section to return to Uhura, specifically as she has been envisioned in the new millennium and the *Star Trek* films of J. J. Abrams and Justin Lin. The original *Star Trek* was canceled in 1969—at the height of the civil rights and feminist movements, in the middle of the Vietnam War, and just weeks before the first moon landing and Woodstock. In her final television episode, "The Savage Curtain," Uhura meets Abraham Lincoln on the *Enterprise*. The "Great Emancipator" exclaims, "What a charming negress." Embarrassed by his own archaic vocabulary, Lincoln quickly adds, "Oh, forgive me, my dear. I know that in my time some use that term as a description of property." Unfazed, Uhura responds, "But why should I object to that term, sir? See, in our century we've learned not to fear words." Appropriately, these are Uhura's last lines in the original series. Her claim to a postracial or perhaps postracist consciousness in the future twenty-third-century universe of *Star Trek* can be read as a social commentary on the racially charged mid-twentieth-century America in which the show was actually produced. But her words are also a poignant reminder to regularly interrogate representations of race, gender, and other identity categories, which continue to evolve in both our so-called realities and our imagined universes.

CHAPTER 1

Seeking a Friend for the End of the World: *28 Days Later*

The premise of Danny Boyle's 2002 horror film *28 Days Later* is that a viral epidemic, simply called Rage, has transformed Great Britain into an island of zombies. The pre-credits opening sequence shows the origin of the epidemic—a trio of animal rights activists, two white men and one white woman, break into a Cambridge research facility to release chimpanzee test subjects. The chimps have been infected through brainwashing—they have been administered "inhibitors," strapped to chairs, and forced to watch endless loops of violent news footage on a bank of television screens.[1] The grainy, flickering shots of riots, explosions, armored police, and dead bodies (accompanied by garbled voice-overs) are also the first images that the viewer sees. The film immediately draws a subtle but acute parallel between the chimps consuming these images and the viewer consuming them by way of an R-rated horror film that promises "strong violence and gore."

The villain in this short sequence is a white male scientist who tries to prevent the activists from setting the animals free. Despite the scientist's warning of a contagious infection, the group opens one of the cages. An imprisoned chimp then leaps forward and attacks the solitary female activist, tearing into her flesh in a series of frenetic close-up shots. In an attempt to save her, one of her comrades bludgeons the chimp with a bolt-cutter, ironically reenacting the violent news imagery on the television screens. "We have to kill her!" yells the scientist, speaking of the woman, who is swiftly transforming into the first human Infected—a bile-spewing zombie with red eyes, jerky movements, and an insatiable compulsion to kill. Of course it is too late. The woman mauls the scientist to death, and the sequence cuts to black and then the film title at the bottom of the screen, followed by ellipses.

As zombie films go, *28 Days Later* is now a bona-fide cult classic. And it contains telltale markers of "classic" horror cinema, as outlined by Robin Wood—a state of so-called normality, the "return of the repressed" in monstrous form, and the eventual conquest of the repressed so that normality can resume. Wood argues that "[t]he definition of normality in horror films is in general boringly constant: the heterosexual monogamous couple, the family, and the social institutions (police, church, armed forces) that support and defend them" (71). All of these signifiers of normality manifest in the film, and all of them are subsequently threatened. Indeed, the footage of riot police facing off against angry protesters in the opening sequence is a microcosm of this battle between normality and the repressed. Wood makes the vital observation that *re*pression is typically reinforced by *op*pression and lists a range of forces and bodies that are invariably repressed/oppressed by bourgeois patriarchal capitalism: sexual energy, bisexuality, female sexuality, and Otherness as embodied by women, people of color, the proletariat, and so on. Appropriately for this particular film about a virus called Rage, Wood observes, "The most immediately obvious characteristics of life in our culture are frustration, dissatisfaction, anxiety, greed, possessiveness, jealousy, neuroticism: no more than what psychoanalytic theory shows to be the logical product of patriarchal capitalism" (64).

In its first five minutes, the film introduces a symbol of patriarchal normality (a male scientist), the rise of a repressed Other (a female activist Infected by Rage), the urgency of patriarchal oppression ("We have to kill her!"), and the implication that these tropes mirror deeply rooted ideologies. Certainly, zombie films reflect all kinds of social conditions and anxieties. As the screenwriter Alex Garland states in an interview, "Lots of stuff was happening in this country that felt like the right kind of social subtext or social commentary that you could put in a science fiction film. Danny [Boyle] was particularly interested in issues that had to do with social rage—the increase of rage in our society, road rage and other things. Also our government's inability to deal with things like BSE [mad cow disease], Foot and Mouth" (Boyle and Garland, "Diseased"). One can thus read the film as a broad allegory for an ailing post-Thatcher Britain whose underlying social and physical maladies have finally erupted.

My feminist analysis of the film begins with the fact that a (white) woman is patient zero for Infection and the figurative mother of the Rage that decimates Britain over the course of twenty-eight days (the length of a menstrual cycle). Although the virus is man-made, it is a female body and female difference that becomes a biological hazard. The film poster and the subsequent DVD cover for the film are bright blood red, with the glowing eyes of an Infected staring out and the film title stamped over a biohazard symbol. As G. Christopher Williams observes, "Boyle suggests a number of cultural assumptions about the linkage between female biology and blood, violence, and pain through this transition between the rage carrying 'Eve', the menstrual 'curse', and the birth of the protagonist that follows the Fall" (37). Blood is everywhere in this film, as are the grotesque Infected, all signaling a primal and abject femininity that transgresses paternal boundaries and laws.[2] Writing specifically of what she calls the monstrous-feminine, Barbara Creed observes, "The modern horror film often 'plays' with its audience, saturating it with scenes of blood and gore, deliberately pointing to the fragility of the symbolic order in the domain of the body which never ceases to signal the repressed world of the mother" ("Horror" 46). For Creed, who builds on the work of Julia Kristeva, horror cinema is about showing the viewer that which patriarchy deems unclean, taboo, and abject, particularly the reproductive female body and the maternal.

If *28 Days Later* conveys the monstrous-feminine by way of its "rage carrying 'Eve,'" its Infected hordes, and its literal bloodbaths, then the film presumably anchors female monstrosity in its lead female character. Selena (Naomie Harris), the only adult female in the film (apart from the activist turned Infected), appears to fit with this reading. G. Williams suggests that her name, "derived from lunar worship and the goddess Selene, [is] yet another figuration that amplifies the 28 day cycle through its lunar and menstrual connotations" (37). She is also the *femme castratrice*, or castrating woman, another variation of Creed's monstrous-feminine: "She assumes two forms: the castrating female psychotic . . . and the woman who seeks revenge on men who have raped or abused her in some way" (*Monstrous* 123). The film blends these two roles for Selena over the course of the narrative. As a "castrating female psychotic," she energetically hacks her initial white male companion, Mark (Noah Huntley), to death while her new white male companion, Jim (Cillian Murphy), watches in shock. Though her actions are prudent—one has mere seconds to kill a newly Infected person—Selena's clinical butchering of the Infected (but not yet transformed) Mark appears "psychotic."

Later in the film, Selena and her white teenage ward Hannah (Megan Burns) experience a near gang rape by a group of soldiers that triggers elements of a rape-revenge film. Each of the would-be rapists is systematically picked off, either dying a bloody death or transforming into an Infected. Carol Clover describes the castrating vengeance of the slasher film heroine, whom she terms the Final Girl: "His eyes may be put out, his hand severed, his body impaled or shot, his belly gashed, or his genitals sliced away or bitten off" ("Her Body" 94). Although Selena is not the direct practitioner of this revenge—Jim and the Infected are the instruments of castration, a point to which I will return—she is at the literal and symbolic center of the culminating revenge sequence, which includes most of the gruesome punishments that Clover mentions. The attempted rape and rape-revenge scenes take place in a labyrinthine gothic mansion, another staple of horror cinema. Clover calls it the "Terrible Place" but notes that it too is an ironic site of female monstrosity: "Nor can we help noticing the 'intrauterine' quality of the Terrible Place, dark and often damp, in which the killer lives or lurks and whence he stages his most terrifying attacks" ("Her Body" 92). If the classic haunted house is built on patriarchal foundations, it can also be an "intrauterine" space in which female and female-allied characters find an "uncanny" agency despite their entrapment.

By virtue of her identity as "last woman," Selena is ultimately a stand-in for the maternal, a role imposed upon her by the adult males in the film but one that she eventually accepts regarding the adolescent Hannah. Although she is neither Eve nor Infected, Selena is also the face of women en masse and thus inextricable from the different manifestations of the monstrous-feminine. And her potential to symbolize monstrosity is amplified by racist ideologies, which have long coded black femaleness as subhuman, primitive, and monstrous in its own right. Signifying practices collude here to produce a heroine who is doubly horrific, especially to a default white male gaze. Jim's stunned, indeed horrified, expression as Selena hacks Mark to death with her trusty machete may well mirror the viewer's expression. Of course, the subversive potential of the horror film lies precisely in its ability to reflect our ideological selves back to us—our deepest fears and our deepest desires. In the tradition of Wood, some critics view the genre as progressive because it exposes the fallacies of such interrelated systems as patriarchy, white supremacy, and capitalism. Other critics argue that Western horror films (and cinema in general) reinforce these systems because the cinematic apparatus is itself a product of these systems and thus inherently patriarchal, racist, classist, and heterosexist. Even when the horror film presents a seemingly active and empowered female character, à la Clover's Final Girl, there is the possibility that she too is simply another version or projection of default white masculinity. In light of these diverse and sometimes divergent theories regarding femaleness, femininity, and the maternal in horror cinema, *28 Days Later* is a provocative (if underdiscussed) case study because it initially aligns the monstrous-feminine with white womanhood but situates a black woman as the primary signifier of heroism and monstrosity.

As a black *and* female main character in a horror film, Selena derives from a few specific American predecessors, including Ben (Duane Jones) in *Night of the Living Dead* (1968), Lisa (Rosalind Cash) in *The Omega Man* (1971), and Ripley (Sigourney Weaver) in the *Alien* tetralogy. Each of these earlier characters was groundbreaking in their own right, if not always successful in subverting white and phallocentric precedents regarding narrative and spectatorship. Much as *Night of the Living Dead* has been lauded for its social critique and its capable black male hero, Ben is still killed in the end and Barbra (Judith O'Dea), the promising white female character who opens the film, is reduced to "hysteria" and catatonia. Lisa, Selena's most obvious forerunner, signals all kinds of potential, but she does not appear until a good thirty minutes into the film and very quickly devolves into a sexual object and spectacle for the white male hero and the viewer. And Ripley, one of the most popular horror heroines of all time, continues to elude staunch feminist claims on her. Clover writes, "To applaud the Final Girl as a feminist development, as some reviews of *Aliens* have done with Ripley, is, in light of her figurative meaning, a particularly grotesque expression of wishful thinking" ("Her Body" 98). Similarly, Thomas Doherty writes of the first three films, "The *Alien* trilogy would not be a pure product of commercial Hollywood cinema if it did not express an ambivalence toward the strong woman at its center. After all, from one vantage, the venerable Hitchcockian formula for gripping drama—'torture the women'—defines the narrative project" (224). Although the fourth installment, *Alien: Resurrection*, undoubtedly evolves the character and her feminist potential, the franchise as a whole does not decenter phallocentrism or hegemonic whiteness.

In *28 Days Later*, the viewer encounters a "different" horror heroine, if not an entirely new one. Selena is a savvy survivor (like Ben), an initial savior (like Lisa), and something of a Final Girl (like Ripley).[3] But hers is also a unique, even unprecedented, narrative arc, especially for a black woman in the genre, and the film models a surprising feminism given the genre's reputation for punishing women. Like so many horror films, *28 Days Later* deals extensively with the family as a primary Freudian trope. Patriarchal myths of the "normal" family unit and a woman's place abound, but Selena regularly complicates these discourses. Although the monstrous-feminine pervades the mise-en-scène of the film, paternal signifiers—the scientist, an Infected priest, Hannah's father, Frank (Brendan Gleeson), and the leader of the soldiers, Major Henry West (Christopher Eccleston)—are themselves rendered grotesque. Barry Keith Grant's comment on the 1990 remake of *Night of the Living Dead* lends itself to my analysis of *28 Days Later*: "[A]t the beginning of the film the zombies are the monstrous threat, but at the end it is hysterical masculinity that is truly horrifying" ("Taking Back" 238).

Granted, Selena's pairing with a white male protagonist seemingly undermines her centrality to the film. But this interracial partnership of a black woman and a white man, which has cinematic roots in not only *The Omega Man* but also American SF films such as *Time Runner* (1993), *Strange Days* (1995), and *Supernova* (2000), is another place where the film pushes boundaries. Although Selena's agency appears to diminish as the narrative progresses, she remains the only constant hero of the film and a powerful embodiment of sexual difference that subverts patriarchal and racist constructions of the monstrous-feminine. If anything, the film shows an exponential association between Selena and Jim as agents of female empowerment who collaborate to undermine "hysterical masculinity."

It bears stating that *28 Days Later* is groundbreaking in British speculative cinema simply for its inclusion of a black female lead. All the obvious predecessors to Selena feature in American films and—aside from examples such as Jennifer Beals's Golden Raspberry Award–winning performance as Eva in the horror flop *The Bride* (1985)—she remains the only black female lead in a British horror film to date.[4] The earliest example of a memorable black female character in a British speculative role may well be the singer Tina Turner as the Acid Queen in Ken Russell's rock fantasy film *Tommy* (1975).[5] As Stephen Bourne emphasizes, however, the role is hardly a subversive one: "With a red neon light constantly flashing, the scantily dressed, oversexed Acid Queen, waving a syringe in the air, attacks the defenceless Tommy, and introduces him to drugs" (147). And Turner is not a primary cast member, in keeping with the marginalization of black women across cinematic genres. Subsequent twentieth-century examples are sparse and similarly problematic. One could include Grace Jones as the villain May Day in the James Bond film *A View to a Kill* (1985), which (like the entire franchise) is loosely speculative.[6] Black British filmmaker Ngozi Onwurah released her SF film debut *Welcome II the Terrordome* in 1995, featuring the unknown Suzette Llewellyn as Anjela McBride. But these kinds of examples are so sporadic that they can do little more than model the mass erasure of black female characters in the majority of British speculative films and the caricaturization of those few black women who do appear on the big screen. The role of Selena in *28 Days Later*, which Tobias Hochscherf and James Leggott hail as "the most significant and influential British science fiction film of recent memory" (3), is a pioneering one by comparison.

Naomie Harris, the actress cast as Selena, is also one of the few black British actresses currently sustaining a high-profile career. Although a relative unknown when she starred in Boyle's film—she appeared in the television adaptation of Zadie Smith's celebrated novel *White Teeth* in the same year—she has since appeared in major British and American productions, most notably *Miami Vice* (2006), two of the *Pirates of the Caribbean* films (2006 and 2007), the James Bond films *Skyfall* (2012) and *Spectre* (2015), the biopic *Mandela: Long Walk to Freedom* (2013), and the recent critical favorite *Moonlight* (2016). In none of these films, however, is she pivotal, despite being a member of the main cast. Harris's role as Tia Dalma, the patois-speaking witch in the *Pirates of the Caribbean* films, is a particularly stereotypical part for black women, namely, that of voodoo priestess, dark arts practitioner, or supernatural sorceress.[7] Her acclamation as the first black Moneypenny is another indicator of the limitations placed on black female actresses. Moneypenny is ostensibly the least important female character in the Bond universe—neither the "Bond girl" nor the villain, she is the secretary who exists only to engage in naughty wordplay with the eponymous hero. Indeed, Harris has had few lead roles since *28 Days Later* that give her as much screen time or as much range. In her 2002 article for the *Guardian*, Dee O'Connell writes, "Danny Boyle believes that [Harris] deserves to be a star of Kate Winslet's magnitude, but doesn't know if this country will propel a black woman into that firmament." Over a decade later, Boyle's prediction has proven to be accurate, and one is forced to look backward for those roles in which Harris truly gets to shine.

Repent—The End Is Extremely Fucking Nigh

Following the pre-title sequence and then the title itself, which doubles as exposition regarding the passage of time, *28 Days Later* introduces its protagonist, Jim. Whereas the viewer is privy to the backstory regarding Infection, Jim has been lying in a coma as a result of being hit by a car. Ignorant of the apocalypse, he wanders out into the familiar, albeit deserted, streetscapes of London, where he gleans from the carnage, missing person posters, and ultimately the Infected themselves that he is in a vastly changed world. Graffiti on a church wall literally inscribes the idiomatic "writing on the wall," even as it provides a version of biblical advice:

"Repent—The End Is Extremely Fucking Nigh." Jim's innocence, in both knowledge and experience, is important because it confuses gendered expectations in this unconventional zombie flick. Jim may be a male hero and, at least initially, a "last man," but he does not adhere to stereotypical paradigms of masculinity in horror cinema. One can bear in mind here the Mulveyan premise of active male spectatorship and passive female spectacle, as well as the traditional horror principle that "the monster is coded as male, the victim, female" (Grant, "Introduction" 5).

When the male lead is not the monster (vampire, werewolf, serial killer, and so on), he is traditionally an authoritative and hypermasculine figure. Consider the British film *The Day of the Triffids* (1962), which Garland cites as another influential source for *28 Days Later*. The hero, a navy officer named Bill Masen (Howard Keel), first appears in a hospital bed (much like Jim), where he is recovering from eye surgery. But Bill quickly compensates for the "lack" of his bedridden status and his bandaged eyes. Leaning back with his hands behind his head, he makes a facetious comment in a booming voice and then lights a cigarette (with the hand of an attractive female nurse to guide the match). Another pertinent example is *The Omega Man*'s Robert Neville (Charlton Heston), a military scientist who believes he is the sole survivor of a global plague. Robert first appears cruising around the empty streets of Los Angeles in a red convertible. Roughly one minute into the film, Robert whips out a submachine gun to shoot at a shadow in an upstairs window and then resumes his afternoon drive as the opening credits appear. In *Night of the Living Dead*, Ben embodies this active masculinity as well. In his first scene, he rescues a terrified Barbra by whisking her into a house, locking the door, and speaking words of reassurance, all while brandishing a tire iron.

These films model a precedent of macho heroism and phallic performance for those male characters who are not busy terrorizing female victims. Building on the same mythological and fairy-tale archetypes that influenced Freud, horror cinema indicates that men can be the Wolf (monster) or the Woodsman (hero), but *not* Little Red Riding Hood (victim). Yet Jim is very much the victim in his opening scene, oblivious to the dangers "out there" and lacking the knowledge into which the audience has already been initiated. For, as Clover puts it, "[w]e are both Red Riding Hood *and* the Wolf; the force of experience, in horror, comes from 'knowing' both sides of the story" (*Men* 12). The fairy-tale undertones of Jim's awakening after a long sleep also align him with female characters such as Sleeping Beauty and Snow White. The camera films him from above—a full-frontal nude shot that captures his pale, almost skeletal, body on dark blue sheets. The scene conveys stillness, passivity, and vulnerability, which is especially poignant because the shot shows an actual penis, rather than phallic substitutes such as Bill's cigarette, Robert's submachine gun, and Ben's tire iron. When Jim eventually stumbles out into the postapocalyptic world in oversized green medical scrubs, he is the "feminine" victim while Selena (who appears soon afterward) is the "masculine" hero.

Jim's investigation of a church leads to his first encounter with the Infected, the moment in which the compromised patriarchal law and the archaic maternal are made visible in the postapocalyptic world. The cavernous interior of the church is completely dark, another Terrible Place filled with death. In the sanctuary, now a misnomer, countless corpses are piled on top of one other, sprawled across pews and beneath stained-glass windows. Like the gothic mansion that serves as a base for the soldiers, the church is old, ornate, and creepy, but also the chosen home for a specific group: "What makes these houses terrible is not just their Victorian decrepitude but the terrible families—murderous, incestuous, cannibalistic—that occupy them" (Clover, "Her Body" 78). When Jim calls out "Hello?" his voice rouses a couple of zombies, who turn and stare at him. But it is the insistent rattling of locked doors that induces fear in this particular scene. An Infected in a cassock—the symbolic patriarch of this particular house—finally bursts into the gallery and spastically advances while Jim slowly backs away. Hesitantly, Jim asks, "Father? Father, are you okay?" Realizing that "Father" is not "okay," Jim uses a plastic bag full of soda cans to hit the zombie and then immediately regrets it: "I shouldn't have done that." The priest is a clear embodiment of diseased patriarchy and the symbolic Name of the Father, which Jim literally invokes here. But like the "Father," the entire paternal law is contaminated and unstable. Jim flees the church and races out into the street with a trickle of zombies chasing after him until Selena and Mark materialize to save him.

It is exclusively as savior, then, that the viewer sees Selena for the first time. Unlike Jim's introduction as naked and passive innocent, Selena (with Mark as *her* sidekick) is active, armed, and informed. Wearing goggles, a bandanna, and an ankle-length leather coat, she races out of the darkness, slinging Molotov cocktails at the zombies while calling out to Jim: "Here! Over here!" She and Mark rush Jim to the safety of a mall shop, close the metal security grill behind them, and then educate him on the apocalypse. Generic horror codes are entirely upturned by the male and female leads. Despite being grouped with two white men, Selena is the authoritative presence, the voice of reason, and the one in charge. If the cinematic apparatus equates agency with white male bodies on-screen and

Figure 1.1. Selena (Naomie Harris) explains the apocalypse to the recently awakened Jim (Cillian Murphy) in *28 Days Later* (2002).

white male spectators offscreen, Selena's black female body immediately disrupts these models. The film encourages the viewer to defer to her authority without attempting to qualify her authority as atypical. She simply leads and "we" (like Jim and Mark) follow.

But Selena also immediately forecloses any easy appropriations of her character by phallocentric systems. A common logic for "explaining" empowered female characters is that they are like men and therefore "phallic women." This reading suggests that audiences (and male audiences in particular) can take pleasure in a "strong" female character because she does not threaten masculinity—she embodies it. Her phallic attributes also serve to alleviate the castration anxiety that "woman" automatically induces. At the same time, the phallic woman is often "re-feminized" at some point in the narrative. Her performance of masculinity is curtailed, and she is returned to a more stereotypical version of femininity. Creed uses Ripley in *Alien* as a prime example—at the end of that film, Ripley becomes "a reassuring fetish object for the 'normal' woman" ("Horror" 65). Her seminudity, clean environment, and symbolic protection of a cat all suggest a safe and comforting maternal figure (rather than the monstrous-feminine that haunts the film).

But Selena is never *quite* a "reassuring fetish object," which is precisely what gives her such remarkable agency in this film. Even when the soldiers put Selena in a slinky red dress so that she embodies the "normal" female role of sexual and reproductive object, she remains dangerous rather

Figure 1.2. Selena kills the Infected Mark (Noah Huntley) with a stoic brutality that shocks Jim.

than comforting to patriarchal discourses. And her heroism is never easily claimed as a "male" victory. Mark's early death is a case in point. The trio is attacked in the night by a pair of frenzied zombies who go straight for Jim, knocking him to the ground and straining to bite him as he screams for help and tries to hold them off. Selena appears out of nowhere, an impressive silhouette with spiky hair, brandishing her machete with both hands. Wordlessly, she dispatches the larger male zombie, hacking into him with weighty blows until he lies still. Mark stabs the smaller female zombie with a hunting knife, and the blood-spattered Jim crawls free. One might argue that Selena is very much the phallic woman here (she has a bigger weapon than Mark and targets the bigger zombie). Her killing of the Infected also positions her as an enemy of the monstrous-feminine rather than its potential incarnation. However, such phallocentric reassurances are quickly negated when Selena kills Mark mere seconds later with the same brutality she used on the zombie.

In this moment, Selena becomes the *femme castratrice*, and her machete—a phallus used to protect a male character (Jim)—is suddenly an instrument of castration that attacks a male character (Mark). Creed argues that the *castratrice* is not simply a phallic woman, as Clover suggests of the Final Girl. Instead, posits Creed, this heroine upsets the male gaze because she causes rather than allays castration anxiety—a fact that is borne out by Jim's shocked expression in the aftermath. After butchering Mark, Selena warns Jim that she will do the same thing to him if necessary: "And just so you know where you stand, if it happens to you, I'll do it in a heartbeat." Her threat is a narrative device, but it is also another layer of male terror in this horror film, the monstrous threat of castration, which Selena now symbolizes. It is no coincidence that when Selena encounters the soldiers, the first thing that they do is confiscate her machete. Clearly, Selena signals multiple, conflicting roles, which makes her especially subversive from a feminist perspective. In these early scenes, she is active hero, phallic woman, Final Girl, and *femme castratrice* interchangeably. The viewer cannot rely on predictable "coping" measures to rationalize her on-screen empowerment.

Of course, Jim contributes to the subversion by way of his own gendered performance, and it quickly becomes evident that both Selena and Jim embody or simply share aspects of the Final Girl and the monstrous-feminine. If Selena's resourcefulness, isolation, wariness, and machete all position her as a Final Girl (even if her feminine name does not), Jim's journey from terrified victim to symbolic castrator is surely a trademark of this heroine as well. He is certainly closer to a Final Girl than to any male paradigms in horror cinema, and his role is one of increasing "feminine" agency, especially in the rape-revenge sequence. Clover makes it clear that the Final Girl's evolution into a vengeful killer begins with terror: "She is the one who encounters the mutilated bodies of her friends and perceives the full extent of the preceding horror and of her own peril; who is chased, cornered, wounded; whom we see scream, stagger, fall, rise, and scream again. She is abject terror personified" ("Her Body" 82). The concept of "abject terror" is pivotal to horror cinema, and it is typically routed through a female character. But abject terror is not a predominantly female experience in this film but a male one—it originates with Jim and later presents in other male characters such as Mark and the soldiers. Jim is terrified for much of the film, regularly on the run, screaming, and pleading for help. Only as a Final Girl does he become fearless and then begin to hunt sadistic and misogynistic male characters: "Tentatively at first and then aggressively, the Final Girl looks *for* the killer, even tracking him to his forest hut or his underground labyrinth, and then *at* him" (Clover, "Her Body" 93). Jim's gaze, originally horrified at the spectacle of Mark's death, becomes a sadistic gaze that delights in the gruesome demise of other men.

Critics tend to read Jim's empowerment at the end of the film as a reaffirmation of stereotypical gender roles—boy saves girl. But *28 Days Later* is hardly that predictable, not least because of its nuanced lead characters and its construction of gendered monstrosities. Jim becomes more like

Selena (not the other way around) as the narrative progresses and is arguably at his *most* feminine in the climactic conclusion when he becomes an agent of the monstrous-feminine. Together, Selena and Jim enact the culminating and castrating revenge of the Final Girl and are aided by the "intrauterine" mansion and the Infected themselves. For all that the monstrous-feminine is seemingly everywhere—a repressed Otherness that has finally ruptured patriarchal boundaries—the film does not reinstate or affirm patriarchal capitalism in its climax.[8] The soldiers, of course, try to do just that, particularly in their treatment of Selena and Hannah. But the soldiers also become the obvious villains and far greater antagonists than the Infected. The viewer's sympathies and gaze may shift between various characters, but the film encourages an alliance with Selena, Jim, and Hannah. And the pleasure of watching the soldiers' graphic downfall is ultimately (whether the viewer consciously acknowledges this fact or not) pleasure in the destruction of a patriarchy.

Family Matters

The patriarchal family, often at the heart of horror cinema, is an aspect of normality that is quickly laid bare in *28 Days Later* to reveal what lies beneath. When Selena and Mark first explain the apocalypse to Jim, he asks them, "Where's your family?" They respond that their families are dead and that Jim's family will be dead too. This prediction is proven accurate when the group investigates Jim's suburban house and finds his parents' corpses rotting in the upstairs bedroom. That night Jim experiences a home movie–style flashback of his parents, a scene shot on Super 8mm film to produce a grainy, dreamlike quality. But the idyllic vision of nuclear family bliss—Mom unpacking the groceries, Dad coming in from the garden, and Jim swigging orange juice—is interrupted when two Infected (recognized by Jim as a father and daughter from "four doors down") crash through the windows. This sequence, which leads to Mark's Infection and consequent death at Selena's hands, reiterates the symbolic death of the "normal" family in this postapocalyptic world.

Through Frank and Hannah, also a father and daughter, the film provides yet another model of family that is initially attractive and familiar in an otherwise monstrous landscape. Selena and Jim see blinking Christmas lights on the balcony of an apartment building and manage to reach the apartment despite the Infected. After welcoming them inside and making introductions, Frank, a middle-aged cab driver, urges them to sit down in the living room. After consulting his teenage daughter, he serves the "guests" his dead wife's crème de menthe in crystal glasses. The four survivors exchange awkward pleasantries and sip their drinks while a tinkly rendition of "Frosty the Snowman" plays in the background. The whole scene is odd, indeed uncanny, and this sense of both normality and strangeness carries through the rest of the group's time together. The foursome, who quickly become their own family unit, decide to pursue the source of a military broadcast claiming to have "the answer to Infection" and drive to Manchester in Frank's taxi. But all the signs of "normal" bourgeois patriarchal capitalism remain slightly off. For example, they stop for groceries in a spotless supermarket and the colorful aisles, endless products, and shopping carts serve as a curious respite in this dark film. The music is catchy and upbeat as they enter the bright, clean, fantasy-like space and Selena declares, "Let's shop." Yet the absence of other people, the rotten produce (aside from a crate of "irradiated" apples), and Frank's laughter as he leaves his MasterCard by the cash register all speak to the incongruity of the entire experience.

The rest of their road trip is similarly tainted. Jim is forced to kill a child Infected when they are filling up on gas. And despite a picnic on lush grass and a night camping out in the open, everyone except Frank takes a Valium to fall asleep. Jim is plagued by nightmares, and the earlier sight of four healthy wild horses, which Frank describes as "like a family," manifests in Jim's bad dreams as an ominous fleeing herd. These scenes are a buildup to their arrival at their destination, the forty-second blockade in Manchester. Expecting to find "the answer to Infection" promised by the broadcast, they instead find a deserted military post. Suspicious (and rightly so), Selena says, "I don't like this. I think we should go." But an incredulous Frank refuses to believe that their journey has been in vain and continues to explore the blockade. When he kicks a corrugated iron scaffold in frustration, a crow takes flight from a corpse and a single drop of contaminated blood splashes into his eye. Thus, even the avuncular Frank, who has become a comforting father figure to all three young people, is transformed into something Other than himself. Camouflaged soldiers then appear out of nowhere, shoot the Infected Frank to death, and bring Selena, Jim, and Hannah back to their base (a Terrible Place).[9]

The tropes of normality, repressed Otherness, and monstrosity coalesce in this final third of the film. What the film shows until this point is a dark reflection of normality and glimpses of families that are not quite what they seem. And the underlying menace throughout is the Infected, the bloody hordes that repeatedly threaten patriarchal institutions like the family—breaking into suburban homes, climbing up stairwells, lurking in churches and dark tunnels, and amassing outside walls and gates. The Infected are coded as monstrous-feminine from the outset, but this meaning becomes more obvious in the climactic scenes involving the soldiers. Notably, the soldiers are the most definitive version of normal patriarchy even as they are the most disturbing. They welcome the three survivors, still reeling from Frank's death, into their gothic home, over which flies another symbol of normality, the Union Jack. Their leader, Major West, highlights the amenities and security features of the base—clean sheets, hot water, a generator, a perimeter wall, land mines, and so on. A warm meal is served in the formal dining room "in honor of [the] guests." These formalities—handshakes, introductions, and hospitality—are familiar in that Frank observed the same conventions when Selena and Jim first arrived on his doorstep. But in this case, appearances of propriety are deceptive.

Part of the point is that etiquette, rules, and "civilized" behavior are themselves a vehicle and mask for repression. West, the epitome of paternal law, plays the authoritarian father in marked contrast to Frank, whom Jim fondly called "a big softie." Wearing his formal dress uniform, West enters the dining room, where he reprimands one of his men for wearing a hat at the table. The men are loud, rowdy, and eager to show off for the newcomers. West's authority keeps the soldiers in check, but just barely. The major commends a young private named Jones (Leo Bill) for preparing a "feast," but then immediately chastises him because the surprise omelet is spoiled. Jones, still wearing a frilly pink apron over his uniform as part of his assigned domestic role, apologetically explains, "I thought the salt might cover the taste, sir." The omelet is an apt metaphor for the soldiers themselves, who are rotten despite their facade of decorum and good manners.

The ensuing dinner conversation further contextualizes the men as the new antagonists of the film, not least because they espouse stereotypically patriarchal views and express a clear nostalgia for bourgeois capitalist normality—Christmas, eggs, and Marks & Spencer. The only voice of opposition among the soldiers is a sergeant named Farrell (Stuart McQuarrie), who declares, "If you look at the whole life of the planet, we—you know—man, has only been around for a few blinks of an eye. So if the Infection wipes us all out, that *is* a return to normality." This comment is telling in light of my own gendered reading of Infection as monstrous-feminine, a repressed force that has returned to threaten patriarchal normality. In response to Farrell, West (as Name of the Father) retorts that "people killing people" has always been the "state of normality." Through this debate, the film reaffirms Wood's basic formula for horror cinema: "normality is threatened by the Monster" (71). Fittingly, the dinner is interrupted when a handful of Infected storm the mansion, racing across the lawn only to be shot down or blown up by the soldiers.

At this stage in the film, the true agenda of the soldiers becomes explicit—they plan to use the females as sexual slaves and breeders. Likewise, the shared feminist agency of Selena, Jim, and Hannah is crystallized. For about ten minutes of screen time, the soldiers have their sadistic fun. Jim (along with Farrell) is beaten up and then taken into the forest to be shot. Concurrently, Selena and Hannah are jostled into a bathroom where the men violently begin to strip Selena. On West's orders, the soldiers attempt to put the two females in "expensive dresses" as a precursor to rape—once again, the male antagonists observe a bizarre sense of propriety, which Selena eventually uses against them. The separation of Jim and Selena, a division of the male and female leads, allows for a rare fluidity on the part of the viewer when it comes to identification and viewing pleasure.

Clover uses the term "victim-hero" to describe horror heroines who get revenge on male characters but still appeal to male audiences. After being brutalized in some way, the victim-hero engages in a retributive justice that is implicitly satisfying for the character herself and for the spectator watching her mete out this punishment. Clover has done much work on why majority-male audiences enjoy watching the castrating vengeance of a female hero or, for that matter, the initial torture of the female hero as a requisite for revenge. Where rape-revenge films are concerned, what does the audience "gain" by watching a rape or an attempted rape followed by comeuppance? There are no easy answers to this question, although Clover notes that vicarious and repressed sadism *and* masochism are possible for all spectators. What is most useful for my analysis is Clover's point that "the center of gravity of these films lies more in the reaction (the revenge) than the act (the rape), but to the extent that the revenge fantasy derives its force from *some* degree of imaginary participation in the act itself, in the victim position, these films are predicated on cross-gender identification of the most extreme, corporeal sort" (*Men* 154).

There are two parallel scenes in *28 Days Later* of victimization being channeled through the gendered bodies and experiences of Selena and Jim. The threat of violation is visceral in both cases, and the sadism of the male perpetrators is meant to alienate the viewer and encourage corporeal identification with the victim position. At the same time, the violence of the soldiers serves the important function of warranting revenge, which the viewer can later enjoy because the revenge is proportional. When Jim is marched by two of the soldiers—Jones and a corporal named Mitchell (Ricci Harnett)—into the forest at daybreak, he is bound, bloody, and terrified. When he trips and falls, he tearfully begs for his life (much like a Final Girl). Mitchell steps on Jim's neck and scoffs, "Believe me, I'm not interested. See, I'm gonna have the black one. And I'm gonna make her squirm."[10] Once again, abject terror is channeled through Jim's male body, complicating notions of who can play what role in a horror film. Mitchell himself is quick to feminize Jim in this moment and to threaten rape, albeit rape by proxy—his promise to make Selena "squirm" is intended to torture Jim. With a sharp kick to Jim's ribs, Mitchell then says, "Get up, you cunt!"

When they reach the place of execution, where bodies are piled up against the perimeter wall, the rhetoric of rape is again explicit. Farrell bravely goads his captors in an effort to protect Jim: "Come on then, you fucking pansies. Do me first." Theatrically, Mitchell attaches a bayonet to his rifle, clearly intending to stab rather than shoot the captives. When Farrell spits in Mitchell's face, the latter declares, "I'm gonna enjoy this." The promise of rape (in the form of a stabbing) is interrupted when a nervous Jones shoots Farrell in order to spare him a painful death. Startled, Mitchell temporarily turns his anger and his weapon toward Jones, screaming, "You stupid cunt!" This distraction facilitates Jim's escape—he is able to flee his captors and symbolically jump over the wall to the Other side. The filming of this entire sequence frames Mitchell's cruelty as ugly and extreme, not only to the spectator but also to all the other male parties involved, including Jones. Mitchell's macho sadism is almost hyperbolic as he waves his rifle around, threatening and feminizing (as "cunts") those who do not practice his violent and misogynistic version of masculinity.

The subsequent sequence with Selena is analogous to Jim's brutalization and near-stabbing but also clearly different. The camerawork is more manic and the pace more urgent than the filming of Jim's death march. The viewer first sees Selena's half-naked torso being literally manhandled, then Hannah screaming nearby while a soldier restrains her, and finally a full-length standing mirror, which contains a reflection of the soldier ripping off Selena's shirt. There is nothing erotic about the sequence, which simulates the gang rape that the men have already declared as their intent. Once again, misogynistic masculinity is ugly, except here it is a group of men who practice it rather than the singular Mitchell. As Clover writes of

Figure 1.3. Selena fends off the soldiers who plan to rape her and Hannah (Megan Burns).

rape-revenge fantasies that interrogate "quotidian patriarchy," the "analysis turns on the dynamic of males in groups—how they egg each other on to increasingly abhorrent behavior, and then, when they are brought to account, how they disavow individual responsibility" (*Men* 144). The men—all dressed alike and filmed in such a way that they briefly become interchangeable—shove Selena's body back and forth between them, practicing and promising violence even as they tell her to "relax."

In the end, Selena's initiative prevents the gang rape, much as Jim's initiative allows him to escape Mitchell. She strategically appeals to the men's hypocritical sense of chivalry to gain a few moments of privacy during which she desperately feeds Hannah drugs to dull her senses. Although the soldiers barge back in, Selena's actions are enough to interrupt the attack and are followed immediately by a distraction of Jim's making. He winds up the siren at the blockade, which puts the soldiers on high alert and facilitates Jim's return to the mansion. Appropriately, Jim and Selena work in tandem here, averting what is ultimately patriarchal violation and instigating the climactic revenge sequence. What follows are the most graphic scenes in the film, scenes in which patriarchy is the obvious evil and the primary target of the gratuitous violence that horror cinema promises. If anything, the monstrous-feminine, especially as embodied by the Infected, is now a necessary means of battling the sadistic soldiers. Jim's visible transformation into a feral killer who is almost indistinguishable from the Infected is key here. Despite his maleness, he is an agent of female power in the conclusion, and his rampage places him in the role of Final Girl and castrator.

Selena simultaneously performs an alternative version of the Final Girl by staying one step ahead of the soldiers. Like Jim, Selena and Hannah undergo a visual transformation that is triggered by the soldiers. Stripped of their regular attire and any potential weaponry, the two female characters are forced into bright red evening gowns and then held under guard in a drawing room. It would be easy to read this compulsory and stereotypical feminization as disempowering, and that is certainly the soldiers' objective. But the mise-en-scène of the entire film allows for more creative interpretations than those proffered simply at a narrative level. The color red has been a sign of the monstrous-feminine from the very beginning, precisely because of its associations with rage, blood, and deviant female sexuality.[11] The soldiers presumably choose red dresses in order to have the female characters "perform" sexual promiscuity. But the dresses, much like Jim's zombielike appearance, instead become visual markers of a primal Otherness that has returned to challenge and defeat patriarchy.

I Haven't Got Any Bullets

The most obvious symbol of a stereotypical and misogynistic masculinity in the film is the gun, which becomes a stand-in for the soldiers in the same way that Selena is associated with a machete. The soldiers first make their presence known by shooting Frank, pumping bullets into his body even after he is dead. At the mansion, they repeatedly parade their guns in front of their captives. When Jim escapes his executioners by climbing over their perimeter wall, he is dismissed as "dead" because "he's got no vehicle and no shooter." But guns are largely impotent (rather than important) in the subsequent battle. Jim picks off the soldiers one by one using the element of surprise and weapons such as a metal pipe, a bayonet, and his bare hands. As Clover puts it, "all phallic symbols are not equal, and a hands-on knifing answers a hands-on rape in a way that a shooting, even a shooting preceded by a humiliation, does not" ("Her Body" 79). These, then, are the "tools" of rape-revenge, which "bring attacker and attacked into primitive, animalistic embrace" (ibid.). Jim fires a gun only once, in order to shoot the chain of a captured Infected and former private named Mailer (Marvin Campbell) and set him free.[12] The fact that Jim does *not* kill Mailer positions the Infected as an ally in the ensuing conflict.

The color red remains prominent throughout the rape-revenge scenes.

Figure 1.4. Selena and Hannah, forced by the soldiers to wear red evening gowns, sit under guard in the drawing room.

Jim's first victim tries to find him amid the army-green tents and trucks of the blockade. As the soldier (clutching his rifle) climbs a ladder with bright red rungs, Jim springs up behind him and bashes in his skull with a metal rod. The next sequence shows Selena and Hannah, now wearing the red dresses and sitting calmly on a settee in the dimly lit drawing room, while Jim frees Mailer in a parallel scene. No longer chained behind a bright red door, Mailer appears outside the drawing room. He stares for a split-second through the windowpanes at the oblivious soldier on the other side and then crashes through the glass, mauling the soldier, and vomiting streams of bright red blood. This attack allows Selena and Hannah to sneak out of the room while Jones, the other soldier on guard, sprays bullets that miss Mailer completely. With a high-pitched scream, Jones then flees to the kitchen, where he hides in a cupboard while one of his comrades succumbs to the Infected. Finally, Jones races down a corridor that is bathed in red (by a flashing emergency light) and runs straight into Jim's bayonetted rifle. The symbolism of Jones's stabbing, a dual act of castration and rape, is captured in the moment of penetration. He is first filmed from the back, so that the viewer glimpses the blood-coated tip of the bayonet jutting through his military fatigues before the camera switches to a close-up of his face, wide-eyed and open-mouthed in shock. A rain-soaked, bare-chested, and blood-covered Jim stands intimately close, his expression gratified as he holds the rifle and savors the moment. Jim then runs off, leaving Jones to collapse.

The Terrible Place is now itself a manifestation of the monstrous-feminine. As Mailer runs amok spreading Infection, Jim spirits ghostlike through the mansion, and Selena and Hannah use the ensuing confusion to their advantage; the power shift from the "bad" soldiers to their captives—"good people" in Jim's own words—is palpable. One of the soldiers hides under a bed in what appears to be a little girl's old-fashioned bedroom until Jim discovers him. The soldier cries, "I haven't got any bullets. I haven't got any fucking bullets." Uninterested, Jim effortlessly slips out a window, while the soldier screams, "Don't fucking leave me!" The irony of the "equipped" (albeit bulletless), uniformed, and helmeted soldier looking to the unarmed and half-naked Jim for protection borders on the comical but also serves as another obvious gibe at West's phallocentric system of power. By the time Mailer and another Infected soldier break into the room and begin to mutilate the man, Jim has vanished.

The slow but steadily building suspense is carried along by John Murphy's instrumental composition "In the House—In a Heartbeat," which relies primarily on just two notes in a fixed tempo of seventy-two beats per minute (a comfortable resting heart rate) that winds tighter and tighter as the soldiers die one by one. Boyle describes the music as "a rhythmic looping track that builds and builds and builds" (Hunter 81). The music complements the gothic atmosphere, the chiaroscuro lighting, the pouring rain and lightning outside, the blurry windowpanes (through which Jim periodically peers), and Jim's fluid but feral movements. Although Selena and Hannah are separated during this sequence, they are now ostensibly impervious to the dangers of the Terrible Place. Hannah returns to the room where she and Selena were forced into the dresses because her discarded clothing contains a family photo. When a newly Infected soldier follows her, she hides behind the same full-length mirror that featured in the earlier near-rape scene. Indeed, it is the same soldier whose reflection appeared in the mirror when he was stripping Selena. Now an Infected, the soldier shuffles to the mirror and stares for a moment at his reflection. The scene is uncanny: the phallocentric male gaze can no longer recognize itself. If anything, the camera's close-up pan from Hannah in the red dress behind the mirror to the blood-soaked Infected in front of the mirror reiterates that they are, at least for the moment, two sides of a coin. The monstrous-feminine is the common denominator as the female characters, Jim, and the Infected methodically destroy West's patriarchy.

In a culmination of the entire sequence, including the music composition, Jim tracks Selena—the red dress bright in an otherwise dark color scheme—to a room where an armed Mitchell is holding her hostage. Dropping down from the rafters, Jim yanks Mitchell away from Selena, ignoring gunfire that is once again futile. Wrestling Mitchell to the ground, Jim forces his thumbs into a screaming Mitchell's eye sockets and viciously claws him to death. This act is the final and bloodiest symbolic castration in the sequence, presumably because Mitchell is the most sadistic of the soldiers and the one most intent on rape. Realism, special effects, and music all work together here to sicken and yet thrill the audience as Jim crushes Mitchell's eyeballs into his skull. But any sadistic pleasure in Mitchell's agony is also pleasure in the demise of the misogyny he represents. Perhaps to reiterate that Jim is simply a vehicle for the monstrous-feminine and that Selena is the original *femme castratrice*, the scene brings the camera's point of view back to her as its climax.

Selena's original threat to kill Jim "in a heartbeat" is now tested since Jim has become indistinguishable from the zombies. The death of Jim at Selena's hands would certainly suggest that they are *not* on the same side after all and that he too must be symbolically castrated by female power. Selena reaches for her machete, which is lying on the nearby bed, and faces Jim, whose expression is blacked out by the shadow. As he advances toward her, she prepares to cut him down, but stops. "That was longer than a heartbeat," he quips, prompting her to drop the machete and tearfully embrace him. The two passionately kiss until Hannah interrupts them by smashing a bottle over Jim's head because she thinks that he is attacking Selena. In his new mock role as father, Jim then sternly reprimands Hannah: "I was *kissing* her. Are you stoned?" Admittedly, the reunion of the three survivors is the re-formation of a vaguely patriarchal family (which I address in the next section), but their survival of the Terrible Place is also a triumph that cannot be attributed to any simple gender dynamics regarding victims and heroes. Nowhere is this point made more clearly than in their collective confrontation with the leader and last survivor of the soldiers, West.

When the group runs out to Frank's taxi, they find West waiting for them in the backseat. "You killed all my boys," he says to Jim, before pointing a pistol and shooting Jim point-blank in the stomach. Here, then, is the "real" climax of the film, a climax in which Jim's heroism (even as an agent of female monstrosity) is curtailed. Appropriately, it is Hannah, still wearing a red gown like Selena, who kills West in the end. She hops into the driver's seat of her father's taxi, calmly throws the gear into reverse, and backs the car swiftly and confidently toward the mansion's entrance. An alarmed West calls out to her from the backseat, but she ignores him, stopping the car almost in the foyer and then turning to purposefully watch as Mailer breaks through the rear windshield and pulls a screaming West out of the car. If, as Clover writes of the Final Girl, "her triumph *depends* on her assumption of the gaze" ("Her Body" 104), Hannah's cold stare as the last patriarch is reduced to abject terror is fitting—she too is something of a Final Girl in the end. After Selena manages to get Jim into the backseat, the trio leaves the estate, with Hannah flooring the gas to propel the taxi through the padlocked gates. The impact throws Selena and Jim forward, where the shot freezes and then familiarly cuts to black and the film title at the bottom of the screen followed by ellipses.

Hello

That the whole thing has been a nightmare is hinted at in the subsequent scene, where Selena rolls Jim down a hospital corridor on a gurney, administers an injection and chest compressions, and screams, "Come on, Jim! Breathe! Fucking breathe!" The camera cuts to an upside-down shot of a beautiful lake and the word "HELL" spelled out in giant fabric letters on the grass. And then, with a sharp intake of breath, Jim opens his eyes, precisely as though waking from a bad dream. Visually, the narrative comes full circle by reenacting Jim's awakening after an injury. But instead of a coma ward in a hospital, he is in a sunlit bedroom. His stomach is covered by a clean bandage, he is clean-shaven, and his odd comment, "Not the curtains as well," suggests that he is awakening, not after a monthlong slumber, but simply from a night's rest. A mechanical whirring sound is audible, and the next scene reveals the source. Selena sits at an old-fashioned hand-driven sewing machine, stitching red fabric—the dress—into something else. Jim joins her, pulling on a bright red sweater as he says of the dress that she "looked all right in [it]."

A quick shot of the exterior shows their location—a rambling white farmhouse in the country. Hannah is outside, on the bank of the idyllic lake, laying out giant bolts of cloth on the grass. And a weaving aerial shot, the view from a jet, shows the verdant landscape of England's Lake District as a pilot speaks over his radio. Although the pilot is speaking not English but rather Finnish, his use of the NATO phonetic alphabet is comprehensible.[13] His flyover also shows a couple of emaciated Infected, which are immobile and on the verge of death from starvation. The implications of this entire sequence are made clear when Hannah bursts into the farmhouse and says, "It's coming." She, Selena, and Jim scramble outside with massive bundles of cloth, which they arrange on the ground alongside the rest of the material. Only when the camera's point of view returns to the jet does the viewer see that the cloth completes the giant message, which now reads "HELLO." The three survivors wave frantically as the jet zooms overhead. Grinning, Selena turns to the others and asks, "Do you think he saw us this time?" These are the final lines of the film, which Jim was orig-inally meant to speak but which Boyle assigned to Selena instead. Reflec-tively, Jim stares up into the sky, and the screen cuts to the closing credits.

The concept of a happy ending is rarely a straightforward one in hor-ror cinema. If normality triumphs over the repressed, then that simply means a return to "the heterosexual monogamous couple, the family, and the social institutions (police, church, armed forces) that support and de-fend them" (Wood 71). The fact that the film concludes with Selena and Jim as a heterosexual couple and Hannah as their adolescent dependent points back to the "normal" archetype of the family, even as the NATO jet signals the "normal" presence of armed forces. At the same time, West's hollow promise of protection is proof that a military rescue does *not* mean safety and that patriarchal systems are themselves repressive and oppres-sive (thus triggering the return of the repressed in the first place). But even in this ambiguous ending, which proffers a reassuring return to nor-mality and a reassuring male gaze in Jim's final shot, the film is progres-sive from a feminist standpoint.

For one thing, Selena remains the same active hero in the end that she was at the beginning. Any concluding reading of Selena as a domesticated or passive figure whose "domesticity is evident in this first domestic ac-tivity we have seen her in—sewing" (G. Williams 43) is problematic. Far from the kind of gender performance that Jones undertakes in his pink apron, a parody of domestic femininity, Selena's focused effort at the sew-ing machine is grounded in her survivalist ethos. She is not darning Jim's socks here—she is manufacturing a distress signal. Once again, Selena leads while her companions follow. The fact that the cloth message is her enterprise is clear not just from the sewing machine but also from Jim's comment about the curtains and the fact that he has been recuperating (mirroring the passivity of his opening scene) while she has been work-ing (mirroring the activity of her opening scene). And when Selena repur-poses the red dress, it is presumably not a coincidence that Jim pulls on a red sweater in the same scene. The Infected and their Rage may be on the verge of extinction, but the vestiges of the monstrous-feminine are not entirely absent, even in the tranquil final scene.

Clover argues that the Final Girl cannot be read as a feminist heroine because she is ultimately masculinized: "The moment at which the Final

Figure 1.5. Selena and Hannah exit the hospital without Jim in the alternative theatrical ending.

Girl is effectively phallicized is the moment that the plot halts and horror ceases. Day breaks, and the community returns to its normal order" ("Her Body" 96). But Selena does not build up to a phallic woman (Jim perhaps does) as her visual and narrative arc. She may originate as a masculinized character, but she is also *femme castratrice*, archaic maternal, and female signifier, as evinced by her name. I would echo Creed's observation that "because the heroine is represented as resourceful, intelligent and dangerous it does not follow that she should be seen as a pseudo man" (*Monstrous* 127). As gender performance goes, Selena's climactic encounter with the soldiers takes place in a different kind of drag (namely, the red dress), and she remains a singular face of womanhood that is not easily appropriated or dismissed, especially by a phallocentric white gaze. Although Jim's comment that she "looked all right" in the dress can be taken as an affirmation of the soldiers' patriarchal efforts, such a reading does not fit with what has otherwise been a powerful feminist subtext. Rather, one might take Jim's observation—by way of his white male gaze—as a subtle endorsement of this nuanced black female hero who can perform such a range of terrifying and yet pleasurable roles.

I want to conclude my discussion of *28 Days Later* by briefly address-ing the alternative theatrical ending in which Jim does not survive.[14] That ending is an extension of the hospital scene, and Boyle and Garland, in their audio commentary on the DVD edition, describe it as "the proper ending" ("Alternate"). Boyle goes on to say, "More importantly [*sic*] was that the sequence in the hospital—it was to do with the women really. Particularly Selena, Naomie's character." After Selena fails to resuscitate Jim, she and Hannah each pick up a gun—thus appropriating that partic-ular symbol of masculinity—and the two female characters exit the hospi-tal, walking back down the corridor and into the light while the swinging doors close slowly behind them. The DVD commentary partially clarifies why this ending was not used. Test-screening audiences were uncomfort-able with the death of the white male protagonist and read the surviving female characters as vulnerable (despite all the evidence to the contrary) rather than resilient.

Yet this alternative ending is especially radical *because* of its refusal to simply resume codes of normality, such as heterosexual romance, patri-archal rescue, and so on. Of course, such filmmaking decisions bring us back to the entire cinematic apparatus and its complicity in creating and disseminating so-called normality at the direct expense of Other possi-bilities. But even in the official (and less overtly feminist) ending, Selena maintains her role as hero right up until the last scene, when she and her companions gleefully jump up and down on their giant cloth message to further attract the attention of the pilot. She is still in charge, still fight-ing to survive, and still an embodiment of both comforting womanhood and subversive monstrosity. Visually and narratively, Selena challenges cinematic horror clichés through her fluidity and multidimensionality. Es-pecially given the paucity of black women in speculative British cinema, let alone in lead roles, Selena is a rare character and one that deserves at-tention. As such, her final lines ("Do you think he saw us this time?") are appropriate and reflect her opening line ("Here!"). Selena's entire perfor-mance is bookended by the pressing need to get noticed, a need that is long overdue for black women in subversive roles across genres.

CHAPTER 2

Last One Standing: *Alien vs. Predator*

Expeditions are a common trope in horror cinema—a small group of people sets out to investigate the unknown, typically at great peril. In *Alien*, the crew of the *Nostromo* receives "a transmission of unknown origin" from a nearby planet and tracks it down, with disastrous results. The elite military team in *Predator* traces a helicopter signal to the jungles of an unnamed Central American country, where they encounter a deadly life form. When Selena and her companions pursue the military broadcast in *28 Days Later*, they too meet with catastrophe. Like these SF horror predecessors, Paul W. S. Anderson's 2004 action thriller *AVP: Alien vs. Predator* opens with an expedition that is doomed from the start. A private satellite belonging to a billionaire robotics pioneer named Charles Bishop Weyland (Lance Henriksen) picks up a strange heat signature underneath Bouvetøya Island, a glacial island to the north of Antarctica. Weyland, a dying man, quickly assembles a team to explore and claim this mysterious find. Alexa "Lex" Woods (Sanaa Lathan) is his first hire and top choice to lead the expedition because she is the most experienced environmental guide for the region. He also hires an archaeologist, a chemical engineer, a drilling team, and mercenaries, all of whom congregate on his icebreaker ship off the coast of the island. The stage is thus set for what Thomas Doherty calls a "science fiction–cum–horror–cum adventure" (209).

By virtue of its name alone, *AVP* is a successor to the *Alien* and *Predator* franchises. And like those franchises, *AVP* engages with questions of race and gender on an allegorical level. Once again, Robin Wood's pioneering work on horror cinema is a useful starting point for framing the various forces represented in this film. Flawed families, monstrous Others, and white patriarchies all feature in *AVP*, which very literally pits patriarchal white capitalism (Weyland Industries) against monsters that are coded as black (Aliens and Predators). The Aliens have long been read along racial lines, as Adam Roberts indicates in his discussion of the first film in the franchise: "Ridley Scott's *Alien* (1979) represents the alien as a black-skinned monster, played, in the original film, by a black actor [Bolaji Badejo] in a suit" (95). And both Roberts and Adilifu Nama deconstruct the blackness of the Predators (also played by a black actor, Kevin Peter Hall, in *Predator* and *Predator 2*)—their dreadlock-like extensions, "tribal" features and markings, ritualistic practices, and so on. The names of these respective monsters, "Aliens" and "Predators," further code them as racialized threats to white bourgeois normality.

In terms of gender, these monsters are also manifestations of what Barbara Creed calls the monstrous-feminine (see chapter 1). In other words, they embody patriarchal anxieties about the maternal and female sexuality. Where the Aliens are concerned, scholars have made much of the vaginal facehuggers, the phallic chestbursters, the dripping Alien maws as phalli dentati, and the Alien Queen as the epitome of the grotesque archaic mother. Its massive, muscular, and implicitly male stature notwithstanding, the face of the archetypal Predator has also been read as vagina dentata, epitomized by the epithet "pussy face" in *Predator 2*. Christopher Sharrett sums up the gendered symbolism of both monsters this way: "Like the emaciated biomechanical body of the Alien, with its enormous phallic head, the Predator is an apocalyptic, monstrous incarnation of sexuality itself. Genital sexuality embodied in these monsters is, however, essentially female; it is subdued and destroyed by phallic authority whose ambition is to reinstate repression and 'order out of chaos'" (300).

Phallic authority—that is, the Law of the Father—takes on various forms in the two franchises. In the *Alien* films, a conglomerate named Weyland-Yutani ("the Company") repeatedly attempts to control and profit from the Aliens. But the true nemesis of the Aliens is Ripley, whose goal is always to destroy them. Creed and Carol Clover both argue that Ripley is herself an ironic agent of phallic authority rather than its opponent. Furthermore, Amy Taubin reads Ripley as a version of acceptable white womanhood that subdues a monstrous black femininity: "If Ripley is the prototypical, upper-middle-class WASP, the alien queen bears a suspicious resemblance to a favorite scapegoat of the Reagan/Bush era—the black welfare mother—that parasite of the economy whose uncurbed reproductive drive reduced hard-working taxpayers to bankruptcy" (95–96). Along with Taubin, critics such as Richard Dyer and Joshua David Bellin argue that the *Alien* franchise is as much about conservative white anxieties regarding black fertility and excess as anything else.

In *Predator*, the hypermasculine white male hero, Dutch (Arnold Schwarzenegger), is the primary stand-in for paternal law and the figure called in to make "order out of chaos." Although *Predator 2* institutes a black male hero and thus complicates notions of a default white paternal law, the battle between Mike Harrigan (Danny Glover) and the Predator in an urban jungle also feeds extant stereotypes. As Roberts writes, "In the first film the *Predator* is destroyed by the Aryan übermann Arnold Schwarzenegger. In the second the casting is even more ingenious: the black actor Danny Glover is pitted against the black-man-as-alien, precisely in the scene where black-on-black violence in contemporary America is at its most acute" (95). In both franchises, then, monstrosity is black, abject, and feminized and must be destroyed at the hands of a masculinized hero with either a military or police rank (Lieutenant Ripley, Major Dutch Schafer, and Lieutenant Harrigan). As I mentioned in the previous chapter, the film in the *Alien* series that most successfully interrogates patriarchal discourses and notions of a normal Selfhood versus a repressed female Otherness is *Alien: Resurrection*. In that final installment of the tetralogy, a resurrected Ripley becomes a hybrid Alien and the monstrous-feminine is not tamed or destroyed by way of a conclusion.

When compared to these cinematic forebears, *AVP* is unexpectedly subversive, especially given its reputation as a formulaic, if not outright "bad," film. Of course, as Clover points out, the aesthetic value of horror cinema ranges from high art such as *Nosferatu* (1922) and *Psycho* (1960) to cult classics such as *Alien* and *An American Werewolf in London* (1981) to slasher films such as *The Texas Chainsaw Massacre* (1974). The question of what makes a horror film "good" is highly subjective, but Clover rightly notes that "its quality as a horror film lies in the ways it delivers the cliché" ("Her Body" 72). The viewer wants to see and experience the sensory hallmarks of horror—terror, shock, and excitement—in a fresh way. As a crossover film, *AVP* promises the bizarre Lovecraftian elements of the *Alien* series, the bloody guerrilla warfare of the *Predator* series, and everything from quiet suspense to campy dialogue. And the film's robust performance at domestic and international box offices indicates that fans were not disappointed (even if film critics were). The website Box Office Mojo lists the worldwide ticket sales of all the *Alien* and *Predator* films and confirms that *AVP* surpassed its antecedents in both franchises by generating roughly $172 million. *AVP* thus bears out Wood's observation that "[m]ost horror films make money; the ones that don't are those with overt intellectual pretensions" (69).

But the most surprising aspect of the film has nothing to do with spine-tingling moments, impressive special effects, or the epic battle between slimy, drooling Aliens and armored Predators. Rather, the film's "difference" from its franchise predecessors lies squarely in its black female hero, a character who immediately complicates notions of authoritative white patriarchy, black monstrosity, and abject femininity. *AVP* affords a narrative in which the protagonist and the monsters are *all* racialized and feminized Others and where white paternal law is systematically dismantled. As a Ripley-esque heroine, Lex is certainly a potential Final Girl, as well as a possible patriarchal projection of "normal" womanhood. But if these readings require either her eventual phallicization or her eventual performance of a comforting (rather than threatening) sexuality and motherhood, Lex resists such interpretations. And where Ripley is gradually revealed to be the hero of *Alien*, Lex is framed as the hero from the outset. Like Dutch in *Predator*, she is called in for her expertise. But hers is not the authority of the military or the armed forces, and despite working for Weyland Industries, one of her primary functions throughout the film is to question and challenge the white patriarchal capitalism for which Weyland stands.

Lex's eventual partnership with one of the Predators and the fact that she is the only member of the expedition to survive also point to the destruction of paternal law and the triumph of a repressed female Otherness. The "real" showdown of the film is Lex and the Predator versus the Alien Queen, a curious battle between parties that are all coded as black, female, and Other. In this finale, there is no white or male hero (as in *28 Days Later*), and the battle does not automatically connote phallic authority versus the monstrous-feminine. One could argue that Lex's eventual conquest of the Queen is a symbolic conquest of stereotypes regarding black femininity, stereotypes that Lex herself consistently disproves over the course of the narrative—black women as savage, primeval, hyperfertile, maternal, and, of course, monstrous. Similarly, the demise of the Predator suggests that even the "friendly" monster is dispatched in the end and the "right" or "normal" hero left standing. But Lex's inescapable Otherness as a black woman *and* the fact that she is not easily claimed or explained by phallocentric models render her heroism unusual and subversive.

AVP even goes so far as to punish the voyeuristic and narcissistic male gaze. Building on the work of Laura Mulvey, feminist film critics Linda Williams and Mary Ann Doane argue that the female gaze is typically punished for daring to look. This punishment extends from the female spectator, who "is often asked to bear witness to her own powerlessness in the face of rape, mutilation, and murder" (L. Williams, "When" 17), to the on-screen female character, whose "active investigating gaze can only be simultaneous with her own victimization" (Doane, *Desire* 136). In horror cinema, the female gaze (as indicative of activeness, curiosity, and desire) is shocked, dismayed, and terrified, especially in the face of monstrosity. The woman who *chooses* to look is punished, sometimes by the horrific knowledge that the monster is merely a reflection of herself. In *AVP*, however, it is the male gaze that is repeatedly punished, either for phallocentric narcissism or for looking directly at the monstrous-feminine. So despite the fact that it was a nominee for a Golden Raspberry Award, or Razzie, in the "Worst Prequel, Remake, Rip-off or Sequel" category, *AVP* tackles the horror genre in a surprisingly creative way and does something truly unprecedented by way of its black female hero and the female gaze.

The production notes for *AVP* indicate that hundreds of actresses auditioned for the role of Lex and that Sanaa Lathan won the part in a last-minute audition just three days before Anderson began shooting the film. The director explains on the 2005 DVD special feature "The Making of *Alien vs. Predator*" that he was not looking for an actress to "compete with Sigourney [Weaver]," but rather trying to find "a new actress for a new kind of film." Lathan had previously appeared in romantic dramas such as *The Best Man* (1999), *Love & Basketball* (2000), *Disappearing Acts* (2001), and *Brown Sugar* (2002), and she went on to star in a 2004 Broadway revival of Lorraine Hansberry's 1959 play *A Raisin in the Sun*. To date, *AVP* remains Lathan's only major foray into speculative cinema (although she had a minor role in the 1998 vampire film *Blade*). Because of its poor critical reception, *AVP* did little for Lathan's career, and she has since returned to dramas such as *Something New* (2006), *Wonderful World* (2009), and *The Perfect Guy* (2015). Lathan even admitted in a 2015 interview with the writer Rachel Handler that she never really wanted to star in *AVP*: "It's almost like I did everything in my power not to get it."

But one could argue that many of Lathan's films, not just *AVP*, have been underwhelming and that her career—like that of Naomie Harris—ultimately showcases the limitations for black women in Hollywood. As Handler herself puts it in a rhetorical question, "Does this swath of unremarkable films and sporadic disappearances reflect the fact that Lathan is a black actress in an industry that's only doled out one Academy Award for Best Actress to a black woman [Halle Berry] in the history of cinema that casts non-white actors in only 16.7 percent of lead roles?" Indeed, none of the black actresses discussed in this book is an A- or even B-list star who regularly lands strong leading roles.[1] Lathan has won two and been nominated for five Black Reel Awards for Best Actress, making her the Black Reel equivalent of Meryl Streep. According to the official website, the Black Reel Awards were launched in 2000 "as a vehicle to recognize African-American achievement in Hollywood." However, the Oscar-distributing Academy of Motion Picture Arts and Sciences has never recognized Lathan in any capacity.[2] These kinds of statistics reiterate why scholarship on black actresses, their roles, and their recognition remains not only compelling but also exigent. And Lathan's understandable qualms about *AVP* aside, I maintain that Lex is her most original and perhaps even her most radical starring role when it comes to creative representations of black femininity.

Hunter's Moon

Like *28 Days Later*, *AVP* has a short pre-title sequence that sets up the symbolic conflict between normality and the repressed Other. A caption introduces the setting as "Antarctica, October 10th 1904," and then cuts to an aerial shot of a deserted whaling station. A solitary white male sailor suddenly appears on-screen, visibly terrified and running away from something. Abject terror, then, is introduced by way of a male character. Accompanied by dramatic music, the man flees into the mess hall and slides the door shut behind him. Only when the camera switches to his attacker's point of view do the circumstances become clear. The man is being hunted by an invisible Predator, which materializes in front of him and targets his chest with a red laser. But the Predator's kill is interrupted when an Alien also appears nearby—the two creatures violently clash, and the screen cuts to black and then the title.

On a narrative level, this sequence introduces the eponymous monsters and the primary setting for the film, Bouvetøya Island. But on a psychoanalytic level, the viewer witnesses the demise of white male industry and the return of the repressed. The snow-covered whaling station, the two-masted ship moored nearby, and the bearded and suspended sailor provide a nostalgic portrait of Euro-American intrepidity, exploration, and enterprise. These are the early-twentieth-century markers of patriarchal capitalism that will reappear with the twenty-first-century Weyland and his conglomerate. And the decimation of the station, reduced to one terrified and doomed survivor, promises a similar fate for the next round of explorers to set foot on the island.

Weyland, played by Henriksen (who appeared as the android Bishop in *Aliens* and the human Bishop in *Alien 3*), forges an obvious narrative link with the *Alien* universe. His company, Weyland Industries, is implicitly the twenty-first-century forerunner to Weyland-Yutani in the *Alien* films. Similarly, Weyland's middle name, Bishop, positions him as a predecessor to the *Alien* Bishops, especially since he is a robotics pioneer. That Weyland is the primary signifier of patriarchal authority is made clear from the outset. Following the pre-title sequence and then the title, the first image on the screen is one of Weyland's satellites orbiting the earth accompanied by the caption "October 3rd 2004, Low Earth Orbit, Weyland Corporation Satellite PS12." Initially, the silhouetted satellite bears an uncanny resemblance to the head of an Alien Queen. Only when the camera rotates around the monstrous black figure with a helmetlike crest and spindly legs does it become recognizable as an "innocent" satellite with the name "Weyland" painted across the side. This early trompe l'oeil is a telling juxtaposition of normality (a floating satellite that blinks and beeps reassuringly) and the repressed Other (an Alien Queen).

Weyland's immense wealth, as evinced by his private satellites and receiving stations, is reaffirmed by his ability to handpick his expedition team and fly each of them to his ship off the coast of Antarctica. His company logo, a yellow "W," quickly becomes familiar to the viewer since it appears on all his products and property. The man himself epitomizes capitalist patriarchal power. Once everyone congregates on the ship, Weyland makes a dramatic entrance, his footsteps loud on an elevated metal walkway as he steps out of the shadows. Standing on the second-story deck and thus literally above everyone else, he uses a headset microphone and a digital projector to explain his discovery of a massive ancient pyramid 2,000 feet below the ice and his desire to reach it immediately. The team listens from below, their folding chairs arranged over the giant "W" painted on the floor. There is general excitement from the almost exclusively white, European, and male team. The archaeologist, Sebastian De Rosa (Raoul Bova), announces that the pyramid may be the first one in existence. The chemical engineer, Graeme Miller (Ewen Bremner), expresses his desire to carbon-date a sample. And the drilling team leader, Rustin Quinn (Carsten Nørgaard), proclaims his men "the best" and promises to "chew to that depth in seven days."

As a unit, Weyland and his team have all the trappings of imperial and phallocentric mastery. Their state-of-the-art equipment, weaponry, and bravado connote the hegemonic authority of paternal law—the same authority claimed by the various teams in the *Alien* franchise. Their pride and faith in phallic firepower is especially noticeable—they exude the same confidence that the commandos in *Predator* and the soldiers in *28 Days Later* express in their guns. The team does include one other woman besides Lex, a white mercenary named Adele Rousseau (Agathe de La Boulaye). But Rousseau, who is the first character to show off her side-arm and who cracks a joke about condoms, is clearly meant to be "one of the boys." She is a vague French incarnation of Vasquez in *Aliens*, the Latina who holds her own on an all-male military team. There is also one other black character on the expedition, Weyland's right-hand man, Maxwell "Max" Stafford (Colin Salmon). But the British Stafford, who makes a similar show of loading his weapon, is hardly a subversive figure where racial representation or phallocentrism is concerned.

The obvious Other in these early scenes is Lex, the solitary black woman *and* the appointed leader of the expedition. From the moment she is recruited, Lex positions herself as Weyland's opponent. In this respect, she is not so different from Ripley, who is also a cautionary voice and an adversary of the Company as much as of the Aliens. But Ripley's relentless quest to destroy the Aliens (as black monstrous-feminine) makes her an ironic practitioner of a white and phallic authority. Lex's resistance to not just guns but other symbols of normality, such as heterosexual partnership, maternity, and the patriarchal family, makes her a more provocative challenger of bourgeois white capitalism. Her scorn for Weyland is established in her very first scene, which shows her scaling Mount Everest.[3] Her precarious climb is interrupted by a phone call from Stafford, who introduces himself as Weyland's representative. Upon hearing Weyland's name, Lex responds, "Let me guess. He's suing us again." Lex's identity as an environmentalist who runs a nonprofit foundation is an immediate foil for Weyland's identity as a capitalist businessman.

When Lex is subsequently flown to Antarctica on Weyland's private helicopter (another symbol of patriarchal authority), her subversive difference is again established. The scene opens with a close-up shot of the magazine *Scientific American*, which features Weyland on the cover. The camera then cuts to an extreme close-up of Lex's eyes, which are closed as she naps during the flight. A flash of bluish light goes off at regular intervals, eventually prompting Lex to open her eyes. The source of the flash is the chemical engineer Miller, who is seated opposite her and taking endless "selfies" with his digital camera. The emphasis on the male gaze is not subtle here. Weyland's solemn picture staring out from the magazine and Miller's self-portraits contextualize the male gaze as a narcissistic one, even as Lex's initially closed eyes connote a familiar constraint of the female gaze. Miller explains that he is "documenting the trip for [his] boys" and then pulls up an image of his two young sons, who sit on either side of

Figure 2.1. Lex (Sanaa Lathan) comfortably scales Mount Everest in her opening scene in *AVP: Alien vs. Predator* (2004).

a woman. Graeme introduces his sons by name (but does not mention the central maternal figure in the picture) and then asks Lex to take yet another photograph of him. Although Lex politely acquiesces in taking the photo, her subtle smirk at Miller, his sons, and his selfies serves to question rather than endorse his performance of patriarchal normality.

On the ship, Lex is the sole detractor of Weyland's plan to investigate the pyramid. Although she agrees to lead the expedition, she does so under specific conditions. Before the group leaves for Bouvetøya Island, Lex makes a brief speech, which showcases her priorities as a leader and guide. Her speech is markedly different from Weyland's, although it takes place in the same room. In a high-angle shot, Lex stands on top of the "W" logo with the team gathered around her in a semicircle. She is dressed entirely in red, which visually sets her apart from everyone else (who wear gray, yellow, or orange), and she is at the very center of the group. The camera zooms in and arcs slowly around her as she lays down "three simple rules" for keeping everyone alive: "One. No one goes anywhere alone. Ever. Two. Everyone must maintain constant communication. Three. Unexpected things are gonna happen—when they do, no one tries to be a hero." Her rules effectively prioritize coalition, communication, and circumspection rather than masculinist bravado and a discourse of individual conquest. Only by following her own rules does Lex stay alive. As Sandra Jackson puts it, "[Lex's] advice proves to be utterly prophetic—indeed ironic. For it is she who will be the lone survivor of the team, a heroic figure" ("Terrans" 246).

The expedition arrives on the island during what the archaeologist, De Rosa, calls "La Luna del Cacciatore," or the Hunter's Moon—another foreboding sign. They set up camp at the old whaling station, descend to the pyramid via a preexisting tunnel created by the Predators, and begin to explore the pyramid's rooms and levels. But their actions, which include accidentally stepping on a trigger stone and impulsively unlocking a sarcophagus to steal the three Predator guns inside, set the interspecies warfare in motion. By this point, the viewer has a better sense of the pyramid's backstory, which is later fleshed out by De Rosa and illustrated with flashback scenes. Hieroglyphics indicate that the Predators came to Earth thousands of years ago in the guise of gods and taught humans how to build pyramids for the purpose of ritualistic hunting. The Aliens, "the ultimate prey," were bred inside the pyramids with a chained Alien Queen laying eggs and humans serving as gestational hosts. Every one hundred years, the Predators send warriors to Earth to hunt the Aliens. The heat signature that Weyland's satellite detected was the power core of the pyramid reactivating in preparation for a centennial hunt. These narrative details are the pretext for the presence of the Aliens in the pyramid and the sudden arrival of three Predators, who quickly slaughter the entire surface team and then descend to the pyramid itself. Between the rapidly breeding Aliens and the seemingly indestructible Predators, the expedition is quickly decimated.

What I want to highlight here is Lex's consistent rejection of patriarchal authority, the film's condemnation of a phallocentric gaze, and the eventual alliance between Lex and the last surviving Predator (Ian Whyte) as mutual Others. For all that Weyland is a patriarchal figure, he is also a dying man, which makes his authority temporary and fallible. Lex bluntly makes this point when she says to Weyland, "There's no room for sick men on this expedition." The film thus portrays paternal law as diseased and moribund despite extravagant displays of power. When Lex asks Weyland not to participate in the expedition because of his health, she mentions her own dead father as part of her warning. She explains that her father "broke his leg seven hundred feet from the summit of Mount Rainier" and refused to stop or turn around. Despite reaching and toasting the summit with Lex, he died shortly afterward from a blood clot. Weyland interprets the story as a victory narrative, but Lex's story is instead a cau-

Figure 2.2. The team of mercenaries inspects the contents of the Predator sarcophagus.

tionary tale regarding the limits of the Father. Lex herself expresses no interest in staking claims and marking territory, refuses to carry a gun, and *sees* differently from Weyland and the rest of the team.

The scene in which the group opens the sarcophagus is particularly relevant from a visual and narrative standpoint. Once the lock on the ancient container is broken, its lid slides dramatically open with a hiss of steam to reveal an interior of bubbling white mist. The mist gradually dissipates to reveal the three identical Predator guns affixed to pedestals. The guns are futuristic, covered in intricate designs, and more phallic than the average firearm with circular stocks and long rectangular barrels. The men immediately congregate around the sarcophagus, spellbound and excited as they inspect the contents. As Miller puts it, "This is like finding Moses's DVD collection." The camera maximizes the suspense and then the revelation, filming the guns first in a bird's-eye shot and then in a slow close-up pan. But Lex steps away from her male companions, all of whom are kneeling reverently around the sarcophagus with their numerous (and also phallic) flashlights trained on the guns in an almost comical tableau of phallic worship.[4]

Like the scene in which Miller awkwardly but compulsively photographs himself, the sarcophagus scene indicts the narcissistic and phallocentric male gaze. The sight of the Predator guns immediately triggers a coughing fit in Weyland, who then inhales a shot of oxygen and explains that he has had "too much excitement." Contrary to the basic tenets of horror cinema, it is the male gaze that is ultimately punished in this film. The men's collective decision to not just look upon but also steal the Predator guns leads directly to their demise. As soon as the guns are detached from their pedestals, the pyramid enters the "fight" mode intended for the Predators. The massive stone doors grind shut, the Aliens are released, and the action sequences of the film begin. From this point on, the humans are caught in the ensuing battle between the Aliens and the Predators and are methodically killed off one by one. Lex now becomes the straightforward hero of the film, but not by performing the macho heroism of Ripley (or, for that matter, Dutch and Harrigan). Instead, Lex's survival hinges on her partnership with, rather than her conquest of, one of the monsters.

Although the Predators are hostile, they are also intelligent and technologically advanced beings that once collaborated with ancient humans. And the Predator code, which is established in the earlier *Predator* films, becomes clear in *AVP* as well—they prefer to attack armed foes during their hunts, and they do not harm "weaker" opponents. In other words, they differentiate between humans rather than seeing them as all the same, a skill that is enhanced by their visual ability to scan organisms right down to the cellular level. In *Predator 2*, the Predator X-rays a female police officer, discovers she is pregnant, and spares her life. This scene is re-created in *AVP*, but here the target of the scan is Weyland. Upon seeing Weyland's damaged cells, the Predator chooses not to kill him and walks away. The scene thus suggests an early affinity between Lex and the Predator, both of whom assess and then dismiss the primary patriarchal figure as terminal and contaminated. The Predator kills Weyland only when the latter demands to look upon the monster ("Don't turn your back on me") and then attacks it with an improvised flamethrower.

Lex is also the first person to see the Predator's true form by spying on it through a rectangular hole in the wall. Oblivious to her gaze, the Predator removes its helmet to reveal its face, which "grotesquely caricatures female genitalia" (Sharrett 300). After watching for a moment, Lex calls her last surviving human companion, De Rosa, to look as well: "Look over here." The pair quietly observe the Predator mark its helmet using the acidic blood of a dead facehugger. Traditionally, the female gaze expresses horror at the spectacle of the monster, but Lex is fascinated rather than

Figure 2.3. Lex secretly observes the last surviving Predator (Ian Whyte).

horrified by this incarnation of the monstrous-feminine. Of course, De Rosa also voyeuristically gazes upon the face of the Predator and is similarly intrigued. But like all the other male characters in the film, he is punished for looking and shortly thereafter gets snatched and "impregnated" by an Alien. However, the Predator spares Lex and even forges an alliance with her. Robyn Citizen rightly argues that "the black woman and the monster recognize their similar places in patriarchal structures of seeing" (195). But where Citizen reads the Predator as "racialized and gendered as a black male" (196), I maintain that both the Predators and the Aliens can be read as manifestations of the monstrous-feminine.

Once all her human companions are gone, Lex herself begins to take on the visual markers of the titular monsters. And the camera clearly endorses her partnership with the Predator and her transition into something monstrous in her own right. After Lex kills a full-grown Alien with the Predator's retractable spear, she becomes an honorary Predator. The Predator then fashions the dead Alien's body parts into weapons and gives them to Lex for the ensuing battle. She fits the Alien's elongated head—complete with bared teeth—over her left arm as a shield and carries the Alien's tail (tied to a wooden staff) in her right hand as a new

Figure 2.4. Lex and the Predator form an alliance and prepare for battle.

spear. Granted, both of these objects are blatantly phallic and seemingly confirm Lex's masculinization as a Final Girl. But the fact that Lex fights the Aliens using their own body parts also suggests a further channeling of the monstrous-feminine rather than the phallic authority of guns and flamethrowers. She and the Predator exchange a look of mutual recognition and then begin to jog in tandem down the corridor. The shot becomes blurry, symbolically melding the two together as they fade into the distance. Here, the film reaffirms that Lex is the definitive hero of the story and the character with whom the viewer must identify, especially in the absence of any alternatives. At the same time, her new identity as a Predator signals a newfound agency and her transition from prey to hunter.

AVP also refuses to endorse familiar "explanations" for female heroism, particularly maternal compulsion and heterosexual romance. Ripley's battles with the Aliens are often inextricable from her desire to protect a surrogate child—the cat Jones in *Alien*, the little girl Newt in *Aliens*, or the robot Call in *Alien: Resurrection*. The possibility of "normal" heterosexual desire also pervades the *Alien* franchise by way of Ripley's interactions with white male characters such as Dallas, Hicks, Clemens, and Johner. Along similar lines, Selena in *28 Days Later* is a maternal proxy to Hannah and fulfills expectations of a heterosexual partnership by way of her relationship with Jim. In stark contrast to these films, *AVP* forecloses any possibility of motherhood or romance for its female hero. Consider Lex's apathetic reaction to the photograph of Miller's young sons, which she later follows up with the comment, "Your kids aren't that cute." Although the film hints at flirtation between Lex and De Rosa, that romantic possibility is also a case of misdirection. Upon finding the missing De Rosa entombed in the Alien nest, Lex shoots him as a "mercy kill" (the only time she ever fires a gun). So Lex exists outside these expectations of normality, and her resolve is never grounded in maternal or heterosexual drives. The viewer must take her at face value and go along with her heroism despite the absence of formulaic cues.

The Bitch Is Back

The Queen is an Alien variant that first appears in *Aliens* as Ripley's final opponent—Ripley saves Newt from the Queen and delivers the now iconic line, "Get away from her, you bitch!" In *Alien: Resurrection*, Ripley and a Queen are symbiotically resurrected two centuries after the human Ripley dies in *Alien 3*. Because Ripley and the Queen share genes as a result of the cloning process, they are both human-Alien hybrids. Creed argues that "Mother Alien represents Ripley's other self, that is, *woman's*, alien, inner, mysterious powers of reproduction" (*Monstrous* 51). The Queen is always a monstrous foil for Ripley, specifically where "powers of reproduction" are concerned. In *AVP*, an Alien Queen once again has the potential to be an "other self" for the female protagonist. Like her predecessors in the *Alien* franchise, the Queen in Anderson's film is a hyperbolic version of the monstrous-feminine. She is a grotesque but pitiable creature, a manacled monstrosity that is forced to breed prey for the Predators. That her offspring are used for target practice by a species that is *also* coded as black complicates the racial metaphor, which conveys both systemic violence against blacks and unmitigated black-on-black violence. But the most interesting aspect of the Queen's racialization as reproductive slave *and* "husbandless, inhuman 'bitch'" (Gallardo-C and Smith 108) is that she must battle "another" black female rather than what Taubin calls "the prototypical, upper-middle-class WASP" (95). Lex, an upper-middle-class African American woman who eschews sexual partnerships and motherhood in favor of independence and career, functions as a very different kind of double for the Queen than Ripley.

From a psychoanalytic perspective, Lex's final battle with the Queen is the most important sequence in the entire film. By that climactic point, all the familiar signs of patriarchal white capitalism and "normal" paternal law are fatally compromised. On the surface, the dead bodies of the drilling team have been strung up by their ankles as the Predators' grisly trophies. In the pyramid, Weyland, Stafford, and the rest of the mercenaries have also been killed by the monsters. When Lex discovers the Alien nest, she finds Miller's digital camera lying on the ground with the picture of his sons still visible on the viewfinder. A few steps later she finds Miller's dead body and then the almost dead De Rosa, whom she tearfully shoots before a chestburster explodes through his ribcage. In the end, equipment, expertise, and guns cannot save Weyland's expedition, and their curiosity regarding the unknown is categorically punished. With the exception of Lex, not a single member is left alive. Indeed, the last thing that Lex and the Predator do before returning to the surface is set off a cataclysmic explosion, which obliterates not only the pyramid below but also the entire century-old whaling station built on the ice. All evidence of the Aliens, the Predators, and the humans is thus erased, leaving only the final three survivors of these respective species to battle for supremacy.

In *Predator*, the final battle between Dutch and the Predator insidiously endorses white phallic authority. Harrigan's subjugation of the Predator in *Predator 2* relies on the feminization of the latter as "pussy face" and perpetuates images of intraracial black violence. And Ripley's battle with the Queen in *Aliens* positions her as a champion of conservative white family values (with Hicks as figurative husband and Newt as figurative daughter) facing off against black female monstrosity. The absence of both white and male characters in the culminating battle of *AVP* allows for subversive readings that are simply untenable in the film's predecessors. The simplistic binaries that so often delineate "hero" and "monster" are far less straightforward. Even if the Queen remains static and familiar as an obvious monster, her "opposites" are now decidedly *un*familiar. Instead of proffering a white female hero as a "reassuring and pleasurable sign" (Creed, "Horror" 65), *AVP* juxtaposes the Queen with a black woman, who is rarely such a sign on-screen. And the formerly antagonistic Predator is now a foil for the Queen as well, despite its own construction as monster. Regardless, then, of who wins this battle, that winner will not easily conform to semiotic codes of white phallic power.

The scenes leading up to the final battle are rapidly sequenced, action-packed, and periodically gauche. The Queen is freed by her adult offspring, who temporarily attack her in order to produce the acidic blood that will burn through her chains. As soon as the last manacle has snapped, she tears away from her massive ovipositor (also featured in *Aliens*) in a gush of liquid and charges down the corridor with a horrific scream. In parallel scenes, Lex and the Predator set a time bomb inside the Alien nest and escape the pyramid. Lex kills one last Alien with a piton gun after she delivers the *Predator* franchise signature line and her final line of the film, "You are one ugly motherfucker." The male heroes of the *Predator* films make this pronouncement upon seeing the unmasked and vaginal faces of the Predators for the first time. Dutch hides behind a tree and watches from a safe distance as the Predator removes its helmet. Harrigan unmasks the Predator himself when the monster is presumed dead. The line thus serves as a telling patriarchal pronouncement on exposed female sexuality and the monstrous-feminine. The male gaze is disgusted in these moments, and the monster is punished accordingly.

However, *AVP* once again complicates its cinematic predecessors in an ostensibly feminist way. Lex does not speak the line upon the unmasking of the Predator, whose true appearance instead triggers her fascination and even desire. Rather, she speaks the signature line in response to the adult Alien that suddenly descends on the Predator near the tunnel exit. It is worth noting that her pronouncement of "ugliness" is not mere voyeuristic observation but coincides directly with the Alien's phallic attack with its internal mouth. Despite the broader implications of the Aliens as monstrous-feminine, this specific evocation of phallus dentatus is what triggers disgust by way of the female gaze. Lex destroys the Alien in a burst of green spatter, and then she and the Predator ride a retracting mechanized sled at high speed back to the surface while the bomb goes off behind them.

Following the shockwave, Lex undergoes a final transformation as a hybrid figure that signals repressed Otherness rather than normality. The Predator removes its helmet permanently and then uses Alien blood to ritualistically scarify Lex's cheek with the same two marks that it wears on its forehead and helmet. Having already appropriated Alien body parts, Lex now takes on Predator markings as well. The scene is a hammy one, but it provides a visual culmination of Lex's metamorphosis into a human/Alien/Predator. One might even go so far as to say that she and the Predator, with their matching scars, are now conclusively one and the same. The Predator is her extension rather than her opposite. Notably, the scarification scene also borders on romantic and would qualify as such if the scene involved a human companion. In this respect, the film continues to resist the normality of the heterosexual couple that even *28 Days Later* caters to in its conclusion. Unlike Selena, whose sequence in England's verdant Lake District with Jim as mate and Hannah as daughter simulates (even if it does not realize) a return to Edenic innocence, Lex's ending is more radical. For Lex, there is no oedipal family or the promise of Eden—there is only her, the last one standing. And whether one reads the Predator as an extension of Lex or her quasi-mate, their alliance flies in the face of patriarchal norms and expectations.

Of course, one obvious risk of Lex's buildup to a scarred and spearwielding warrior is the simultaneous reduction of her character to a clichéd version of savage black womanhood. Just as Selena and her machete may appear to endorse myths of black primitivism, Lex's adoption of Predator symbols also has the potential to reinforce stereotypes. What undercuts or at least moderates this risk is Lex's definitive status as hero and protagonist rather than sidekick or foil for someone else. The film intimates that she now has all the agency and power of a Predator and that she is as formidable an opponent as the iconic Ripley (who puts on a robotic Power Loader exoskeleton to fight and defeat the Queen) or the hard-bodied strongman Dutch. On cue, the Queen suddenly bursts forth from the snow, the last member of her kind. The DVD scene selection menu provides a title for each scene, which the viewer can see when scrolling through to select a particular scene. The Queen's battle sequence is titled "The Bitch Is Back," a title that should immediately be familiar to fans of the *Alien* franchise. Gallardo-C and Smith note that the preliminary marketing of *Alien 3* was built around this tag line, but the question of which "bitch" (the Queen or Ripley) was intentionally left ambiguous. In *Alien 3*, an adult Queen never makes an appearance, confirming that "[t]he 'bitch' who is 'back' must then be Ripley" (Gallardo-C and Smith 120). But the use of this line on the *AVP* DVD edition is not quite so equivocal. The Alien Queen, who seemingly returns from the dead, is definitively the "bitch" that is "back." With the size and gait of a Tyrannosaurus rex and the skull frill of a Triceratops, she advances menacingly, still dragging her chains behind her.

The Queen is ultimately *the* monster in *AVP*, and her death is requisite in the context of two franchises that demand the monster's demise, even if that demise is temporary. Accordingly, the Queen fights Lex and the now symbolically unmasked Predator but is drowned in the Atlantic Ocean. What is remarkable here is the inversion or absence of those semiotic clues that "explain" the battles in the earlier franchise films. Writing of the Queen versus Ripley in *Aliens*, Doherty cites the classic interpretation: "In the duel scenes between Ripley and the alien mother, the

Figure 2.5. Lex and the Predator face off against their ultimate enemy, the Alien Queen.

visual parallel is unmistakable: two queens fighting for their respective offspring" (223). But such a reading does not apply in *AVP*, where neither "queen" has any offspring to protect. Nor does the final battle occur in a space that suggestively reinforces patriarchal authority. The jungle imagery in *Predator* contributes to the role of the Predator as a product of feminized chaos. In *Predator 2*, Harrigan kills the Predator in its own spaceship, a dark and mist-filled craft with labyrinthine tunnels, intricate carvings on the rounded walls, and both human and nonhuman skulls (including that of an Alien) on display. And Ripley's final battle with the Queen occurs in the dim and claustrophobic space of a cargo bay.

In *AVP*, however, the last battle takes place out on the tundra amid the last remnants of the whaling station. And the wrecked station, the last vestige of white male industry, is entirely destroyed in the battle, which culminates with the Queen being chained to a giant elevated whale-fat cauldron that Lex tips over into the water. The heroism of the protagonist (and her Predator sidekick) does not reinforce a symbolism of white male order and black female chaos. Like Ripley, Lex saves the world by killing the Alien Queen, but she does not pay the typical female price for such a victory—either a reentry into the symbolic patriarchal order or death. Nor does the film subtly condemn blackness in its finale, as the *Alien* and *Predator* franchises are guilty of doing. Granted, both of the monsters, which are coded as black and female, die in the end. Having fulfilled its own novel role as sidekick, the Predator expires from its wounds. These respective manifestations of the monstrous-feminine are thus dispatched and the viewer is left with Lex. But if the Queen and the Predator are racist and patriarchal constructs, then their deaths at the hands of and in the service of a black female hero are provocative. For Lex is also a repressed Other and an emblem of difference, and her victory hardly signals a return to normality.

The sudden materialization of a giant Predator spaceship and an entire platoon of Predators, who arrive to collect the body of their comrade, further reinforces her Otherness. As *28 Days Later* effectively demonstrates, horror cinema often points to the end of the nightmare by way of "comforting" symbols of normality. Thus, the NATO jet is meant to reassure the survivors and the viewer that everything is now (or will be) okay. The helicopters in the final shots of *Predator* and *Predator 2* serve the same function. The *Alien* tetralogy provides a range of endings, but they frequently involve an escape craft as a haven from which the monster is ejected. However, there are no evacuations in *AVP* by way of helicopters, squad cars, or armed forces. Instead, the film introduces more monsters, which temporarily decloak themselves in order to claim their dead and to honor Lex by giving her a ceremonial spear. Far from the classic, albeit ambiguous, horror ending in which there is at least the appearance of a return to normality, *AVP* remains grounded in the repressed until the very end. And Lex's final scene with the Predators reaffirms an alliance of mutual Others *and* the fact that the Predators remain a thriving species rather than an eradicated one.

Because Lex is a Final Girl, one must still consider Clover's point that this horror heroine is always a phallic woman (and thus herself a patriarchal construct) in the end: "Her symbolic phallicization, in the last scenes, may or may not proceed at root from the horror of lack on the part of audience and maker. But it certainly proceeds from the need to bring her in line with the epic laws of western narrative tradition" ("Her Body" 106). But I am not convinced that Lex is merely a proxy for a male audience. Like many a Final Girl (including Ripley), she uses a range of phallic tools and weapons over the course of the film—an ice ax, a flare gun, a spear, a handgun, and a piton gun. And there is something potentially unsettling about the shot in which the Predator leader brusquely hands Lex the ceremonial spear as a final gift and rite of passage (thus re-creating the scene from *Predator 2* in which a Predator leader gives Harrigan an antique eighteenth-century flintlock pistol as a reward). The scene implies that Lex's ironic reward for her singular victory is nothing less (or perhaps nothing more) than a symbolic phallus.

But like the Alien head and tail that become Lex's primary weapons, this Predator weapon is also an extension of the monstrous-feminine. Just as Jim and Selena resist guns in their battle against the soldiers, Lex largely rejects Weyland's symbolic firepower in favor of Other weapons. And if she is phallicized in her final shot, it is precisely a ceremonial gesture that has little bearing on either her narrative journey or her conquest of the Queen. The film's consistent indictment of the phallocentric male gaze also subverts a final reading of Lex as phallic woman. The last gaze of the film is Lex's as she stares up at the departing Predator ship before walking purposefully toward a snow vehicle that is idling nearby. Notably, the subsequent and very last shot of the film shows the dead body of Lex's comrade, now lying in state on the Predator ship. The body spasms when a new breed of Alien, a chestburster with a Predator face, explodes out of the Predator's chest before the scene cuts to black and the closing credits. The film thus leaves the viewer with a hybrid of phallus dentatus and vagina dentata, a new species of monster that promises a sequel and guarantees the return of the repressed.

Last One Standing

Like the entire *Alien* franchise, *AVP* is loosely inspired by the work of H. P. Lovecraft, particularly his novella *At the Mountains of Madness* (1936). Lovecraft, a literary pioneer in horror fiction, has long been a source of notoriety and debate owing to the explicit racism in both his personal and professional writing.[5] As Charles Baxter puts it in his review of Lovecraft's oeuvre, "Racism is not incidental to Lovecraft's vision but is persistent and essential to it. Ethnic minorities and monsters are, for him, often interchangeable." Baxter further points out that "[m]ixed in with the racism is the inevitable misogyny, which is not scary but horrifying. Progressing through the eight hundred pages of *The Annotated Lovecraft*, the reader is likely to notice the general absence of women and of any female protagonists." In *AVP*, Lex's identity as a black female hero *and* the one who lives to tell the macabre tale flies in the face of Lovecraft's original racist and misogynist mythology.

A heroine like Lex is ultimately out of place, whether on Mount Everest or in the entire Lovecraftian world in which she finds herself. Considering that none of the films in the *Alien* and *Predator* franchises includes a black female character (although black male characters play prominent roles in both franchises), she is also out of place in these specific SF universes. But it is her very "out-of-place-ness" that renders her subversive and complicates perceptions about what is "normal," especially in the speculative genre. In her book *Purity and Danger: An Analysis of the Concepts of Pollution and Taboo*, Mary Douglas makes an observation about dirt: "[I]f uncleanness is matter out of place, we must approach it through order. Uncleanness or dirt is that which must not be included if a pattern is to be maintained" (41). The cultural theorist Stuart Hall has extended the symbolism of Douglas's "matter out of place" to social constructs like race and gender: "[Y]ou don't worry about dirt in the garden because it belongs in the garden but the moment you see dirt in the bedroom you have to do something about it because it doesn't symbolically belong there." Lex, a black woman, is "matter out of place" because she "doesn't symbolically belong" in a SF action thriller or a Lovecraftian horror tale, genres that prioritize white male subjectivity and heroism. If she disrupts these patterns of representation by her mere presence, then she surely implodes them by being the hero.

For speculative heroines writ large, the trade-off for being *the* protagonist in a film is often nudity, objectification, and a thin plot. The female predecessors to a groundbreaking SF heroine like Ripley are sex symbols such as Loana (Raquel Welch) in *One Million Years B.C.* (1966) and Barbarella (Jane Fonda) in *Barbarella* (1968). And sexuality continues to be a prerequisite for modern SF heroines, as Jeffrey Brown notes in his study: "The leather-clad or wife-beater wearing heroine armed to the teeth is such a cliché that films like *Barb Wire* [1996], *Catwoman* [2004], *Aeon Flux* [2005], *Elektra* [2005], *Ultraviolet* [2006], and *Bloodrayne* [2005] offer little else to viewers other than the sexual spectacle of a beautiful woman doing backflips, throwing punches, and firing weapons" (244). Brown argues that the few exceptions to the cliché are "all featured in well-written and directed movies" (245) and cites Ripley, Sarah Connor in *Terminator 2* (1991), and Beatrix Kiddo (Uma Thurman) in *Kill Bill: Volumes 1* and *2* (2003 and 2004). One could presumably add more recent examples like Katniss Everdeen (Jennifer Lawrence) in *The Hunger Games* tetralogy (2012, 2013, 2014, and 2015) and Ryan Stone (Sandra Bullock) in *Gravity* (2013).

These exceptions demonstrate that black actresses are still waiting to be cast in "good" speculative films as primary or solitary protagonists, even in the new millennium. Whereas black actors such as Wesley Snipes, Will Smith, and Denzel Washington have appeared in successful big-budget productions such as the *Blade* franchise (1998, 2002, and 2004), *I, Robot* (2004), *I Am Legend* (2007), and *The Book of Eli* (2010), the same cannot be said of black actresses. One must turn either to Razzie nominees and critical failures like *AVP*, *Gothika* (2003), and *Catwoman*—"bad" movies that have unambiguous black heroines—or to "well-written and directed movies" such as *28 Days Later* (or a twentieth-century predecessor like *Strange Days*), which relegate the black heroine to secondary status. But its faults notwithstanding, *AVP* remains a singular example of a blockbuster SF horror film that portrays a black woman as a serious and primary hero without resorting to sexual spectacle or a default white male partner. Anderson's directorial vision aside, Lex also embodies difference in a way that challenges, interrupts, complicates, and subverts hierarchal identity categories and dichotomies.

Lex is the obvious hero right up to her very last shot, when she marches alone across the snow, the camera filming her from a zooming-out bird's-eye view until she is a tiny red-clad form in the desolate glacial landscape. The scene mirrors her opening shot, where she is also a tiny figure methodically making her way up a glacial wall. In both cases, her isolation in a hostile environment connotes neither weakness nor the need for immediate rescue. Rather, she seems entirely self-sufficient, a default persona for white male characters on the big screen since the earliest days of Western cinema but still a rare one for black women. Jackson writes of Lex's concluding scene, "Given her survival skills, one can surmise that [Lex] will make her way to some rescue point, and that she will be able to tell her story. And perhaps, prepare for the next encounter, another visit from the Predators" ("Terrans" 251). The shooting script itself promises that "Lex will return in: A-P-A: Alien/Predator: Annihilation" (Anderson, *AVP*). But Lex does not return, despite Anderson's teaser. As Jackson points out, the 2007 sequel, *Aliens vs. Predator: Requiem*, directed by the Brothers Strause, never refers or returns to Lex in any way. But Lathan's performance in *AVP* illustrates her ability to carry a film and to keep audiences invested in a narrative with a black female hero. One cannot dismiss the film's critical weaknesses, but its worldwide financial success still stands. And its ability to show a black female character in new and creative ways without resorting to blatant stereotypes is unprecedented.

CHAPTER 3

The Black Madonna: *Children of Men*

In their analysis of the 2006 dystopian film *Children of Men*, Terryl Bacon and Govinda Dickman censure director Alfonso Cuarón for his portrayal of Kee (Clare-Hope Ashitey), the central black female character: "Cuarón knows, he has to know, how racist and sexist the whole notion of Kee-the-fantasy-slave-girl-lost is, how perfectly she plays the role of abjected Child-Mother-of-the future" (157). Especially when read with two of the film's most memorable scenes in mind—the revelation of Kee's pregnancy and the birth of Kee's child (both in the presence of the white male protagonist)—this condemnation is understandable. It is almost impossible to dissociate Kee from centuries of racist and sexist Western iconography concerning the black female body. Unlike Selena and Lex, the respective black heroines of *28 Days Later* and *AVP*, Kee does not model "feminist bad-ass" (Siegel 124). If anything, she reinforces myths of black female sexuality, fecundity, primitiveness, and naïveté. As Sayantani DasGupta puts it, "Kee is all fertility, 'savage' simplicity, bestiality, and childlike trust" (188).

Although Cuarón's film is a loose adaptation of P. D. James's 1992 novel *The Children of Men*, his screenplay (cowritten with Tim Sexton) makes a number of major changes, including the creation of Kee's character. Kee, an "African" refugee (her country of origin is never explicit) and the only reproductive female on the entire planet, does not appear in the novel. Human infertility is certainly a dominant theme in James's work, but she imagines the future of the species through a pregnant white British woman. Cuarón rewrites this role specifically for a black African woman, in part because of the standing "Out of Africa" or single-origin theory that humankind originated on the African continent. As he states in an interview, "We wanted her to be a black African. There are many different reasons—one is, that as far as we know, human life sprang out of Africa. There is the notion that the future of humanity resides on the dis-possessed—the lumpen of the lumpenproletariat on that continent" (Wagner). Drawing on a Marxist vocabulary, Cuarón situates Kee (implic-itly a genetic "key") as both an originary Eve and a symbol of the future, an African subaltern who will ultimately save a decaying postmodern planet. As such, the director deploys a form of Afro-optimism in which Africa is the once and future "cradle of civilization." Readings of Kee, a black woman, as a last hope, messianic figure, and Madonna all have sub-versive potential.

And yet, her visual performance on the screen rarely fulfills that po-tential. Kee's importance to the plot is consistently eroded by her unim-portance in almost every other aspect of the film. To briefly illustrate this point, let me use the original film poster, which features a close-up of the white male hero, Theo Faron (Clive Owen). The unshaven hero frowns slightly as he gazes stoically at the viewer through a broken pane of glass. Owen and costars Julianne Moore and Michael Caine get top billing on the poster—the unknown Ashitey is not included. Indeed, Ashitey, nineteen years old at the time of filming and in the middle of her university stud-ies, had acted in only one other film before *Children of Men*. The names of the starring actors and the film title are printed in white below a series of short narrative teasers in red block capital letters: "The year 2027: The last days of the human race. No child has been born for 18 years. He must pro-tect our only hope." The 2007 DVD cover has a slightly different design—instead of gazing through broken glass, the hero peers furtively around a corner. But the teasers on the DVD cover are identical to the poster. The blurb on the back similarly highlights the roles of Owen and Moore and relegates Ashitey's part to a nameless "young pregnant woman" whom the hero must save in order to "deliver the miracle the whole world has been waiting for." Without belaboring the point, suffice it to say that the film's marketing captures Kee's ironic insignificance (given her role as "only hope" and "miracle") throughout the film. And as Bacon and Dickman in-dicate, the scenes in which Kee does take center stage are fraught, to say the least. Their point that "Cuarón *knows*" (157, emphasis added) is a fair one given the lengths to which the camera seems to go to fetishize Kee's black female body.

In my first chapter, I noted both the absence of black women in Brit-ish speculative cinema and the spectacularization of the few black women who do appear in lead roles. Cuarón's new millennial representa-tion of Kee simultaneously shows the viewer something new in the con-text of British speculative films and something very old in the context of the white Western imaginary. If one reduces the pregnant Kee's story arc to its most basic terms—pre-birth, birth, and post-birth—she is (to my knowledge) the first black female character to perform that arc in a British speculative film. Her childbirth scene, the subject of a special feature on the DVD edition ("Visual Effects: Creating the Baby"), involves prosthetics, animatronics, and revolutionary computer-generated imagery (CGI). Framestore, the British special effects company charged with making the birth sequence and the baby look as real as possible, describes the process on its website as "one of the most demanding VFX [visual effects] briefs of 2006."[1]

As part of the broader theme of fertility, pregnancy and childbirth are familiar tropes in speculative cinema, and these tropes have become more overt with the evolution of production codes, rating systems, and special effects.[2] Pregnancy and birth often serve as metaphors, and *Children of Men* is no exception. Especially in the context of global infertility, Kee's singular ability to conceive and give life has all kinds of allegorical possibilities, including the Afro-optimism that Cuarón intimates. In this respect, Kee is a notable departure from earlier models of black womanhood in British speculative films (and speculative cinema more widely). Of course, mother figure is a role commonly ascribed to black female characters, including those in speculative films. Mace in *Strange Days* (1995) has a young son. Kaela Evers, also played by Angela Bassett, in *Supernova* (2000) becomes pregnant at the very end of the film. Selena in *28 Days Later* is targeted for her reproductive ability and periodically performs maternity, even as the film evokes themes of female creation and destruction. But pregnancy and childbirth are never more than vague histories or prospects in these films. Although Tania Modleski rightly argues that the black woman in film is often "too literally a woman (reduced to her biology and biological functions)" (133), explicit portrayals of the pregnant black female body and the black female body in childbirth are quite rare in speculative cinema, in keeping with the rarity of the black female body writ large.

The closest cinematic predecessor to *Children of Men* in terms of visually foregrounding black female reproduction is Jonathan Demme's 1998 adaptation of Toni Morrison's award-winning 1987 novel *Beloved*. Faithful to Morrison's original plot, the film version features pregnancy and childbirth through Sethe (Oprah Winfrey and Lisa Gay Hamilton) and Beloved (Thandie Newton). Both *Children of Men* and *Beloved* are film adaptations by male directors of speculative novels by celebrated female authors. But where Demme's film is at least grounded in a neo-slave narrative about the horrors of racism and sexism, especially against the black female body, Cuarón's film is a more generic critique of what he calls "the state of things" ("Interview"). As much as *Children of Men* tackles xenophobia, police brutality, and violence against Others, it never targets specific histories of prejudice against black women. Thus, Kee's originality as a black Madonna is again ironic—her graphic reproductive role, which sets her apart in speculative cinema, is the same role that has stigmatized black women for centuries.

As Jennifer Morgan observes in her discussion of early modern travel writing, "English writers regularly directed readers' attention to the sexually titillating topic of African women's physiognomy and reproductive experience. In doing so, they drew attention to the complex interstices of desire and repulsion that marked European men's gaze on Amerindian and African women" (178). Kee's body, particularly as seen through the gaze of the white male hero, is precisely all of these things—titillating, desirable, and repulsive. Is it possible, then, to track agency, empowerment, and/or subversiveness in Kee? To do so, one must begin with the fact that she is, to borrow Zahid Chaudhary's words, "too much: Eve, Madonna, Earth Mother, figure of subjection, animal-like black woman, humanity's last and only hope, excessively fertile black woman, damsel in distress" (96). Multiple and fluid identities can result in a more nuanced portrayal of black womanhood, as a character like Selena demonstrates. But all of Kee's signifiers are hyperbolic, and it is only as hyperbole, then, that she can shed light on and perhaps critique racist and sexist histories.

A useful psychoanalytic concept here is the fetish, which Anne McClintock discusses at length in her work *Imperial Leather: Race, Gender and Sexuality in the Colonial Contest*: "Far from being merely phallic substitutes, fetishes can be seen as the displacement onto an object (or person) of contradictions that the individual cannot resolve at a personal level. These contradictions may originate as social contradictions but are lived with profound intensity in the imagination and the flesh" (185). McClintock examines the ways in which imperial discourses fetishized blackness and Africanness, and how such fetishism became inextricable from phallocentric Freudian readings of the female body. Kee is very much *the* fetish in *Children of Men*, although there are certainly other examples, which I will discuss. Chaudhary makes this point as well, observing that Kee is "the fetish object of the film's liberatory narrative" (96). First as pregnant Madonna and then as Madonna with child, she functions as an object of awe, confusion, power, and worship but always on decidedly male terms. Since her pregnancy is a divine mystery, she is also the fetish as enigma: "Women became the Dark Continent, the riddle of the Sphinx—exoticized and implicitly racist images drawn from an Africanist iconography. Constructing women and colonized people as a riddle ('the Woman Question,' 'the Native Question') allows privileged European men to answer the riddle in terms of their own interests" (McClintock 193). Even behind the camera, this dynamic plays out in the relationship between the white director Cuarón and the black teenage newcomer Ashitey. When asked about how she chose to portray Kee, Ashitey implied that she had little room for interpretation: "Alfonso comes in and won't play games with you and tells you this is who she is, which makes my job a bit easier" (Morales).

This chapter situates Kee as a multilayered metaphor for "Africa" and, simultaneously, a powerful example of the fetishized black female body, a reading that acknowledges the film's evocation of historical stereotypes and Eurocentric models of power. Cuarón may or may not be aware of the fundamental ironies in his representation—indeed, his *invention*—of Kee. She is the most important character in the film and yet the least important character in the marketing of the film. She is only ever truly seen through a white and/or male gaze, and the film both models and encourages voyeurism where her body is concerned. Certainly, the film channels what E. Ann Kaplan calls the imperial gaze, which "reflects the assumption that the white western subject is central, much as the male gaze assumes the centrality of the male subject" (*Looking* 78). A number of Kee's primary scenes recall offensive nineteenth-century discourses regarding black femininity. But these ironies and contradictions become part of her hyperbolic excess, which arguably transcends the director's intentions. It is her *over*determination as signifier and fetish that makes Kee a compelling metaphor, particularly for "Africa."

In his work *The Idea of Africa*, V. Y. Mudimbe writes, "Only from the eighteenth century on is there, thanks to the Enlightenment, a 'science' of difference: anthropology. It 'invents' an idea of Africa. Colonialism will elaborate upon the idea. But one could continue the declension. Out of the idea, Africa has become a metaphor" (30). Cuarón extends the eighteenth-century "science," the nineteenth-century "invention," and the twentieth-century "metaphor" of Africa into the twenty-first century. Critics stress that Kee is, by turns, silenced, spoken for, and fought over, but also radical and quite literally heavy with promise. On the one hand, she models Africa's historical role as a resource to be mined and the stereotypical projection of Africans as parasitic refugees whose primary gift or curse is the ability to reproduce. Yet the much-discussed conclusion to the film also hints at a newfound independence for this African mother and her newborn daughter. It is in Kee's ambivalence as a signifier that we can find her agency. And reading her as a stand-in for "Africa" yields new insights into and new allegorical possibilities for her character.

The background and cultural heritage of an actor adds another layer to the performance of Otherness. Like Naomie Harris, Clare-Hope Ashitey was born in London to immigrant parents. Although Harris plays a British woman in *28 Days Later*, using her own English accent, she is well known for her Jamaican accent in *White Teeth* (2002) and the *Pirates of the Caribbean* films (2006 and 2007).[3] Similarly, Ashitey admitted in an interview that she auditioned for Cuarón's film with her own English accent but was asked by the director to "have this African accent" for the role (Morales). Drawing on her Ghanaian heritage, she cultivated a generic "African" accent, but she also admitted in the interview that "the dialogue isn't conducive to what I feel is [an] African accent." This detail reminds us that "Africa" is *always* being imagined, invented, and performed and that such performances do not necessarily line up with a so-called reality.

Last One to Die Please Turn Out the Light

Given that the film is set in 2027 but draws heavily on contemporary discourses about immigration and border protection, it is worthwhile to consider how Africa as a geographic location features in this futuristic narrative. Long before Kee's first appearance, the viewer is introduced to the dystopian setting through the protagonist, Theo Faron—a jaded, disheveled, middle-aged white man living in Britain, which is now a visibly decaying police state. Shot entirely on Super 35mm film, *Children of Men* has a documentary-style look, which is partially achieved by Cuarón's trademark use of handheld cameras and long takes. Even before the opening scene, while the screen is still black, two alternating male and female English voices narrate the news: "Day 1,000 of the siege of Seattle. The Muslim community demands an end to the army's occupation of mosques. The Homeland Security bill is ratified. After eight years, British borders will remain closed. Deportation of illegal immigrants will continue."[4]

The voice-over news continues as the camera captures the first shot—a bleak but crowded coffee shop. Everyone is gazing up at the mounted television screen, which is broadcasting the day's top story, the death of the planet's youngest citizen, eighteen-year-old "Baby Diego." An apathetic Theo shoulders his way to the counter and orders a coffee that he takes out into the busy London streets. Like *28 Days Later*, which includes markers such as the London Eye and an overturned red double-decker bus in its postapocalyptic world, *Children of Men* makes London instantly familiar. Red double-deckers roll by, and St. Paul's Cathedral is just visible in the distance above the white smog. The brief shot of the famous cathedral is not unlike the iconic photographs of it during the Blitz. As if to invoke that World War II history, a bomb goes off in the next shot as the camera shifts fluidly from the cathedral to Theo spiking his coffee with whiskey and then back to the coffee shop, which explodes. As a woman stumbles out screaming and clutching her severed arm, the title appears, accompanied by a high-frequency whine that simulates tinnitus for both Theo and the viewer.

This introduction to Britain as a violent but recognizable dystopia is quickly expanded to include the rest of the world, which is also in a state of ruin. Theo boards a train, which coasts past angry protesters and darkly humorous graffiti: LAST ONE TO DIE PLEASE TURN OUT THE LIGHT. A television screen on the train provides a quick summation of the world's state of affairs. The names of cities flash across the screen over a montage of burning buildings, marching protesters, corpses, and explosions. The city names begin to appear in rapid succession accompanied by dramatic music: Paris, Moscow, Washington, Kuala Lumpur, Tokyo, Brussels, Hong Kong, and so on. Eventually, the names appear so quickly that they cannot be read. The music climaxes with the words "The world has collapsed." The montage cuts to footage of Big Ben and the slogan "Only Britain Soldiers On" emblazoned across the Union Jack as the famous bell tolls. Of course, this propagandist claim to British exceptionalism has already been rendered hollow by the opening explosion and will continue to be contradicted by the subsequent images of the death and destruction taking place on British soil.

Aside from contextualizing the postapocalyptic landscape, this government propaganda video serves another interesting purpose. If one were to pause the DVD in order to back up and review the names of all the cities in the video, one would find European capitals, Asian capitals, and North and South American capitals and metropolises represented.[5] Each city name is accompanied by brief footage appropriate to that city—the Eiffel Tower, the Kremlin, the United States Capitol, and so on. Although these sites are all under siege—smoke billows from the Petronas Towers and rioters swarm the Coliseum—they remind the viewer of humanity's accomplishments, even as they signal humanity's demise. However, not a single African city appears on the screen—not Cairo, or Lagos, or Johannesburg—nor does the video include the Giza Plateau or, say, Nelson Mandela Square. Does this mean that Africa—the second-largest continent, the second most populous continent, and the continent with the most nation-states—is exempt from the so-called collapsed world? Or does Africa not merit representation because its collapse is somehow always already implicit? Whatever the logic for this directorial decision (or oversight), the absence of Africa in this video on "the world" sets the ironic tenor for the entire film where representation of the continent is concerned.

Once again, Africa is "dark" and exists outside time and space. One can recall here Georg Hegel's dismissal of Africa in his introduction to *Lectures on the Philosophy of History*: "At this point we leave Africa, not to mention it again. For it is no historical part of the World; it has no movement or development to exhibit. Historical movements in it—that is in its northern part—belong to the Asiatic or European World" (117). Cuarón seemingly takes Hegel's snub a step further since Africa is *not* mentioned in the video—its presence is signaled only through its absence and omission. The only time Africa is explicitly mentioned ("not to mention it again") is when Theo is kidnapped by his former romantic and activist partner, an American woman named Julian Taylor (Julianne Moore). He is held in a small room that has been completely pasted over with newspapers. One headline in particular stands out at the beginning of the scene: "Africa Devastated by Nuclear Fall Out." As a signifier, Africa plays a familiar part in this Western film—a vague and monolithic place that appears in a fleeting reference but does not merit the inclusion or heterogeneity that is afforded other parts of the world.

The primary manifestation of Africa, then, is the pervasive presence of refugees, or "foogies" as they are called, in detention camps and ghettos. At this early stage in the film, Africa seems to have little to offer the dystopian world except its stereotypical lumpenproletariat, what Frantz Fanon terms "the wretched of the Earth." These are the "illegal immigrants" described by the newscaster in the opening voice-over, the ones trying to get into Britain despite its closed borders. Fanon, writing in the early 1960s when the decolonization of Africa was at its height, argues that "[t]he lumpenproletariat constitutes a serious threat to the 'security' of the town and signifies the irreversible rot and the gangrene eating into the heart of colonial domination" (81). This mid-twentieth-century image of African masses rising up against their European colonizers translates to this futuristic film, where African masses rise up again, this time in a symbolic postcolonial return to Britain, which is still "the heart of colonial domination." *Children of Men* renders these masses nameless and faceless. They are filmed in washed-out colors, wearing nondescript clothing, rounded up in cages and buses, kneeling before police on sidewalks, or marching in the streets. Granted, the foogies of the film are not only from Africa. The viewer gets hints of the diversity contained within the masses throughout the film. When Theo walks past a cage full of detained people, one woman calls out in Serbian and another woman in German. Later, when Theo smuggles Kee into Bexhill, a refugee camp, the viewer is immersed in a cultural crucible—sights, sounds, and languages blend together in a nighttime cacophony. But Kee becomes the symbolic face of the masses—the one foogie who matters and who represents the people outside the system and outside representation.

Kee is already mythical even before she appears on the screen. Julian and her underground militant group, the Fishes, kidnap Theo because he has government connections and can procure transit papers for Kee. As Julian explains to Theo, "A girl. She's a foogie. Need to get her to the coast. To pass security checkpoints." Baffled, Theo responds, "I haven't seen you for nearly twenty years and you come asking me for transit papers." The strangeness of Julian's request suggests that this "girl" is not just any refugee. And it is here that Theo's own symbolic significance begins to take shape, especially as a foil for Kee, the film's metaphorical "Africa." As a civil servant who works for the Ministry of Energy, Theo is easily read as a representative of government bureaucracy. His character is distanced from the more violent performances of masculinity that take place throughout the film. Despite the omnipresence of security police, Islamist militants, and terrorist groups, all of whom carry guns, Theo never handles a weapon in the film.

His closest friend, Jasper Palmer (Michael Caine), is a former political cartoonist who now lives secretly in the forest with his disabled and catatonic wife Janice (Philippa Urquhart).[6] As a couple, the Palmers represent a history of activism (much like Theo and Julian), as well as a bygone era, which is captured in Franco Battiato's melancholy cover of the 1966 song "Ruby Tuesday." The chorus appropriately coincides with a shot of Jasper and Theo flanking Janice's wheelchair and draping a scarlet shawl around her neck. Their triangular formation is mirrored in the next close-up shot—an old photograph of Theo and Julian holding their long-dead toddler son, Dylan. In his DVD commentary on the film, Slavoj Žižek describes Jasper as an "old, obscene, impotent, retired hippie person," a description that loosely extends to Theo as well. For Theo is similarly cast as an aging man who has effectively checked out of life and left his sexuality and activism behind, largely because of personal tragedy. In a curious inversion of the 1960s hippie slogan "make love, not war," Theo and Jasper do neither.

Figure 3.1. Theo (Clive Owen) enters the Ark of the Arts, where his cousin Nigel (Danny Huston) has preserved Michelangelo's *David*, in *Children of Men* (2006).

This aging and impotent version of white British masculinity, which arguably stands in for "Britain" itself despite the fact that it is a police state, manifests in another key scene—the Ark of the Arts. Tempted by Julian's promise of £5,000 for the transit papers, Theo arranges a meeting with his cousin Nigel (Danny Huston). Nigel is the affluent Minister of Arts who can arrange the papers but who doubles as a postmodern Noah figure, rescuing (Western) masterpieces from the unfolding apocalypse. This entire sequence is a commentary on the end of "civilization" as it exists in Britain. Theo is driven by a chauffeur in a luxury Rolls-Royce to the Ministry of Arts, which is located in the recognizable and long-defunct Battersea Power Station, and then ushered into Nigel's penthouse foyer. Here one finds a provocative moment of intertextuality between *Children of Men* and *28 Days Later*. The latter film features a copy of the Greco-Roman sculpture *Laöcoon and His Sons* in the foyer of Major Henry West's commandeered mansion. In that film, the sculpture is an implicit symbol of West and his performance of a violent and misogynistic masculinity.

Children of Men also includes a famous marble sculpture as a stand-in for masculinity, albeit a different kind of masculinity. As Theo enters Nigel's "sterile" home, something brings a cryptic smile to his face. Only when the camera rotates around to his back, so the viewer sees what he sees, does the source of his smile become clear. Michelangelo's towering sculpture *David* stands at the end of the corridor in front of floor-to-ceiling windows. The sculpture's left calf is missing and has been replaced with a metal rod, but it looks otherwise intact. Nigel then materializes in a white T-shirt and jeans and stands in front of the statue. His appearance puts the size of the sculpture in perspective—his head does not even reach its knee. "Couldn't save *La Pietà*," says Nigel. "Smashed up before we got there." He then glances proudly up at the *David*. "Pretty rummy, huh?" The camera continues to follow Theo as he approaches Nigel and the sculpture. "My mum had a plastic one in the bathroom," Theo observes. "It was a lamp." Since the camera cannot contain the entire fourteen-foot sculpture in its close-up shot of the two men, the *David* is gradually minimized to its lower half, its genitals hovering above them until their embrace obscures it entirely. The entire sequence is accompanied by the 1969 song "In the Court of the Crimson King" by the British rock band King Crimson, whose lyrics further convey loss and disenchantment.

If the sculpture *Laöcoon and His Sons* in *28 Days Later* connotes a violent but condemned patriarchy, then *David* in *Children of Men* suggests another kind of condemnation. The sculpture—a personification of Western male youth and beauty—is damaged and obsolete in this dystopian world. Theo's Baudrillardian comment implies that the worth of the "real" *David* and that of his mother's plastic *David* lamp are now one and the same. The occlusion of the sculpture's genitals, cut out of the frame in an act of visual castration, is another reminder of the impotence that marks even the young men of the world. Indeed, the very next shot is an extreme close-up of a young man's face, his neck and jawline occupying the whole screen. Pimples are visible on his hairless cheek, and a graffiti-style tattoo of the word CRAZY is inked across his neck. Another close-up shows his tattooed right hand controlling a small video game monitor by way of a wired wristband. The hand moves robotically beside an untouched plate of prime rib. Finally, the camera reveals the young man himself, an attractive teenager in an argyle sweater who ignores everything except his video game. Seated beneath Picasso's *Guernica* on the wall, he completely tunes out the multicourse meal and the dinner conversation between Theo and Nigel. The only time the young man stirs, at Nigel's insistence, is to take a series of unidentified pills with his left hand (and without looking away from the monitor). Like the beautiful *David*, the young man (typically read as Nigel's son but sometimes as his lover) is damaged and disconnected.

In *28 Days Later*, West says to Jim, "Women mean a future." And these words resonate in *Children of Men* as well, which associates male characters in particular with death and endings. Following the stabbing of eighteen-year-old "Baby Diego" at the very beginning of the film, the newscaster announces that "the mantle of the world's youngest human has passed to a woman—eighteen years, five months, and eleven days old." Since Kee herself is about eighteen years old, she is also one of the planet's youngest people and another potential, albeit undocumented, contender for the "youngest" title. But this announcement foreshadows the miraculous birth of her child, a girl. The future, then, does not lie with the males of the species, a point that Theo sums up when he stands with Nigel in front of a window overlooking the city: "A hundred years from now there won't be one sad fuck to look at any of this." Two things are visible outside in the gloomy industrial landscape—a giant inflated pig and one of the four white Battersea chimneys.

Much has been made of this pastiche, which simulates the cover of the 1977 Pink Floyd album *Animals*. Critics read it as another Orwellian layer to the film, a playful symbol of apocalypse (pigs fly), a gibe at the police state, and, as Samuel Amago writes, "an ironic synecdoche for Great Britain" (222). To these creative readings I would simply add the phallic symbolism of the chimney, which (like the entire power station) no longer serves a purpose beyond the decorative. Theo's pronouncement on an almost extinct humanity is also a pronouncement on masculinity. In this respect, the phallus is a dominant fetish in the film, whether it manifests as the disabled sculpture of *David*, the obsolete Battersea chimney, a bus advertisement for Niagra (an erectile dysfunction pill), or Theo's cigarettes, which he lights but never finishes. The phallus as fetish is ultimately a source of self-deprecation and mockery, even as it conveys a predictable castration anxiety.

But the film's strategic devaluation and displacement of the phallus opens up a space through which to find feminist agency in Kee, the "other" and most powerful fetish in the narrative. Undoubtedly, Kee's fetishization as black Madonna reinscribes racist and sexist discourses, as I have already noted. She is the *object* of white male fetishism rather than the *subject* of black female fetishism. But she also demonstrates McClintock's point that, "[a]lthough the fetish is a compromise object [between castration or denial], it does not necessarily embody only two options. Fetishes can involve triangulated contradictions, or more than three. . . . Considerable theoretical rigor and subtlety are lost if all fetishes are reduced to the magisterial phallus" (202). To locate these contradictions, one must look not just at Kee's objectification but also at her subjectification—her moments of voice, choice, and resistance (however fleeting) outside Eurocentric and phallocentric systems of representation. Her ambivalent role as Other and "Africa" can facilitate this reclamation of female and feminist agency.

My Baby Is Not a Flag

The MacGuffin of the film is something called the Human Project—a mythical group of scientists who are "out there" searching for a cure. The viewer learns that this clandestine group has a sanctuary in the Azores, can only be contacted via a medical ship named the *Tomorrow*, and can only be reached by boat. Like everyone and everything in the film—Kee, Theo, mass infertility, and so on—the Human Project can be read as metaphor. As a final destination for Kee (a black female fugitive and a stand-in for "Africa"), the Human Project is ostensibly freedom and independence. I will return to the implications of the Human Project in my discussion of the film's ending, which (like *28 Days Later* and *AVP*) is ambiguous. But in this section and the next, I want to chart Kee's symbolic journey to the *Tomorrow*.

The main players in helping Kee reach the coast are Theo, Julian, an eccentric but grandmotherly white British midwife named Miriam (Pam Ferris), and Julian's second-in-command, a young black British man named Luke (Chiwetel Ejiofor). Each of these characters has a different stake in Kee, and *all* of these characters lose or sacrifice their lives because of her. As a dispirited colonial figure, Theo initially has a financial incentive to help Kee. The only reason he physically accompanies her is that he has procured joint transit papers, which necessitate his presence. Julian, the leader of the Fishes, presents herself as an egalitarian freedom fighter who will facilitate Kee's path to freedom in the same way that she champions democratic rights for all foogies. Julian functions as both white American savior and white Western feminist, emblematic roles that arguably contribute to Kee's objectification as a black African woman. Miriam, a dreadlocked spiritualist who practices what Kee calls "voodoo woodoo," is charged with the safe delivery of the baby. And Luke, despite pretending to believe in the Human Project, soon reveals his true agenda, which is to appropriate Kee's child as a political bargaining chip for the Fishes. Luke is the primary antagonist of the film, a figure comparable to Major West in *28 Days Later* in terms of his deception and eventual use of force. But the fact that the villain in *Children of Men* is a black Brit is significant, a point to which I will also return.

The journey begins with the nostalgic tenor of a family road trip, another detail that echoes *28 Days Later*. The host on the car radio station even proclaims, "The afternoon is looking good here on Radio Avalon. And now one for all the nostalgics out there. A blast from the past all the way back, from 2003. That beautiful time when people refused to accept the fu-

Figure 3.2. Kee (Clare-Hope Ashitey) is escorted to the Human Project by her various self-appointed guardians.

ture was just around the corner." The song is "Wait" by the indie rock duo The Kills, which features an American female vocalist and a British male guitarist. This British-American band merely complements what the camera is already showing the viewer—this trip is initially about Theo and Julian. Although Kee appears on camera for the first time (thirty minutes into the film)—a sullen teenager wearing a gray cloak, matching hairband, and white earphones—she is visually marginalized. Wedged alongside Miriam and Theo in the backseat, while Luke and Julian ride in front, Kee is a "minor" in both age and importance. However, she engages in an early act of resistance here when she speaks her opening line to Theo: "What the fuck are you staring at?" Theo dismisses Kee's question as teenage rudeness, but in the context of cinematic ideologies that regularly conspire to objectify the black female body, her question is an urgent one that extends to the viewer as well. This fleeting challenge to the imperial white male gaze notwithstanding, the primary subjects on the road trip are Theo and Julian, who quickly lapse into silly flirtation, much to Kee's amusement.

I need not oversell the symbolism of this British-American partnership, two "benevolent" and historically allied white guardians with an African child under their aegis. Captivated by the mouth-to-mouth Ping-Pong ball trick that Theo and Julian play ("Do it again!") and by their consequent kiss ("That's disgusting!"), Kee embraces her infantilized role. And when Julian is unexpectedly and violently assassinated in a coup secretly planned by Luke, Theo instinctively becomes Kee's protector, dutifully taking up the "white man's burden." This concept, named for Rudyard Kipling's 1899 poem, has long been what David Spurr calls "a metaphor for the civilizing mission [and] a recurring theme in colonial writing" (111). It portrays colonialism as a benevolent enterprise—an onus on the white West to lift its black brethren out of literal and metaphorical darkness and into the light of "civilization." Such rhetoric, which became a pretext for physical and psychological colonization, extends from the earliest days of colonialism in Africa to the mid-twentieth-century decolonization of the continent. The logic of all the European colonial powers, including Britain, was that African colonies could not manage without their more "civilized" colonial masters.

Western cinema regularly facilitates this logic by way of the imperial gaze, as Kaplan points out: "Even reformist thinkers, missionaries and educators are incapable of understanding the position of the Other and their own gaze structure vis-à-vis them. Anxiety, in this case, is displaced into a condescending paternalism" (*Looking* 78–79). In *Children of Men*, Theo's original identity as a self-serving and financially motivated chaperone for Kee gradually morphs into an identity of moral guide, voice of reason, and representative of knowledge and progress. And in another of the film's great ironies, it is not Theo who initially claims the "white man's burden" but rather Kee, who foists this role upon him by observing that only *he* has the power to save her now that Julian is dead. Even Theo's initial plea of ignorance regarding the *Tomorrow* is not enough to weaken Kee's conviction that he can and will get her to the boat. Writing on Kipling's representations of white masculinity, Edward Said eloquently observes, "One became a White Man because one *was* a White Man; more important, 'drinking that cup,' living that unalterable destiny in 'the White Man's day,' left one little time for idle speculation on origins, causes, historical logic" (227). Theo implicitly has no choice—he *is* the White Man (not Miriam, Luke, or, for that matter, Julian) and *must* take on that "burden" or "destiny."

After Julian's death, Miriam, the midwife, also adopts a new role as spiritual guide to Kee. She prays over Julian's body in the forest, repeating the Sanskrit mantra "Om Shanti," which is spoken at other points in the film.[7] She then instructs Kee, who is kneeling beside her, to raise her hands over the body as well. In the car, Miriam chants another mantra, "Om Mani Padme Hum," which Kee begins to parrot. If Theo is now responsible for guarding and guiding Kee's body to safety, then Miriam seems loosely responsible for her soul. Indeed, when speaking of Miriam's spiritual practices, Kee says to Theo, "She smited me with that. Said it was good for my baby." Of course Miriam does not present colonial Christianity here but a kind of Asian fusion of Buddhism and Taoism, as well as a professed belief in the paranormal. Neither does she model the genteel and domestic femininity that was part of the colonial message to African women. However, she functions in much the same way that white British women did when they were stationed among the indigenous peoples of the Empire as teachers, nurses, and missionaries. Together with their "menfolk," these women were responsible for the "uplift" of their colonial charges, especially other women. As Patricia Grimshaw and Peter Sherlock observe, "The female missionary organizations pursued the ideology of separate spheres of activity, focusing on the tasks of teaching girls, domestic training, modeling Victorian and Edwardian womanhood, providing medical care in the form of nursing, and entering exclusive female spaces" (184). As a midwife, Miriam already functions as a practitioner of specialized knowledge on women. But she symbolically becomes Kee's white female "guru" as well, thus complementing (but not upstaging) Theo's role as white male hero.

Theo and Miriam are also set up in direct contrast to Luke and the rest of the Fishes, who very quickly become the obvious enemies in the film, even more so than the hostile police presence. Despite his Britishness, Luke aligns himself with the oppressed foogies for whom he is fighting. As a black man, he cannot represent colonial Britishness in the same way as Theo. Instead, he functions more like the vanguard of anticolonial African nationalist leaders—men who were raised and educated in a colonial tradition but who served as the first agitators for independence and the first leaders of the decolonized nation-states. My emphasis on men here is intentional, since women, despite being crucial participants in nationalist movements, were rarely the public faces of these movements and not a single newly independent African nation appointed a woman as its head of state. Luke's interest in Kee is similarly suspect and recalls what Amina Mama describes as the "betrayal of women's interests by the [African] nation-states" (54) after independence.

As an antigovernment rebel who is willing to resort to extreme violence, Luke's politics also reflects such militaristic (and masculinist) freedom movements as South Africa's Umkhonto we Sizwe (MK), Kenya's Mau Mau, and Mozambique's Liberation Front (FRELIMO). Part of Luke's logic for seizing power is precisely that Julian's philosophy of peaceful activism does not work. As he declares to Theo near the end of the film and just before his own death, "Julian was wrong. She thought it could be peaceful. But how can it be peaceful when they try and take away your dignity?" Luke further demonstrates the ambivalence of representation since he is

both a sincere freedom fighter and a "savage" killer who murders inno-
cents (including the pacifist Jasper). The safe house of the Fishes, a remote
farm out in the country, can be read along similar lines—as both an idyllic
retreat removed from the smog and squalor of London *and* as an indicator
of the group's primitivism. The farm is pastoral but also primal—mud, animals, and "nature" abound.

It is on the Fishes' farm that Kee makes her infamous revelation to
Theo, summoning him to the barn where she stands amid hay, cows, and
milking machines.[8] After declaring that she does not trust anyone except
him (on Julian's advice), Kee disrobes before a stunned Theo, who ultimately proclaims, "Jesus Christ!" at the sight of her swollen belly. Indeed,
there are resonances of the virgin birth as a mezzo-soprano sings a sacred aria in John Tavener's original composition "Fragments of a Prayer."
The camera maximizes the suspense by first shifting from Kee's ample
breasts, which are visible for only a second, to her naked back. From that
angle, she faces away from the viewer and toward Theo, whose expression
is awestruck. The camera zooms in on his face, but the viewer cannot yet
see what he sees. As with the scene in the Ark of the Arts, where the *David* is revealed to be the source of Theo's smirk, the viewer must again *see*
in order to understand. And the viewer is not disappointed. The camera
returns to Kee, panning leisurely across the black-and-white cows before
traveling up her body to take in her short white undergarments, her pro-
truding belly, her breasts (now discreetly covered by her left arm), and
her frightened expression. Neither the death of "Baby Diego" ("a wanker"
in Theo's words) nor Michelangelo's masterpiece of the male nude could
move Theo, but Kee's pregnant female body does. As such, her body fig-
uratively displaces the phallus but in so doing becomes its own powerful
fetish.

Laura Mulvey's psychoanalytic work on film situates "woman" as a
source of anxiety for the male gaze because she lacks a penis and thus signals castration. Mulvey further argues that the two coping measures for
the male unconscious are either voyeurism—"investigating the woman,
demystifying her mystery"—or "fetishistic scopophilia, [which] builds up
the physical beauty of the object, transforming it into something satisfying in itself" ("Visual Pleasure" 64). In a fitting illustration of this point,
Luke and another male Fish come racing into the barn to check on Kee,
while Miriam trails behind them. For a split-second, the three men stand
together and stare unabashedly at Kee, performing a combination of voyeurism and fetishistic scopophilia. For Kee is demystified, at least for Theo
("She's pregnant!"), even as she is rendered erotic and miraculous by the

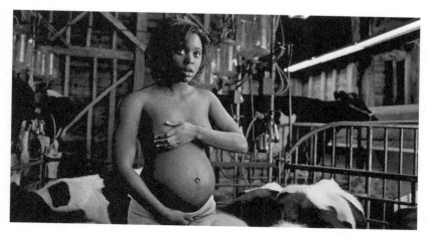

Figure 3.3. Kee reveals her pregnancy to a stunned Theo.

camera and the collective male gaze. Miriam then bustles past the men and into the cow pen, which she enters by raising a symbolic barrier and then closing it behind her. The men remain outside the pen while Miriam stands inside amid the cows helping Kee to put her dress back on. In this ambivalent moment, Miriam enacts her own female and perhaps feminist interruption of the male gaze, but she simultaneously showcases her privileged access to Kee's body as an authoritative white woman.

Remarkably, however, this controversial scene may also be the first sign of agency for Kee. The sign is tenuous, to be sure, but Kee has extended dialogue here (she educates Theo on the mutilation of dairy cattle) and she makes an independent decision by choosing to reveal her pregnancy to Theo. If Kee's reliance on Theo as the one true guide to safety is clichéd and replicates the "white man's burden," then it at least precipitates the finding of her voice. In the very next scene, the Fishes sit around a large kitchen table debating what to do next. When one woman declares, "This baby is the flag that could unite us all," Kee retorts, "My baby is not a flag." This exchange takes on greater significance in the context of the African nationalist movements that the Fishes emulate. If Theo, the aging white colonial presence, represents one kind of patrimony for Kee, then Luke and the Fishes represent another. McClintock, for example, cites Fanon (whom she admits sometimes "knew better") as an example of gendered nationalism: "For Fanon, both colonizer and colonized are here unthinkingly male, and the Manichean agon of decolonization is waged over the territoriality of female domestic space" (154). She further notes that "[w]omen are typically constructed as the symbolic bearers of the nation but are denied any direct relation to national agency" (154). Kee's value to the Fishes lies in her reproductive body and her potential to bear a son (as Luke wrongly predicts) who can serve as a symbol of unity. A reading of Kee as a metaphorical "Africa" encourages one to revisit the "value" placed on black women and their bodies not only by patriarchal white colonialists but also by patriarchal black anticolonialists. The subtext here is that true independence for Kee lies with neither Theo nor Luke. In explicitly rejecting the Fishes' claim on her child as a flag (another kind of fetish), Kee finally begins to articulate her own aspirations for herself and her unborn baby.

It's a Girl

In Bexhill, the seaside town turned refugee camp, Kee gives birth to her daughter and eventually boards the rowboat that will take her to the *Tomorrow*. The events leading up to the birth scene crystallize Theo's role as paternal white male hero and Kee's role as his dependent. Despite Cuarón's comment on the DVD edition that "from the standpoint of an action hero, [Theo] is the most clumsy action hero you could ever see" ("Theo"), there is little to detract from Theo's patriarchal authority on the screen. Props like his whiskey bottle and the fact that he spends much of the film in flip-flops are cosmetic and hardly unsettle his newfound role as hero. Once Luke's intentions are clear, Theo becomes the agent of action and movement in the film, in keeping with what Mulvey considers the classic male role in cinema. He orchestrates an escape from the farm with Kee and Miriam in tow, moves them to his own safe house (Jasper's hideaway), and then smuggles them into Bexhill.

It is not in action, then, that one will find the strongest examples of Kee's agency. For the entire second half of the film, she is swept along by the plans of others. When her contractions begin on the bus into the camp, Theo and Miriam consult and advise in their joint roles as informed guardians. At a checkpoint, Kee is almost seized by a guard with a sniffer dog, but Miriam quickly distracts the guard and gets taken instead. In Bexhill, Theo finds them temporary housing with a Romanian foogie named Marichka (Oana Pellea) and then delivers the baby that night. The one name that Kee calls out on a regular basis, particularly during her labor, is "Theo." When the guard who smuggled them into the camp returns the next morning and discovers the newborn infant, Theo and Marichka (a new ally) attack the guard and then rush Kee to safety in a wheelchair.

And when Luke and the Fishes storm the camp and briefly kidnap Kee and her daughter in the midst of a gun battle with government troops, Theo braves the bullets and explosions to locate her. In another of the film's memorable scenes, Theo escorts Kee and the newborn out of a crumbling tenement that has become the primary combat zone. The infant's cries are enough to cause a temporary ceasefire, and soldiers on both sides of the conflict fall to their knees in awe until a mortar shell breaks the spell and the battle resumes. With Marichka's help, Theo then finds a small rowboat and rows them out to sea and the buoy that is the rendezvous point for the *Tomorrow*.

In none of these moments is Kee particularly active. Even in the climactic birth scene, she is strangely secondary as Theo lays down his coat, washes his hands, calls out encouragement, and ultimately holds the squalling newborn in the lamplight, pronouncing it a girl. Over the course of the film, Kee shifts frantically from one location to another—pursued, harangued, and literally manhandled. She is always in motion but always propelled by others, who lead, drive, support, wheel, cajole, and row her along. The literal scrambling for Kee is all too reminiscent of colonial powers and their historical "Scramble for Africa," but she also embodies "the white man's burden" of colonial rhetoric and the "mother of the nation" of black nationalist rhetoric. Again, she hyperbolizes some of the historical and decidedly contradictory ways in which "Africa" has been imagined. At the same time, however, she encourages us to look for those rare moments in which she imagines and invents herself. It is in *those* moments, when she expresses creative resistance to her own overdetermined role as object and fetish, that one can arguably find her agency. I will briefly highlight three interconnected scenes in the film that constitute such understated but critical moments of agency. These are also scenes of stillness and calm in which Kee and the viewer get a break from the frantic nonstop action. Since Kee is not a particularly active heroine like Selena and Lex, her moments of resistance take place in quiet private spaces where she is in a state of repose. But these spaces are strategically coded as safe, female, and removed from violent performances of masculinity. Kee finally says and does things that are of her own volition, demonstrating her histories and knowledge as a black female subject rather than a black female object.

The first scene takes place in Jasper and Janice's house, where Theo, Kee, and Miriam temporarily hide when they escape the Fishes' farm. Kee, still pregnant here, reclines on the couch beside Janice, whose long hair she is braiding. After teasing Theo (who stands at a distance) that she is a virgin and then laughing at his confusion, Kee announces that she will

"name [her] baby Froley." The second scene takes place in the home of another elderly couple, Russian foogies who live in Bexhill and who provide
food and shelter for a few hours. Kee has given birth by this point and lies
on an antique double bed with the baby beside her. The Russian woman
sits nearby in a wheelchair and sings a lullaby while offering Kee sections
of a peeled orange. Marichka also hovers over the baby girl, tickling her.
Laughing, Kee declares to Theo (who is again across the room), "I want to
call her Bazooka." The third and final scene takes place in the rowboat,
where Kee and Theo wait for the *Tomorrow*. As Theo slowly bleeds to death
from a gunshot wound, Kee says to him, "I'll call my baby Dylan. It's a
girl's name too." By the time she spots the *Tomorrow* on the horizon, Theo
is dead. But Kee is able to smile to her daughter and promise that they are
"safe now" before singing her own Ghanaian lullaby.

There is continuity between these scenes, all of which involve a provi-
sional safety, a sympathetic older generation (particularly women in the
first two examples), and a new name for the baby girl. Notably, women
like Janice, the anonymous Russian woman, and Marichka create a female
sphere for Kee without objectifying or patronizing her in the ways that
Julian and Miriam do. Among these women, all Others like herself, Kee
is more confident and more outspoken but also more of a person. In other
words, her hyperbolic excess is suspended and her character is given more
depth. She demonstrates a clever sense of humor by pretending to be a virgin and then laughing infectiously. The rituals of braiding hair and singing lullabies become part of the female sphere but also a reminder that
Kee has her own cultural practices to draw upon, which are not inherited
from the West. Thus, the scenes challenge that "gaze structure which fails
to understand that, as Edward Said phrases it, non-American [and non-
Western] peoples have integral cultures and lives that work according to
their own, albeit different, logic" (Kaplan, *Looking* 78).

Kee's ritual of choosing a name for her child is especially important because naming has historically been a male ritual. McClintock discusses
the colonial practice of naming "discovered" or "virgin" lands at length,
and her observations are useful for contextualizing the naming of Kee's
daughter:

Historically, the male desire for a guaranteed relation to origin—secur-
ing, as it does, male property and power—is contradicted by the sexual
doubling of origins, by women's visibly active role in producing a child and
men's uncertain and fleeting contribution. To compensate for this, men
diminish women's contribution (which, as Irigaray notes, can hardly be

Figure 3.4. Kee finds a brief moment of rest with her newborn daughter, Dylan, and Other women who are "foogies" like herself.

questioned) by reducing them to vessels and machines—mere bearers—without creative agency or the power to name. The insistence on the patrimony marks a denial: that something different (a woman) is needed to guarantee the reproduction of the same—the son with the same name as the father. The sexual scene of origins, I suggest, finds an analogy in the imperial scene of discovery. By flamboyantly naming "new" lands, male imperials mark them as their own. (29)

Here McClintock pinpoints the ways in which territory was claimed, much like offspring, by imperial powers. Female genesis is both irrefutable and threatening to patrimony, which then stamps its own proof of origin and strips the woman of her creative role. For Kee, the first pregnant woman in almost two decades and a metaphorical "Africa," an "insistence on the patrimony" is inevitable, which is why her reclamation of "creative agency [and] the power to name" is significant.

Luke, of course, continues to connect Kee's child explicitly to maleness by predicting that it will be a boy. Even after the birth, he says to Theo, "We need the baby. We need him." Theo's correction that the baby is a girl stuns Luke, who has clearly not considered how a girl will serve his cause. But Theo himself invokes patrimony early on by asking Kee, "Who's the father?" Her answer—"Fuck knows"—undoubtedly contributes to the stereotype of black women as "naturally" promiscuous. She even admits, "I don't know most of the wankers' names." However, this absence of a fa-

ther or even the potential name of a father also disrupts the male imperial narrative of staking a claim. Certainly, there is room here to read the
anonymity of Kee's sexual partners and her ignorance of their names as
a direct rejection of the Name of the Father. Kee flippantly dismisses the
name of her baby's father and, in so doing, dismisses a paternal claim on
her child. Even Kee's joke that she is a virgin becomes a gibe at the imperial myth of empty and untouched "virgin" territory waiting to be pen-
etrated. Kee's invention of the name "Froley," her first creative act, forecloses the possibility of "the son with the same name as the father."

Once Kee gives birth to her daughter, she rejects "Froley" as "a man's
name" and comes up with another name, "Bazooka." Whether or not Kee
is serious about this possibility is not the point. Her new choice extends
her creative agency but also indicts the war that is now literally raging
all around her and the phallocentric system that underpins that war. She
chooses "Bazooka" in Bexhill, which is being overrun by troops and tanks.
Even in the peaceful Russian apartment, where the strains of the second
movement of Sergei Prokofiev's Violin Concerto No. 2 fill the room, mixing
with the women's laughter, gunfire and heavy shelling is still audible outside. As a phallic instrument of war, "Bazooka" is a powerfully ironic name
for a baby girl. If "Froley," a made-up name, is a commentary on the baby's
nameless and thus claimless biological father, then "Bazooka" is a commentary on the more symbolic patriarchy that threatens to destroy Kee
and her child rather than save them.

In the rowboat, Kee settles on her final choice for her daughter's name,
"Dylan." This choice is another provocative example of ambivalence in
the film. On the one hand, her decision to name her daughter after Theo's
dead son seemingly brings us back to patrimony and the legacies of colonialism. Theo expresses staunch disapproval of Kee's previous name
choices, but "Dylan" is her last gift to him—he smiles peacefully and then
dies. Despite Theo's role as an aging and obsolete white guardian, a dying British presence, the naming of Kee's daughter suggests that his legacy
continues. But Kee's gesture is not only about honoring Theo, Julian, and
their child. It is also about self-invention and adaptation. As Kee rightly
observes, again showcasing her own knowledge, "It's a girl's name too." Instead of the Father claiming a son, we have a mother claiming a daughter
and choosing a name that does not only belong to boys, or only belong to
Theo, or only belong to the West. Patrimony is inverted here as Kee takes
Theo's legacy and makes it her own.

Žižek is enthusiastic about the film's ending, where freedom and safety
lie in the rootlessness of a boat on the open sea. As he puts it in his DVD

Figure 3.5. Kee and Dylan on the rowboat waiting for the *Tomorrow*.

audio commentary, "The condition of the renewal means you cut your roots—that's the solution." Kee has left her pursuers, her guardians, and British soil behind. Just as the rowboat arrives at the buoy, government bombers fly overhead and destroy Bexhill with warheads. So there is no going back for Kee, only forward. But Sarah Trimble provides a necessary admonition to overly optimistic readings of the ending: "A transnational alternative to the English state's insular authoritarianism, the Human Project is nonetheless fraught with peril for a black stateless woman whose value inheres in her reproductive body. What will Kee exchange for safe passage on the *Tomorrow*? How does the spectre of a deferred transaction haunt the ending of *Children of Men*, implicating its vision of (renewed) futurity in a history of transatlantic trafficking in bodies?" (258). Trimble rightly highlights the historical dangers of seas and boats for a black woman like Kee, whose metaphorical significance as "Africa" makes her final scene in a rowboat waiting to be picked up by the *Tomorrow* all the more haunting. The gray fog blankets the waters, and the dead Theo slumps to one side. Kee looks small and lost, particularly in relation to the *Tomorrow*, a large vessel with only white male sailors visible on deck. As with the NATO jet in *28 Days Later*, the Human Project is hardly a guarantee of protection and safety.

The viewer must look to the last image of Kee herself, because the aptly named *Tomorrow* is merely on the horizon and yet to arrive. For the immediate present, then, Kee is "safe now," as she puts it. "Now" is the here, the present, and the moment. With her child, she is not alone and her resources are her own. Much like the African continent, she is still physically and symbolically connected to Europe, if only because Theo haunts the boat. But Kee is finally her own keeper, and the rowboat, not the *Tomorrow*, is our final and perhaps definitive image of her. Trimble writes of this shot that Kee and Dylan "are adrift between two already unfolding processes . . . the destruction of Bexhill and its inhabitants by a violent state apparatus and the 'rootless' isolation of the Human Project" (267–268). Indeed, this mother and daughter are between spaces and processes, but they are also, for the first time, free. Throughout the film, Kee is "too much." But in this concluding scene, she is arguably just enough as she sits calmly on the water, the light of the buoy flashing nearby as she sings to her daughter—an appropriate final image and metaphor for Africa as the once and future "cradle of civilization" in a lost world.

CHAPTER 4

Thank Heaven for Little Girls:
Beasts of the Southern Wild

The opening scene of Benh Zeitlin's 2012 fantasy film *Beasts of the Southern Wild* features a ramshackle trailer sitting precariously on top of two massive oil drums. The trailer is silhouetted against a gray sky, and thunder rumbles in the distance. The scene is literally a dark one until a light goes on inside the trailer. Someone is apparently home inside the curious structure. That someone is a little girl named Hushpuppy (Quvenzhané Wallis), the African American child protagonist of the film. As the wind howls outside, Hushpuppy sits cross-legged on the floor, fashioning a mud perch for a baby chicken. The bird cheeps as she places it atop the mud—it seems satisfied, in the same way that Hushpuppy seems satisfied with her own perch, suspended above the land. The viewer quickly learns that, despite being only six years old, Hushpuppy claims ownership of this house and lives there alone. But the viewer also sees the fragility of her house and, by extension, her sense of place and belonging in the wider world.

Although this book focuses primarily on black women in speculative cinema, I have a number of reasons for including a child protagonist. Hushpuppy provides a unique opportunity to explore representations of black girlhood in the genre. I have already emphasized the absence and erasure of black women in British and American speculative cinema. Characters such as Selena in *28 Days Later*, Lex in *AVP*, and Kee in *Children of Men* are rare, not least because they have central parts in their respective narratives. But if adult black women in major roles are scarce, then black female children are all but invisible. A 1992 episode of *Star Trek: The Next Generation*, "Rascals," includes a twelve-year-old version of the black female character Guinan (Isis Jones), who experiences age reversal as a result of a transporter glitch. An episode of *Doctor Who: Series 2* (2006), suggestively titled "Fear Her," also features a twelve-year-old black girl, Chloe

(Abisola Agbaje), with the ability to trap people inside her drawings.[1] In the film adaptation of book 1 of *The Hunger Games*, which came out the same year as *Beasts of the Southern Wild*, twelve-year-old Rue is played by a black actress (Amandla Stenberg). But Rue is a minor character, despite the lasting impression she makes on the white heroine Katniss. And even the casting of Rue as black was a troubling source of controversy on Twitter as so-called fans of the book expressed their "disappointment" in Rue's ethnicity. Lastly, the obscure 2016 zombie film *The Girl with All the Gifts*, in starring a black female child protagonist, Melanie (Sennia Nanua), is an extraordinary example in British horror cinema.[2]

So black girls (like their adult counterparts) are rarely the center of a cinematic narrative, rarely featured on a film poster, and rarely visible in the imaginary worlds that speculative fiction brings to life. For this reason alone, *Beasts of the Southern Wild* merits inclusion. The fact that Hushpuppy is a very young child is especially unusual considering that the aforementioned examples all feature adolescents. The memorable film poster and subsequent DVD cover image, which function as a "first look" for the film, set up a powerful visual dynamic in terms of what to expect. In a blurry impressionistic shot, a solitary Hushpuppy runs straight toward the camera with a Roman candle firework in each outstretched hand. Nighttime colors, deep purples and greens, swirl around her and blend with the white light of the fireworks to convey a sense of magic. Even without seeing the film, one can take something away from this image, namely, that it places a young black girl at the center of things. Although Hushpuppy's domineering father, Wink Doucet (Dwight Henry), is a main character, the story is always and unambiguously hers. Cinematographer Ben Richardson even describes the camera's perspective as an extension of Hushpuppy: "I tried to just be Hushpuppy's sense, if not literally her eyes." And instead of materializing at a later point in the narrative, as Selena, Lex, and Kee do, Hushpuppy is the first character to be seen and heard on-screen. Thus, she shows us something surprisingly radical where representations of black femininity in speculative cinema are concerned.

Shot on location in Louisiana, *Beasts of the Southern Wild* invokes the recent memory of Hurricane Katrina and the ongoing aftermath of that storm. But the film does not have the dark look of the digitally filmed *28 Days Later*, the Lovecraftian atmosphere of *AVP*, or the hyperrealism of *Children of Men*. (The last two were produced with Super 35mm cameras.) Instead, the grainy Super 16mm film conveys an aesthetic as gritty and vivid as the central characters themselves. Hushpuppy is part of an iso-

Figure 4.1. The memorable film poster for *Beasts of the Southern Wild* (2012) places the young protagonist Hushpuppy (Quvenzhané Wallis) literally front and center.

lated multiethnic community called "the Bathtub," which is located on a bayou and cut off from the mainland by a levee. Much of the film deals with the threat of displacement for this small community (with a population of eighty-seven, according to the town sign) and for Hushpuppy in particular. A primary goal for this child protagonist is to eke out a place and identity that cannot be easily uprooted. As she states early on in a voice-over, "They think we all gonna drown down here. But we ain't going nowhere." She models a bold resistance to different symbolic forces: her violent alcoholic father, the apocalyptic storm that is about to descend, the prehistoric aurochs that climate change has released from polar ice caps, and the government workers who threaten a forced migration for the Bathtub residents.

On the one hand, the Bathtub is a fierce, proud, and vibrant community—a magical place with a seemingly infinite supply of parades, seafood, and moonshine. The Bathtub residents celebrate everything, including the pending storm season. Yet the opening shot of Hushpuppy's trailer and subsequent scenes of the Bathtub also convey abject poverty and a sense of exposure, whether to the elements or to other dangerous forces. The film thus operates along the lines of the "ethnographic" in that it presents a mythologized people in their so-called natural habitat. Even the title of the film is reminiscent of an early-twentieth-century ethnographic "classic" like *Nanook of the North* (1922). In both cases, the title implies a documentary-style focus on a specific Other body (Beasts/Nanook) *of* a specific Other place (the Southern Wild/the North). The emphasis on "Beasts" of the "Southern Wild" obscures the fact that there are human characters and pitches the film more like a wildlife documentary. The "Beasts" here have a double meaning since they connote both the aurochs of the South Pole *and* the inhabitants of the Bathtub.

In her study *The Third Eye: Race, Cinema, and Ethnographic Spectacle*, Fatimah Tobing Rony writes, "The people depicted in an 'ethnographic film' are meant to be seen as exotic, as people who until only too recently were categorized by science as Savage and Primitive, of an earlier evolutionary stage in the overall history of humankind: people without history, without writing, without civilization, without technology, without archives" (7). Although *Beasts of the Southern Wild* is not quite the "ethnographic film" that Rony describes, it nonetheless invokes the codes of ethnographic cinema. The Bathtub appears to exist outside (Western) time and space and to function without the telltale markers of (post)modernity—radio, television, computers, cell phones, Internet, "modern medicine," governance, currency, and so on. The people themselves embody cultural "authenticity," closeness to nature, and naïveté, in keeping with the generic role of "natives" in ethnographic spectacle.

At face value, then, the film appears to be about "noble savages" on an inevitable collision course with "civilization," or what Hushpuppy calls "the Dry World." Bell hooks interprets the film in much this way, declaring in her review that she is "deeply disturbed and militantly outraged by the images [she has] just seen" ("No Love"). Hooks argues that Hushpuppy is stereotyped, eroticized, and marginalized and that the film is guilty of simply regurgitating old myths of black primitivism, black violence, black sexuality, and so on.[3] But I submit that Hushpuppy effectively interrupts the ethnographic spectacle, rendering it a pseudo- or faux-ethnography, by functioning interchangeably as voice-over narrator, active screen subject, and returner of the gaze. If, as Rony puts it, "the 'ethnographic' in film works to deny the voice and individuality of the indigenous subject" (71), then *Beasts of the Southern Wild* inverts that model by hinging entirely on Hushpuppy's voice and individuality. Hushpuppy practices what Rony describes as "third eye" perception by looking back at and even appropriating those external gazes that attempt to negate or exoticize her presence. As a speculative narrative, the film already complicates the semblance of scientific documentation promoted in early ethnographic cinema. But since Hushpuppy herself identifies as a keeper of cultural records, indeed an ethnographer, she becomes the definitive teller of her own story and that of the Bathtub.

In psychoanalytic terms, the film also provides a provocative cinematic example of a mother-daughter relationship that confounds the patriarchal Law of the Father. In her discussion of the "maternal melodrama" *Stella Dallas* (1937), Linda Williams asks, "What happens when a mother and daughter, who are so closely identified that the usual distinctions between subject and object do not apply, take one another as their primary objects of desire? What happens, in other words, when the look of desire articulates a rather different visual economy of mother-daughter possession and dispossession?" ("'Something Else'" 5). Hushpuppy's love-hate relationship with her father dominates the screen, but her mother drives the story and functions as her primary object of desire. Feminist film critics have long grappled with the oedipal function of the maternal and the mother's "unrepresentability in any but patriarchal terms" (L. Williams, "'Something Else'" 16). Initially, Hushpuppy can *only* know her absent "Mama" through the memories and stories of her present father.

In her seminal work "Mama's Baby, Papa's Maybe: An American Grammar Book," Hortense Spillers suggests that the African American female has long occupied a singularly misrepresented position because she displaces the Law of the Father yet lacks legitimacy and authority: "[T]he African-American woman, the mother, the daughter, becomes historically the powerful and shadowy evocation of a cultural synthesis long evaporated—the law of the Mother—only and precisely because legal enslavement removed the African-American male not so much from sight as from *mimetic* view as partner in the prevailing social fiction of the Father's name, the Father's law" (80). Spillers is clear that this imposed historical role on African American women is a cruel distortion but one that might be reclaimed from a feminist perspective. Notably, *Beasts of the Southern Wild* inverts the stereotypical model of an African American family by showing a present father and an absent mother. But this inversion of the mother in the film doubly negates her—she does not embody the misleading but potentially recoverable Law of the Mother, and she can only embody lack under the patriarchal Law of the Father. Hushpuppy's symbolic repossession of her nameless African American mother complicates both of these maternal misrepresentations and is arguably the main investigative project for the protagonist and, by extension, the viewer.

The entire film is a steady buildup to the meeting and the look of desire between Hushpuppy and her mother—a moment that permanently destabilizes Wink's patriarchal versions of these female characters. Citing the work of Julia Kristeva, E. Ann Kaplan argues that patriarchy both fetishizes the female form and represses the maternal as a means of foreclosing "the aspects that would bind woman to woman" (*Women* 6) and daughter to mother. Wink dresses Hushpuppy in what the screenplay describes as "boys' underpants and a child-sized wife-beater" (Alibar and Zeitlin 1) and treats her exclusively as a son. She is permitted to perform only stereotypical masculinity in his presence—displays of physical strength, periodic alcohol consumption, and "no crying." As Kaplan puts it, "Woman qua *woman* thus disappears, rendered as she now is in likeness to man" (*Women* 5). Since Wink is dying of a mysterious illness, his interest in Hushpuppy is also inextricable from his own mortality and his desire to leave something behind. The Bathtub thus functions as a patrilineal inheritance, which Wink impresses upon Hushpuppy. "Someday when I'm gone," he says, "you're gonna be the last man in the Bathtub." Later, he solemnly vows to his daughter, "You're gonna be king of the Bathtub."

If Wink fetishizes his daughter's female form by "deny[ing] its *difference*; he incorporates it into his own body in addition by dressing the female in male attire" (Kaplan, *Women* 5), then he also fetishizes Hushpuppy's mother, albeit in a more predictable fashion, in his erotic flashbacks. Until Hushpuppy meets her mother, the only visual images of Mama are filtered through Wink. He relates the story of Hushpuppy's conception, which allegedly took place after Mama (Jovan Hathaway) single-handedly killed an alligator with a shotgun and then served the gator meat for lunch. Mama is filmed exclusively from the back, naked except for her white underwear. She cocks the (phallic) shotgun in slow motion, shoots one round, and then rotates to one side. The camera zooms in on her underwear, which is now covered in the alligator's bright red blood. The camera then zooms out so that a profile of her lower body fills the screen. She silently poses for both Wink and the camera, her right hand leaning casually on the shotgun, her left hand on her hip, and blood staining her inner thighs. Wink grins, and the camera provides an extreme close-up of Mama's right eye as she coquettishly winks at him. This scene epitomizes Laura Mulvey's argument that the cinematic female body is "bearer of the bleeding wound" ("Visual Pleasure" 58), a manifestation of male castration anxiety. This fragmented and blood-spattered image of Mama is pure fantasy and pure symbolic lack.

But the film models a feminist reclamation of mother and daughter by way of its confrontational female subject and a gaze that subverts the (dying) father and his self-professed kingdom. Hushpuppy seeks not only symbiosis with her mother but a means of speaking and representing her own subjectivity outside a patriarchal language and ideology. Also citing Kristeva, L. Williams indicates that a complete break from patriarchal systems of representation may be impossible but that certain films afford female spectators "moments of resistance in which two women have been able to represent themselves to themselves through the mediation of their own gazes" ("Something Else" 21). Although Hushpuppy is a little girl, a fact that situates her even more squarely within an oedipal framework, she consistently attempts to represent herself and her mother in ways that are not defined by her father. The conclusion, as in *28 Days Later*, *AVP*, and *Children of Men*, is ambiguous. Yet again, one is unable to categorically pronounce a happy ending. But also like the previous films I have discussed, the lack of a happy ending for the black female character is not the same as the lack of possibility. Like Selena, Lex, and Kee, Hushpuppy has the literal and figurative last word in the narrative and a concluding agency that at the very least conveys change, if not outright hope.

Incidentally, *Beasts of the Southern Wild*, like *Children of Men*, is a loose adaptation of a literary work, in this case Lucy Alibar's one-act play *Juicy and Delicious* (2012). And the character Hushpuppy was originally "a sweet little Southern boy" (Alibar 6). But Alibar, who cowrote the screenplay with Zeitlin, reinvented Hushpuppy as a little girl, "an unkempt and seemingly uncared for six-year-old with a gaze of unmistakable wisdom" (1). The DVD feature "The Making of *Beasts of the Southern Wild*" also clarifies that the open casting call for the role of Hushpuppy did not specify race, much like the part of Lex in *AVP*. Quvenzhané Wallis, five years old when she auditioned in 2009, made the strongest impression and won the part despite no previous acting experience. She went on to become the youngest nominee for the Best Actress Academy Award, and her performance is regularly credited with making the film a success. As Roger Ebert writes in his glowing review of both Wallis and the film, "Here is a case of a great role finding the perfect actress to play it." Wallis has since proven to be more than a proverbial one-hit wonder by garnering similar acclaim for her starring role in an otherwise unremarkable cinematic remake of the musical *Annie* (2014).

The Bathtub

The first five minutes of the film immerse the viewer in Hushpuppy's world. After the opening shot of Hushpuppy's trailer, the camera takes the viewer through a typical morning for its child protagonist. Wearing a white undershirt, orange underwear, and white rubber boots, she wanders out into a makeshift yard of hay and old tires where pigs, chickens, cats, and dogs roam free. These initial shots of a poor and unkempt black child in rural Louisiana certainly border on white ethnography. But Hushpuppy's voice-over immediately and literally interrupts that facade and continues to do so over the course of the film. Rony points out that in 1920s Western ethnographic cinema, "the filmmaker speaks for native peoples, raising the problem of the ethics of ventriloquism" (154). Implicit and explicit narration, including the expository intertitles of silent films, contextualized and "translated" the film images for a target white audience. Even the present-day infomercials of humanitarian organizations, which "document" child poverty in non-Western nations, require a Western voice to raise funds on behalf of the "natives." As Rony puts it, "Ethnographic ventriloquism *assumes* the inarticulateness of the Native" (155).

The fact that Hushpuppy relates her own story in her own words affords her that authoritative voice typically reserved for an adult, white, and often male presence. She picks up a baby chicken and places it against her ear, listening to its heartbeat, which is amplified so that the viewer also hears it. "All the time, everywhere, everything's hearts are beating and squirting and talking to each other in ways that I can't understand," she states confidently in the voice-over. Although she is implicitly talking to the viewer, her words are an internal monologue that functions independently of an audience. For Hushpuppy, the world itself is a subject of study, and she spends her time listening, exploring, and sometimes cataloging what she finds. The camera follows her, rendering her its subject, but also regularly cuts to her perspective so that the viewer sees what she sees. Hushpuppy is the documenter rather than the documented, and her habit of drawing her findings and her allusions to "the scientists in the future" position her as the ethnographer of the film.

As she absorbs and records her world, Hushpuppy also questions it, and she expresses curiosity about life outside the Bathtub. The film clearly evokes the trope of Primitive versus Modern in its juxtaposition of the Bathtub and the Dry World. Writing of ethnographic "racial films" such as *Moana: A Romance of the Golden Age* (1926) and *Stark Love* (1927), Rony notes that "the distant Primitive is set explicitly in uncomfortable prox-

Figure 4.2. Hushpuppy serves as the primary subject of the film.

imity to emerging modern industrialism, providing the context for a rumination on loss and the passing of time" (132). The underlying question in these films is whether the Primitive can coexist indefinitely with or transition into encroaching modernity. Even if the Primitive is idyllic, as in *Moana*, its beauty and simplicity are inextricable from its placement in a prehistory that is out of touch with the realities of Western progress. *Beasts of the Southern Wild* explores these tensions through Hushpuppy's eyes. In one early scene, she and her father sit contemplatively in Wink's boat and float peacefully along the water. Across from them are the massive concrete levee and an industrial wasteland of factories and smokestacks. "Ain't that ugly over there?" asks Wink, before pronouncing, "We got the prettiest place on earth." The stark contrast between the "ugly" Dry World and the "pretty" Bathtub is an aesthetic and narrative device that the film repeatedly employs. But Hushpuppy's perspective allows the film to evade simplistic answers and solutions, in part because she questions everything, including her father's rigid dichotomies, which extend to gender roles as well.

If the Bathtub is a figurative Eden, then it is also an oedipal patriarchy in which Wink considers himself king. Hushpuppy and her father live in equilibrium, and their mutual understanding is epitomized by their demarcation of space, their respective houses, and the clothesline that they share.[4] Wink instills a sense of identity in his daughter that is inextricable from the Bathtub. But Hushpuppy also expresses that something is missing in her world and that her father is unable or unwilling to fill that void.

When Wink mysteriously disappears one day, the viewer gets to observe Hushpuppy in her own private rituals of self-sustainment, which are deeply rooted in fantasies of her mother. In the absence of what her father calls "feed-up time," Hushpuppy must feed herself. But instead of messily consuming a roast chicken among the household pets, she attempts to cook a meal that is inspired by Mama. She announces in her voice-over that "[e]verything we still got from Mama, I keep in *my* house." Her emphasis on the possessive pronoun conveys a sense of pride and ownership. She distinguishes herself from her father and *his* house, while simultaneously claiming her mother's things as her own.

This scene speaks to that "dialectic between the maternal unrepresentable and the paternal already-represented" (L. Williams, "Something Else" 11–12). Without the father's phallocentric system of representation, the mother cannot exist. Nonetheless, Hushpuppy *tries* to imagine and represent her mother in ways that are separate from Wink. Although Hushpuppy's trailer is cluttered with old furniture and knickknacks, there is an order and intentionality to it as well. A red basketball jersey with the number 23 on the back hangs ceremoniously on the wall, surrounded by Christmas lights that Hushpuppy turns on, transforming the jersey into a shrine. The jersey is a stand-in for Mama, whose head has been crayoned onto the wood paneling above the neckline. That Hushpuppy chooses a sports jersey to signify her mother is telling precisely because the woman-as-fetish is often a hyperfeminine spectacle, at least via the heterosexual male gaze. But since Hushpuppy herself dresses like a boy (at her father's behest), her equation of her mother with a "masculine" basketball jersey becomes a curious point of affinity between their female bodies. Kaplan argues that "male attire 'permits' female–female bonding because it pays lip service to a sexual difference we have all come to believe is necessary" (*Women* 5). Ironically, the jersey allows Hushpuppy to connect to her mother in a way that is premised on their shared femaleness *within* patriarchal traditions.

Draping the jersey over a kitchen chair for company, Hushpuppy makes dinner, reaching for pots and pans and holding an imaginary conversation with her imaginary mother. "Hi, my sweet baby," croons her mother in a playful but disembodied voice. "You being good like I taught you?" Hushpuppy is shy but enraptured with this maternal presence, and the entire scene is accompanied by a gentle jazz melody and soft translucent light.[5] Hushpuppy's mother even sings a simple but poignant ditty to match the jazz tune: "You're good. You make me happy." Certainly, there is something pre-oedipal or simply embryonic about this scene, which models what Kaja

Silverman describes as "the maternal-voice-as-sonorous-envelope" (73). The maternal voice is the initial and omnipresent voice for the child. As Silverman puts it, "[T]he mother's voice is a fantasy of origins—a fantasy about precultural sexuality, about the entry into language, and about the inauguration of subjectivity" (74). Hushpuppy's trailer (a space that Wink is not allowed to enter) becomes a private fantasy where she attempts to reconstitute her mother's body and voice. While her mother sings, Hushpuppy stares reflectively into the saucepan of cat food that she is frying for dinner. The close-up shot of the bubbling cat food frying in lard is itself vaguely primordial. Indeed, the screenplay calls it "a surreal churning vision, like the bubbling lava at the center of the earth" (Alibar and Zeitlin 13). The entire scene frames Hushpuppy's story as one of self-discovery that hinges upon the recovery of the primordial mother.

The viewer is reminded that this scene of maternal light and love is a fantasy when Wink's aggressive (and also disembodied) voice interrupts the reverie, shouting at an unseen pet outside. His sudden materialization restores patriarchal order to Hushpuppy's fantasy world and negates the already absent mother in the process. At the sound of her father's voice, Hushpuppy races out of her house to meet him and declares, "Daddy! Daddy! I learned lots of things while you were gone." One of her newly acquired skills is to "burp like a man," which she immediately demonstrates despite her father's obvious lack of interest. Wearing a hospital gown and bracelet, Wink ignores his daughter and stalks angrily through the high grass toward his tree house. Hushpuppy then asks derisively why he is wearing a "dress" and a "bracelet." This moment again showcases Hushpuppy's own indoctrination where symbols of maleness are concerned. Even her father's unintentional performance of femininity is inappropriate to her because it upsets those patriarchal systems of representation that he himself put in place. Indifferent to Hushpuppy's over-eager performance of masculinity in "burp[ing] like a man" and angered by her questions, Wink turns around just long enough to snarl, "Get out of here!" She retreats to her house while Wink returns to his own shack, gets dressed, throws a chicken on the grill, and yanks the clothesline to indicate "feed-up time."

But their brief altercation also triggers Hushpuppy's first overt act of rebellion. Because she is unable to win her father's approval, despite her adherence to his rules, she protests by turning up the flames on the gas stove, which ignite the saucepan of cat food and eventually her entire trailer. Hushpuppy's oppositional third eye perspective *and* her female gaze within a patriarchal system coincide and collude here. As flames engulf her house, she hides under a large cardboard box with a peephole. Resolutely, she crayons on the inside of the box while her father bursts into the trailer, frantically looking for her and calling out her name. After peering for a moment through the peephole, she returns to her drawing as her voice-over states, "If Daddy kill me, I ain't gonna be forgotten. I'm recording my story for the scientists in the future. In a million years, when kids go to school, they gonna know once there was a Hushpuppy and she lived with her Daddy in the Bathtub." Hushpuppy's practice of autoethnography again positions her as narrator and storyteller in this pseudo-ethnographic film. She wishes to preserve her story even if, as she ominously puts it, "Daddy kill me."

But her act of placing an eye at the peephole to look at her frantic father, who cannot see her, takes on more symbolic implications in the context of feminist film theory. Cinematic voyeurism has long been considered a male purview, but Hushpuppy temporarily usurps the gaze, quietly observing her "hysterical" father, who is now the spectacle as he blunders around the room looking for his daughter. The moment reiterates a classic dilemma of feminist film theory, namely, that it is only by way of masculine identification that the female spectator gains subjectivity. Yet Hushpuppy's ability to see without being seen lies very much in her identity as a little girl, one who can choose to disappear inside a box and thus secretly wield the power of the gaze. The traditional invisibility and erasure of black femininity also becomes ironic as Wink desperately yells, "Where you at?" Of course, the price of Hushpuppy's rebellion against the paternal is her house, which has been her primary, even sacred, site of maternal reclamation. Clenching the jersey in one hand, she sneaks out the door and into the woods with a furious Wink chasing after her while the trailer explodes in the background. In response to his verbal threats, she yells, "I'm tearing off just like my Mama!"

The incineration of Hushpuppy's house also leads to her first physical contact with her father, a telling detail given that the two of them spend most of the first twenty minutes of the film together. He roughly grabs her arm, prompting her to scream "no," and then he slaps her hard enough to knock her down. In retaliation, Hushpuppy stands up and proclaims, "I hope you die. And after you die, I go to your grave and eat birthday cake all by myself!" With a glare, she hammers her small fist once against his chest. Hushpuppy's threat of celebrating her father's death with birthday cake is easily read as childish spite, but it also symbolically equates his end with her beginning. Her actions also cause the first fantastical elements of what has so far been a realist narrative. When Hushpuppy strikes Wink, he collapses and begins to have a seizure while, in a parallel shot, an ice shelf collapses into the ocean. Hushpuppy is imbued here with the supernatural power to break the universe itself. Terrified and still clutching her mother's jersey, she runs through the trees and down to the shoreline, where she cries over the sudden thunder, "Mama! I think I broke something!" Hushpuppy now creates a new signifier for Mama in a remote beacon that blinks at regular intervals far out on the water.

One can draw a few conclusions by this point in the narrative. The film firmly aligns the viewer with its young black female protagonist and encourages the viewer to see and experience the speculative world entirely through her eyes. Although the film seemingly caters to a patronizing white gaze by way of ethnographic imagery *and* a male gaze by way of the fetishized female form—the protagonist, the absent mother, and even Hushpuppy's schoolteacher, Miss Bathsheba (Gina Montana), whom the screenplay describes as "sexy like a lady bullfighter" (Alibar and Zeitlin 8)—Hushpuppy's voice and gaze continue to interrupt and deflect hegemonic perspectives. And the symbolic power of the father begins to erode as the symbolic power of the mother increases. Admittedly, Mama remains disembodied and reduced to implicitly masculine symbols such as the basketball jersey and the beacon. The film continues to model that "dialectic between a maternal body that is too diffuse, contradictory, and polymorphous to be represented and a paternal body that is channeled and repressed into a single representable significance" (L. Williams, "Something Else" 11). In other words, Hushpuppy has yet to imagine the maternal body outside of a patriarchal language and a phallic economy. But her quest for a vocabulary and gaze that transcend the father remains subversive, especially in terms of a spectatorship that prioritizes black female subjectivity. Mama (a black female) is a powerful object of desire, but the desire is always mediated through Hushpuppy (another black female), which immediately complicates traditional white and male ways of seeing black femininity.

The landing of the apocalyptic storm arguably crystallizes Hushpuppy's oppositional female gaze. Wink allows his daughter to take shelter in his house but immediately undertakes precautions to prevent her from disrupting his male space. After pasting a long strip of duct tape down the middle of the floor, he lays down the new ground rules for their living arrangement: "Just because you burnt *your* house down, don't mean you can walk in here and take over. This side of the house is still Wink's side. No toys. No girl stuff over here. If I wanna come over there and smack you in the face, that's against the rules. So that's a plus for you." Wink retains control here and continues to embody the Law of the Father. His vague reference to "the rules," including the rules for when he can "smack [Hush-puppy] in the face," is a chilling reminder of the patriarchy that he repre-sents. As the storm rages outside, Wink barks orders to his visibly afraid daughter; his only means of comforting her is to resort to his own predict-able sense of patrimony and masculinity. "No storm can't beat no Doucet," he drunkenly brags. "We Doucets, we're not scared of no damn storm!" Arming himself with a headlamp, a shotgun, and a bottle of moonshine— the phallic props of his performance—Wink makes his way outside, where he shoots shell after shell into the dark sky. "Look at me! Look at me, Hushpuppy!" he yells over the storm.

In another important act of voyeurism, Hushpuppy puts an eye to a hole in the corrugated iron wall and watches her father "fight" the storm.[6] Granted, her gaze is invited, even demanded, this time by her father, who now intentionally makes a spectacle of himself. In his essay "Masculinity as Spectacle: Reflections on Men and Mainstream Cinema," Steve Neale notes that male bodies can certainly be put on display, but they are not typically eroticized in the same way as female bodies: "We are offered the spectacle of male bodies, but bodies unmarked as objects of erotic display. There is no trace of an acknowledgment or recognition of those bodies as displayed solely for the gaze of the spectator" (18). While the black male body undoubtedly has a different history of cinematic spectacle than the white male body, Wink evades an objectifying or eroticizing gaze in this scene. He is filmed in the darkness and rain, a combative and active fig-ure that the camera has trouble tracking. Nonetheless, Hushpuppy's act of "peeping" once again complicates notions of a default male spectatorship and a female "*to-be-looked-at-ness*" (Mulvey, "Visual Pleasure" 62). Notably, Hushpuppy looks for only a brief moment at her father's spectacle of mas-culinity. And then she disobediently backs away from the wall, withdraws deeper into the now-rattling shack, and twice calls out, "Mama!" In this instance, she chooses *not* to look, because her father's spectacle does noth-ing for her. At the height of his performance of masculinity, the father is rendered inadequate, an ironic symbol of lack for a daughter who desires her mother instead.

In Search of Our Mothers' Gardens

The storm destroys the Bathtub, at least as a physical location. When Hushpuppy and Wink climb through a hole in the roof the next morning, the town is entirely underwater.[7] The screenplay describes the postapocalypse landscape as follows: "Everything is submerged. Every organism is dead or has fled. The quiet is overwhelming" (Alibar and Zeitlin 25). But the survivors, who include Miss Bathsheba, a handful of Wink's friends, and three girls around Hushpuppy's age, quickly band together. In Hushpuppy's mature words, "It wasn't no time to sit around crying like a bunch of pussies. We were gonna make a camp right on top of the Bathtub." Incidentally, her vocabulary is taken directly from Miss Bathsheba, who delivers a mini-lecture on prehistoric cave dwellers to the children at the beginning of the film and concludes with a rhetorical question: "Who up in here think that the cavemens was sitting around crying like a bunch of pussies?" There is an inescapable irony in Miss Bathsheba and then Hushpuppy (mimicking her) using the word "pussy" as misogynistic slang for a weak person. The association of femaleness, specifically female genitalia, with weakness demonstrates the pervasiveness of phallocentric discourse, which even the fierce Miss Bathsheba resorts to and then passes on to the next generation. But the subtext of Miss Bathsheba's lesson, which Hushpuppy has clearly absorbed, is that hardship must be faced head on. The survivors congregate on the school-boat, which they patch up and then expand into what the screenplay calls "a ramshackle Ark" (37).

This section of the film clearly dwells on the small collective of female characters—Hushpuppy, her three school friends, and the schoolteacher Miss Bathsheba. It is not a coincidence that the Ark belongs to Miss Bathsheba, the only black woman in Hushpuppy's life other than her imaginary mother.[8] The camera pans over caged chickens and bright green jalapeño plants before switching to a shot of Miss Bathsheba teaching a medical lesson to the four girls still in her charge. One of the girls rests her head in Miss Bathsheba's lap with her eyes closed. Miss Bathsheba shows the other girls how to massage the sleeping girl's heart by gently rubbing her chest in a circular motion. Hushpuppy raptly listens and then practices the technique as Miss Bathsheba says, "This is the most important thing I can ever teach y'all. Y'all gotta learn how to take care of people smaller and sweeter than you are." In the very next shot, Miss Bathsheba shows Hushpuppy how to plant herbs in their makeshift floating garden. These scenes are brief but important to Hushpuppy's evolving subjectivity as a young black girl and her symbolic quest for a repressed maternal despite a seemingly pervasive paternal law.

From the outset, Miss Bathsheba promotes self-reliance, much as Wink does. She introduces her students to the concept of natural selection by describing everything as "meat" in the "buffet of the universe." She is also the first person in the film to introduce the prehistoric aurochs, which she calls "a fierce, mean creature that walked the face of the earth back when we all lived in the caves." To illustrate her point, she models her right outer thigh on which is tattooed a mock cave painting of three tiny stick figures battling two giant aurochs. The aurochs, like the zombies in *28 Days Later* and the Aliens and Predators in *AVP*, are the literal monsters of this speculative film. As such, they also carry symbolic potential and invite a psychoanalytic reading. Familiarly, Hushpuppy uses Wink's vocabulary of kingship to describe these creatures. Early on, she states, "Way back in the day, the aurochs was king of the world." And about halfway through the film—which is also a halfway point for the aurochs on their journey from the South Pole to Louisiana—she observes, "Strong animals got no mercy. They're the type of animals that eat their own mommas and daddies." Accordingly, the camera provides a close-up shot of an exhausted aurochs collapsing and its herdmates immediately devouring it in a frenzy of hunger.

Cannibalism features strongly in psychoanalytic theories, and this image of the cannibalized parent seemingly speaks to the father-son relationship that Wink has attempted to cultivate with his daughter. As Shuli Barzilai puts it, "Freud never yields ground about the desire for identification through oral ingestion—in a word, cannibalism as an early expression of the relation toward the *father*" (119). Hushpuppy is expected to be king after her father, whom she is not supposed to mourn, and to perform a brutal and unapologetic strength. Yet the aurochs are just as easily read as projections of the maternal. In his work "Family Complexes in the Formation of the Individual," Jacques Lacan argues that the mother, rather than the father, is the primary object of a child's cannibalistic fantasies. Like the pre-oedipal mother, the aurochs is large, mythic, powerful, and supposedly extinct. Granted, this "fierce, mean creature" is a very different embodiment of the maternal than the basketball jersey and the beacon. The aurochs recalls Barbara Creed's concept of the monstrous-feminine, a primal, dangerous, and patriarchal version of the mother. Nonetheless, this monster is another important counterforce to the paternal—Miss Bathsheba inscribes the aurochs on her thigh (in battle with the phallic spear-wielding stick figures), and Hushpuppy resurrects these mythical creatures by striking her father and thus causing the "break" that sets them free. Released from the ice that has trapped them for millennia, the aurochs lumber in a herd straight toward the Bathtub.[9] Hushpuppy's climactic encounters with both her mother and the aurochs are thus culminations of her quest to rediscover and reclaim the maternal.

As in the tattooed scene on her thigh, Miss Bathsheba, an obvious figure of opposition to Wink, engages in symbolic battle with the Law of the Father. Where Wink prioritizes Hushpuppy's survival as the last Doucet in his genealogical line, Miss Bathsheba encourages collective survival and creative resourcefulness. Her lessons of unapologetic strength are tempered by what she calls "the most important thing," namely, the need to protect others as well as yourself. Creativity is central to Miss Bathsheba's lessons of survival and manifests in everything from her tattoo to her purveyance of folklore and herbalism. Hushpuppy is eager to practice creativity and does so in a myriad of ways—the lore that she invents about the universe, the shrine that she makes of her mother's jersey, the dinner that she cooks using lard and cat food, and her "ethnographic" drawings. One can recall here Alice Walker's essay "In Search of Our Mothers' Gardens," which explores the oppressed but indomitable creative spirits of black women. Walker observes that black women historically had to find alternative outlets for their creativity in a world that denied and hindered their talents. Singing, storytelling, quilting, cooking, gardening, and so on, became expressions of creativity for women who were barred from literacy, education, and the fine arts. In her own small expressions of creativity, Hushpuppy emulates the "magic" of her black foremothers, whether Miss Bathsheba's creation stories or her mother's mythical cooking.

The symbolic differences between Wink and Miss Bathsheba are epitomized in the scene where Wink decides to blow up the levee in order to drain the floodwaters. Hushpuppy's voice-over explains to the viewer that, "two weeks [after the storm], everything started to die." The brief optimism of the survivors gives way to despair as their entire ecosystem collapses. Dead fish and fowl float on the water, and a bloated cow carcass is visible on the shore. Hushpuppy's faith in both the Bathtub and her father is shaken, which she demonstrates by covertly asking her father's friend Walrus (Lowell Landes), "You want to leave the Bathtub?" Viewing this question as an act of betrayal, Wink angrily says, "I heard that. Nobody's leaving the Bathtub. You don't know nuthin'!" Although Miss Bathsheba does not present an alternative plan for saving the Bathtub, she does articulate the fact that sabotaging the levee is not a solution: "You so much as piss on that wall, you know what them people gonna do? They gonna find us and stick us in a damn shelter." Both Wink and Miss Bathsheba want to preserve their community, but Wink's motivation remains grounded in his one predictable purpose—to bequeath the Bathtub to his heir.

Hushpuppy is ultimately forced to choose between her father and Miss Bathsheba when she secretly follows the adults to the levee by hiding on

Miss Bathsheba's motorboat. The question of choice is once again significant for the protagonist, who is regularly presented with hierarchical dichotomies by her father—she must choose the Bathtub (not the Dry World), she must be "the man" (not "a stupid little girl"), and she must follow the Law of the Father (not the Law of the Mother). Part of Hushpuppy's motivation is precisely to see and experience what is on the Other side. She watches for a moment as her father wrestles with Miss Bathsheba for control of the trip-line and detonator that will set off the nearby explosives. "What are you doing, woman?" splutters Wink, to which Miss Bathsheba responds, "I'm hauling your ass home, little boy." Significantly, Miss Bathsheba remains "woman" here while Wink is reduced to "little boy." Again, this "battle" models a struggle between the maternal and the paternal, as well as a gradual shift in power as Miss Bathsheba gains the literal upper hand. But when the trip-line falls across Hushpuppy's path, she is the one who has the final choice of whether to destroy the levee or leave it in place. Out of loyalty to her father, Hushpuppy pulls the rope, triggering a cataclysmic explosion that knocks her off her feet, destroys the levee, and immediately drains the Bathtub (much like an actual bathtub). But her decision is also a means of eradicating the massive boundary that isolates her community from the rest of the world.

On the spectrum of ethnographic imagery, this sequence returns the viewer to the Primitive/Modern dichotomy and the inevitable confrontation between the two. The survivalist ethos of all the Bathtub residents is put to the test when Miss Bathsheba's prediction comes true and government workers forcefully relocate everyone to a shelter. Despite the drained floodwaters, the Bathtub is irredeemable—a wasteland of muck and debris. As Hushpuppy observes, "Sometimes you can break something so bad that it can't get put back together," a truth that speaks to not only the Bathtub but also her dying father. The shelter is the only close-up version of the external world that Hushpuppy gets to see. And it is clearly meant to convey desolation, especially when compared to the original vibrancy of the antediluvian Bathtub. Filmed in washed-out whites and grays, the shelter is a warehouse-style building where medical personnel and volunteers tend to the refugees. But everything from the processed food served in Styrofoam containers to the sleeping cots, fluorescent lighting, and terrazzo floors is lifeless and cold.

Zeitlin openly acknowledges that his film is making a political statement about shelters: "It's not good for people to be put in a shelter in the middle of nowhere. That's not better than them fending for themselves in their homes, even if it threatens their lives. It threatens their lives much more to be removed than it does to stay" (Butman). As such, the consequent images of a sullen Hushpuppy in a frilly blue dress and neatly plaited hair are meant to evoke a sense of pathos. In the same way, the relegation of a now deathly looking and semicomatose Wink to a hospital bed is intended to be poignant. These are the "sad" images of the tamed "Beasts" of the "Southern Wild," their wildness broken by their inevitable encounter with "civilization." However, neither extreme—the ruined Bathtub or the desolate Dry World—is ideal for Hushpuppy, and neither is rendered a "right" choice. She may not be able to thrive in the shelter, which she describes as "a fish tank with no water" and which is implicitly a microcosm of the "real world." But neither can she continue living in the Bathtub, now a condemned space whose ecosystem can no longer sustain its inhabitants. The film does not offer Hushpuppy, and thus the viewer, an obvious solution to these two extremes. But the absence of a tidy solution is appropriate in this pseudo-ethnography, which suggests that both the Primitive and the Modern are fraught spaces. Again, one must look to the protagonist herself to negotiate and destabilize these kinds of dichotomies. It is *only* through Hushpuppy's perspective that one sees the ambiguities of the Bathtub and the Dry World and the deceptiveness of boundaries like the levee or Wink's duct tape down the middle of the floor.

Notably, the beacon that symbolizes Hushpuppy's mother exists outside both the Bathtub and the Dry World. The unknown mother thus becomes not just an object of desire for her daughter but a place unto herself, a curious alternative to the physical locations of the Bathtub and the Dry World. Hushpuppy has already experienced alternative power systems and vocabularies to those of her father, and she has challenged symbolic boundaries. Through Miss Bathsheba, as well as the three girls who serve as a newfound posse, Hushpuppy discovers ways of seeing and experiencing the world that transcend Wink's projections of "boss," "king," and "the last man." Her gaze now turns entirely to the absent mother figure in what is arguably the film's most subversive scene where a black female gaze is concerned. It is the mutual mother-daughter recognition and Hushpuppy's reclamation of the maternal that facilitates a more empowered subject position for this black female protagonist.

Elysian Fields

Hushpuppy's physical journey to her mother involves swimming out to sea and thus away from the Dry World and the Bathtub. By this point, she and her father have returned to the ruined Bathtub along with the rest of the survivors and Wink is literally on his deathbed. Accompanied by her three friends, whom the screenplay describes as her "girl gang" (Alibar and Zeitlin 34), Hushpuppy splashes into the Gulf of Mexico and begins to swim steadily toward the blinking light that she associates with her mother. Her journey takes her first to a tugboat where an old white sailor watches her and her friends climb aboard. Defiantly, Hushpuppy says to him, "I'm going by my Mama," to which the sailor replies, "That's a good place to go." Her mother does indeed represent "a good place" in Hushpuppy's imagination. And when the sailor later tells her that the smell of chicken biscuits makes him feel "cohesive," Hushpuppy replies, with profound gravity, "I wanna be cohesive." Both Miss Bathsheba and Hushpuppy describe the universe as a fabric that depends on cohesion. While the theme certainly speaks to the impact of our individual actions on the planet as a whole, Hushpuppy's desire for cohesion is inextricable from her desire for her mother. In a strip club called Elysian Fields made out of an old barge, Hushpuppy finds a beautiful woman cooking in the back kitchen. And for the duration of their meeting, Hushpuppy enjoys what the Elysian Fields in classical Greek mythology promise—paradise.

That Hushpuppy has effectively "arrived" at her mother is signaled by the close-up shot of the beacon, which flashes reassuringly atop the barge. The camera then switches from the beacon to a close-up of Hushpuppy's face, which is awestruck. The club's marquee advertises "girls, girls, girls," and its interior is a blend of Christmas lights, metallic fringe curtains, and the same soft jazz music that accompanied Hushpuppy's earlier fantasies of her mother. At the sight of the children, the "girls" of the club materialize. Clad in negligees, these women of various ages and ethnicities affectionately surround Hushpuppy and her friends. The camera lingers on the women, slowly panning across their smiling faces as they reach out to the four female children with unbridled love. As Hushpuppy makes her way past the women, they touch her almost reverently. But she ignores them and scans the room instead, clearly looking for someone very specific—her mother. Again, Hushpuppy's gaze is important because the viewer *looks* with her, just as eager to see this enigmatic African American woman finally represented on-screen.

Until this moment, the viewer, like Hushpuppy, has had only Wink's erotic flashbacks to go by in imagining Mama—her lean brown back, dark ponytail, and bloodstained thighs. The screenplay stipulates that "we never see [Mama's] face, it's always covered, shot from the back, or out of frame" (Alibar and Zeitlin 32). The alligator scene and a subsequent kitchen scene, where Mama ignites the stove just by touching it, prioritize what the screenplay calls her "supple curves" (32). The camera gravitates to her buttocks, outlined by her translucent white slip, and stays close to her as she bends over to inspect the smoking contents of the oven. These shots easily bear out hooks's claim that, "[w]hen calling attention to the body in a manner inviting the gaze to mutilate black female bodies yet again, to focus solely on the 'butt,' contemporary celebrations of this part of the anatomy do not successfully subvert sexist/racist representations" (*Black Looks* 64). Hooks rightly connects the present-day emphasis on black women's buttocks in popular cultures to the nineteenth-century pseudoscientific practice of reducing black female bodies to their sexual parts. And she further grounds this figurative mutilation of the black female body in slavery, under which black women were bought and sold as sexual objects.

Admittedly, Wink's version of Mama is also impressive in the sense that she rescues a sleeping and vulnerable Wink: cocking the shotgun with one hand, she shoots the alligator and then fries it up for lunch. But she is the same kind of impressive as the blaxploitation divas of the 1970s—women who are infinitely "cool" but also hypersexual. These black female characters are heterosexual male fantasies, as Donald Bogle emphasizes in his discussion of "supermamas" such as Coffy (Pam Grier) and Cleopatra Jones (Tamara Dobson): "[E]ach was a high-flung male fantasy: beautiful, alluring, glamorous voluptuaries, as ready and anxious for sex and mayhem as any man. They lived in fantasy worlds—of violence, blood, guns, and gore—which pleased, rather than threatened, male audiences" (*Toms* 251). Mama is this kind of fantasy—she lights up the screen with "sex and mayhem," and both Wink and the camera are infatuated with her. That the sequence culminates in sex is the entire point of the flashback, which Wink introduces as Hushpuppy's conception story. Still lost in his memories, Wink concludes the narration for these scenes: "Your Mama battered that gator up and set it to frying. Then Hushpuppy popped into the universe about four minutes later."

Again, a feminist reading of the film encourages the viewer to look for alternatives to Wink's patriarchal version of things, including his fantasy of Mama. Hushpuppy's climactic encounter with Mama is crucial to displacing the mother's earlier incarnation as a male fantasy. On the barge, Hushpuppy and the viewer finally get to *see* Mama, not as a series of isolated and sexualized parts but as a whole person. The jazz music winds down for the slow-motion shot in which a slender, out-of-focus woman appears in a blaze of light through swinging double doors. The camera

Figure 4.3. Mama (Jovan Hathaway) appears clearly on-screen for the first time in Elysian Fields.

zooms in on her face and sharpens into focus—a beautiful thirty-some-thing black woman in an orange tank top and an apron tilts back her head and drains a bottle of beer. She peruses the room until her gaze falls on Hushpuppy, who is staring at her with an expression of shy wonder. "You need something, baby?" the woman asks with a gentle drawl. When Hushpuppy is unable to reply, the woman considers her for a moment and finally says, "Get in here. Lemme show you a magic trick." The woman leads her into the luminous kitchen.

This moment may be as close as the viewer gets to what L. Williams calls "the illusion of a pre-Oedipal space between women free of the mastery and control of the male look" ("Something Else" 2). The look between mother and daughter allows for a mutual representation, however temporary, without the mediation of the male gaze or the presence of the father. Hooks's description of a scene involving an older and younger black woman in Julie Dash's *Illusions* (1982) is apt here: "It is this process of mirrored recognition that enables both Black women to define their reality, apart from the reality imposed upon them by structures of domination" (*Black Looks* 129–130). Whether or not this woman is Hushpuppy's biological mother is immaterial in this speculative film. Billed as "the Cook" in the screenplay, she is everything that Hushpuppy imagines her mother to be—not a male fantasy, then, but a female fantasy and, more precisely, a daughter's fantasy. The same actress, Jovan Hathaway, plays both parts, thus explicitly connecting the two roles.[10] Mama's mystical presence in the Elysian Fields is no more fantastical than the aurochs that eventually arrive on Hushpuppy's doorstep. And in the short but unspecified time that Hushpuppy spends with her mother, she experiences that seemingly impossible symbiosis with the maternal.

Inside the golden world of the kitchen, Mama dishes out wisdom, humor, and perfectly battered gator meat with a side of grits. Instead of the shotgun and sex of Wink's fantasy, she proffers another kind of magic, opening a fresh bottle of beer with her teeth and splitting a raw egg in half by expertly spitting the bottle cap at the egg. As she cooks for and feeds Hushpuppy, she says, "When you're a child, people tell you that life is gonna be all happy and hunky-dory and all that bullshit. But I'm here to tell you that it's not. So you need to get that out your head right now." Hushpuppy watches and listens, enraptured by the entire experience. In a culmination of her maternal work, Mama emphasizes the challenges of life from a distinctly female perspective: "'Cause yeah, life's some big ole feast. But you ain't nuthin' but a stupid little waitress. One day everything on your plate gonna fall on the floor. And nobody gonna be there to pick it up for you. One day, it's gonna be all on you." However, she balances this dose of pragmatism with equally firm encouragement: "You understand what I'm sayin'? So smile, girl. Smile!" She winks at Hushpuppy, not as the coquette of Wink's fantasy but as one black female affirming another.

Although her emphasis on being a "stupid little waitress" in the "feast" of life may seem harsh (much like Miss Bathsheba's lecture on being "meat" in the "buffet of the universe"), Mama's life lesson is a necessary counterpoint to Wink's promises of kingship. Even within the Bathtub, Hushpuppy's life was not "hunky-dory," and she will face greater challenges as an orphaned black girl living outside the Bathtub. Yet her mother illustrates that a black woman can still find autonomy in that outside world and even do so with a smile. The next scene returns to the dance floor of the club, where each of Hushpuppy's friends dances with one of the strippers. The women cradle the girls, ambling slowly in time to the music. As the screenplay puts it, the girls "are orphans in a heaven of mothers" (Alibar and Zeitlin 68). Mama and Hushpuppy are also on the dance floor, holding each other tightly in a more literal enactment of their symbiosis. When Hushpuppy asks Mama if she can take care of her and her father, Mama declines: "Don't know nuthin' 'bout your daddy. I can't take care of nobody but myself." The invocation of the Father is firmly rejected here, although Mama immediately adds, "You can stay if you want."

For the space of the dance, these two black female characters—mother and daughter—cling to each other. And Hushpuppy is finally able to reclaim her mother, who has been a basketball jersey, a beacon, and even an aurochs, but never a body. Teresa de Lauretis points back to Spillers when she notes that the African American mother is "always already expropriated and lost," and thus the project for the black female subject is "to re-member, re-find, or reconstitute a female-sexed body as a body for the subject and for desire" (200). Granted, this "heaven of mothers" is itself an illusion, in keeping with the repression of the maternal and the question of whether women can ever exist outside a phallic economy. Being held by her mother triggers an infant memory for Hushpuppy—the only other time she has ever been held was at birth. A flashback shows a young Wink holding his newborn daughter and carrying her outdoors despite the loud protests of an unseen Mama. This memory of Wink breaks the spell of the dance, and Hushpuppy gravely states, "I need to go home." Much as the voice of Wink interrupts Hushpuppy's re-membering of her mother in the trailer, the memory of Wink disrupts even this faraway paradise where the maternal body can exist.

Hushpuppy whispers something into her mother's ear, and Mama nods before spinning her around, placing her gently on the ground, and melting into the crowd. Hushpuppy stares hard for a moment before turning around and marching purposefully back "home" to the Bathtub. But Hushpuppy now carries some of her mother's philosophies on life, her mother's fried gator in a brown paper bag, and a sense of self that is less contingent upon the Father. She has successfully repossessed her mother—who is now more than a mere fetish or an erased body—and in so doing found a new model for her own subjectivity. This reclamation of the mother is also important for the viewer, who has been aligned with Hushpuppy all along. The film suggests that a shared gaze of affirmation between black female characters not only is possible but can be the driving force of a cinematic narrative.

The Aurochs

That Hushpuppy transcends or reimagines her father's patriarchy and her father's patrilineal legacy is symbolized by her confrontation with the aurochs, which charge into the Bathtub at the same time as Hushpuppy and her gang. In one of the film's most iconic shots, Hushpuppy stands in tiny profile to the right of the screen, still wearing the white nightdress from the shelter and clutching the brown paper bag containing her mother's gator nuggets. She stares at the leader of the aurochs, a mammoth beast that takes up the rest of the screen. For a moment, Hushpuppy and the aurochs

Figure 4.4. Hushpuppy confronts the aurochs in the Bathtub.

gaze at each other—another moment of "mirrored recognition"—and the only audible sound is the aurochs' heavy breathing. Wink sits up from where he is lying on a mattress in his ruined shack and stares in disbelief. A close-up shot pans from a defiant Hushpuppy to the moist black snout of the aurochs. The tension is finally broken when the aurochs' leader kneels reverently before Hushpuppy and its herdmates follow suit.

Given my interpretation of the aurochs as yet another manifestation of the maternal, albeit the monstrous maternal, it is significant that Hushpuppy finally meets these mythical creatures in the Bathtub. They are not the golden fantasies of Hushpuppy's imagination, which culminate in her finding her mother in the Elysian Fields. Rather, the aurochs are darker projections of the maternal, a product of the patriarchal imaginary as much as anything else. So her subjugation of these "Beasts" is another act of reclamation. With an air of familiarity, Hushpuppy says to the aurochs' leader, "You're my friend, kind of." Instead of an epic battle, as the aurochs seem to bode throughout the film, Hushpuppy's encounter with these creatures results in mutual affirmation and a form of triumph for the protagonist. Writing of the repressed maternal, Kaplan argues, "Patriarchy has worked hard to prevent the eruption of a (mythically) feared return of the matriarchy which might take place were the close mother-child bonding to return to dominance, or allowed to stand in place of the Law of the Father" (*Women* 205). In the wake of Hushpuppy's magical encounter with her mother, the arrival of the aurochs constitutes such a "feared return of the matriarchy," which takes place in full view of the slack-jawed and dying Wink.

Figure 4.5. Hushpuppy leads her small group of followers out of the Bathtub.

However, the fact that the aurochs are fantastical, much like Mama in the Elysian Fields, also reiterates the limits of trying to imagine or resurrect the maternal outside of patriarchy. Indeed, Hushpuppy parts ways with the aurochs in much the same way she parted ways with Mama in the Elysian Fields—that is, by naming the Father. She says to the aurochs, "I gotta take care of mine," and the aurochs slowly rise and walk away while Hushpuppy does the same. The Law of the Father remains in place for the black female protagonist, and she is compelled to return to Wink. But there is still room in this conclusion for a feminist identification with the protagonist by way of her third eye and oppositional gaze. In situating the maternal as a site for disrupting patriarchal paradigms, Kaplan reminds us, "This is by no means to argue that return to a matriarchy would be either possible or desirable. What rather has to happen is that we move beyond long-held cultural and linguistic patterns of oppositions: male/female (as these terms currently signify); dominant/submissive; active/passive; nature/civilization; order/chaos; matriarchal/patriarchal" (*Women* 206). Although the film presents highly provocative versions of the maternal and centralizes a mutual desire between mother and daughter, it does not attempt to simply "swap" power dynamics.

Wink's quiet death certainly speaks to an erosion of patriarchy, but it does not signal a return to matriarchy or the Law of the Mother. There is even the subtle hint that Hushpuppy finally adopts the "normal" oedipal role prescribed for daughters in relation to fathers. No longer dressed in boys' clothing and no longer called upon to perform a stereotypical masculinity, Hushpuppy temporarily becomes the nurturing mother by feeding Wink a last meal of Mama's gator nuggets. At his funeral, his shrouded body is placed on his boat, which has been transformed into a floating pyre. Solemnly, Hushpuppy lights the pyre and pushes the boat out to sea while the surviving members of the Bathtub recite a dirge in Wink's honor. Hushpuppy and her small band of neighbors then march purposefully out of the Bathtub along a narrow stretch of road, the music uplifting as the ocean licks at their feet. Hushpuppy's final voice-over, an echo of her voice-over when she set her trailer on fire, is very much about her life in the context of Wink and the Bathtub: "When I die, the scientists of the future, they're gonna find it all. They gonna know. Once there was a Hushpuppy, and she lived with her Daddy in the Bathtub." The music swells triumphantly as the camera provides the last long shot of the group and the scene cuts to black.

But even if Hushpuppy names "Daddy" one last time, the final scene itself complicates the Law of the Father. The viewer sees a black female child in charge of her small band—black and white, female and male, young and old, marching together and in solidarity. They carry with them the last remnants of the Bathtub, pieces of wood, the odd stray animal, and homemade flags. Miss Bathsheba and Wink's other friends rally around Hushpuppy, and her three schoolmates also march at her side, seemingly undeterred by the unknown future before them. Hushpuppy's closing narration once again gives her the last word, the authoritative commentary, as her determined gaze, looking into an unknown future, challenges the dismissive or patronizing spectator. Psychoanalytic feminist theories posit that "woman" outside patriarchal discourses and binaries remains difficult to imagine. That difficulty is exacerbated in the case of black womanhood. Similarly, spaces outside Western iconographies of Primitive/Modern or "nature/civilization" are hard to represent. What *Beasts of the Southern Wild* provides in its concluding image is a black female subject on a literal threshold, an in-between space of transition (neither the Bathtub nor the Dry World) where the unknown lies before her.

On a symbolic level, this conclusion makes for a powerful sense of possibility where black female subjectivity is concerned. The viewer has already seen glimpses of what is possible through not only the protagonist herself but also her fantasies of the maternal, the female, and the feminine as presented on-screen. And the viewer has experienced Hushpuppy's returned gaze but also seen the world through Hushpuppy's eyes. The film, like all the preceding case studies, hardly guarantees a happy ending. But it concludes with a black female character who has survived an apocalypse and modeled agency and autonomy in the process.

CHAPTER 5

Intergalactic Companions:
Firefly and *Doctor Who*

It was on the small screen, rather than the big screen, that a black female character in a speculative narrative first gained international celebrity. And a book like this one would be incomplete if it did not address television, the medium that launched Uhura into stardom. Nichelle Nichols, the actress who played Uhura on the NBC series *Star Trek* (1966–1969), tells a popular anecdote about the impact of her iconic role on the next generation of black women: "I met Whoopi Goldberg when Gene [Roddenberry] was doing *The Next Generation* and she had told me when *Star Trek* came on she was nine years old and she said she turned the TV on and saw me and ran through the house screaming: Come quick, come quick. There's a black lady on TV and she ain't no maid" (Martin). Goldberg, who went on to play the character Guinan on *Star Trek: The Next Generation* (1987–1994), credits the original show with imagining a future where black people are both present and empowered.

Uhura's impact is inextricable from the historical period during which *Star Trek* was aired. Especially in light of the civil rights and feminist movements, her role as a black female military officer (rather than a maid) cannot be overstated. Beretta Smith-Shomade cites Diahann Carroll's title character Julia Baker on the NBC sitcom *Julia* (1968–1971) as "the first Black nondomestic female character on television" (*Shaded* 13). But Uhura antedates Julia by two years, having first appeared in the *Star Trek* premiere, "The Man Trap," on September 6, 1966. This chapter returns to the trailblazing concept of a black woman in SF television, albeit in the new millennium.

My approach to the television case studies is not radically different from my approach to the film case studies. In a 1986 article, Patrice Petro addresses the budding anxiety among film theorists regarding the inclusion of television in the field. One concern that she cites is "the 'number crunching' empiricism of communication research, [which] was seen by some to threaten the already beleaguered position of film study within the university by moving it further away from the humanities and in the direction of the social sciences" (5). Petro also mentions a second concern, namely, the fact that television facilitates a different kind of spectatorship and viewing experience than film: "[T]he debate over television's place in film studies came to rest upon the (unexamined) assumption that while film encourages attention to the work itself, television merely contributes to the tendency toward distracted and indiscriminate reception" (5–6). Goldberg's first glimpse of Uhura is an appropriate illustration here. Precisely because Uhura was on television, Goldberg could "[run] through the house screaming," something she presumably would not have been able to do in a movie theater.

Thirty years later, these concerns about television studies are worth revisiting, and in fact they shape my own approach to the medium. The first concern has proven to be fair if only because scholarship on television is now almost exclusively produced by social scientists. Virtually every study of blackness in relation to television comes out of communication, sociology, and anthropology. Whereas literary theory has been instrumental in the evolution of film studies, the same is not demonstrably true of television studies. But textual and semiotic approaches to this medium can still enrich conversations regarding representations of race and gender in popular cultures. The increasingly blurry distinction between film spectatorship and television spectatorship also merits reconsideration in the new millennium. Petro outlines a few of the ways in which film and television were distinguished in 1986—high art versus mass culture, masculine versus feminine, collective versus private, gaze versus glance, and so on. But postmodern epistemologies and new technologies, having all but collapsed these kinds of binaries, encourage critics to engage with television in much the same way that they might engage with film. Undoubtedly the episodic nature of television is relevant, as are the differences in production, marketing, and circulation. But textual and psychoanalytic readings can still be brought to bear and may yield insights regarding the coding of black femininity in specific SF series. Thus, my approach to these shows relies on many of the same analytical tools and the same oppositional gaze in order to tease out meaning.

Both of the television shows that I discuss in this chapter, *Firefly* (2002) and *Doctor Who: Series 3* (2007), feature a black female character in a futuristic SF narrative involving space travel. And both of these shows expand on the possibilities for such a character, something that the 1960s *Star Trek* was unable to do despite its originality. Although Nichols's pioneering role was championed by Martin Luther King Jr. and single-handedly changed the cinematic iconography of black women, the role was still a product of its time. Often reduced to her signature line, "hailing frequencies open," Nichols had very limited screen time, especially compared to her white male costars William Shatner and Leonard Nimoy. In her autobiography, *Beyond Uhura: Star Trek and Other Memories* (1994), Nichols recalls the regular cutting of her script lines and the overall erosion of her character and concludes that "a strong, independent Black woman was not welcome as an equal" (160). In those few episodes where she has more than a few seconds on-screen ("The Man Trap," "Charlie X," "Mirror, Mirror," "The Gamesters of Triskelion," and "Plato's Stepchildren"), Uhura performs an exoticized femininity and looks to male characters for rescue and affirmation. Indeed, it is to Nichols's credit that Uhura became such a popular cultural icon given the constraints of the role.

Since Uhura's presence on the bridge of the *Enterprise*, few black female characters have played memorable television roles in an outer space context. The BBC show *Blake's 7* (1978–1981) introduced the character Dayna Mellanby (Josette Simon), a resistance fighter, in its third season. Goldberg made her first appearance as Guinan, the Ten Forward Lounge bartender, on *Star Trek: The Next Generation* in 1988 and remained on the show until its conclusion in 1994. The Fox show *Space: Above and Beyond* (1995–1996), canceled after a single season (much like *Firefly*, which aired on the same network), included former marine and engineer Vanessa Damphousse (Lanei Chapman) in its main cast. The contemporaneous show *Sliders* (1995–2000) added the black female physicist Diana Davis (Tembi Locke) in its fifth and final season. The now-defunct UPN network aired *Mercy Point* (1998–1999) with a black female psychiatrist, Rema Cook (Gay Thomas), as a pivotal character. The short-lived *Crusade* (1999), a spinoff of the series *Babylon 5* (1993–1998), had a black female medical officer, Sarah Chambers (Marjean Holden). And Gina Torres played her first central television role as Helen Carter, a member of a trio of female resistance fighters, on *Cleopatra 2525* (2000–2001). Also worth mentioning are communications officer Anastasia "Dee" Dualla (Kandyse McClure) on the rebooted *Battlestar Galactica* (2003–2009) and astronaut Molly Woods (Halle Berry) on *Extant* (2014–2015).

However, none of these black women in space has had the same cultural resonance as Uhura, perhaps because none of these shows has had the same impact as *Star Trek*. Although these deep-space dramas imagine black women in creative and empowering ways—as resistance fighters, engineers, physicists, psychiatrists, doctors, military officers, and astronauts—they did not gain traction with audiences. The exceptions are *Star Trek: The Next Generation* and *Battlestar Galactica*, but Guinan and Dee are hardly major players on those series. The most compelling examples, then, of popular new millennial space shows with primary and subversive black female characters are *Firefly* and *Doctor Who: Series 3*. This chapter examines these characters—Zoë Washburne (Gina Torres) and Martha Jones (Freema Agyeman)—as figurative descendants of Uhura who have had an identifiable cultural impact in the twenty-first century. Certainly, there are familiar limitations to these characters, not least the fact that they are "isolated from other members of their racial community" (Citizen 194) and paired with dominant white male leads. But my goal is to once again situate these women as crucial and empowered figures on these shows (both of which, like *Star Trek*, purport a postprejudice humanity and yet imply the supremacy of whiteness and maleness).

Roddenberry's original *Star Trek* ushered in a brand of SF optimism and excitement that channeled the nineteenth-century "manifest destiny" ideology and the twentieth-century space race. The *Enterprise* crew is the diverse face of the United Federation of Planets, and their overarching objective is to peacefully explore the universe. But as M. Keith Booker discusses, the show is rife with contradictions and leaves viewers with "a thoroughly Americanized global culture" (199). In Joss Whedon's *Firefly*, one sees a compelling inversion of the *Star Trek* narrative. Instead of being representatives of a vast interplanetary government called the Alliance, the crew members of the *Serenity* are outlaws living on the fringes of society. The show thus indicts the colonialist power structures that would invariably underpin a bloc like the United Federation of Planets. *Firefly* is less about naive optimism and more about rebellion and the rights of the disenfranchised. But even as *Firefly* imagines a dystopian future when Earth is obsolete and the two dominant languages are English and Mandarin, it glosses over its own need (like *Star Trek*'s) to place a white man at the helm to speak and act for everybody else.

The original *Doctor Who* (1963–1989), which antedates *Star Trek* and was branded as a children's show, sustained an all-white cast and a clear nostalgia for a diminishing British Empire (much as *Star Trek* betrayed nostalgia for an American frontier). Where *Star Trek* projected "a walking icon of Americanism" (Booker 197) in Captain Kirk, *Doctor Who* projected "an upper-class Englishman" (Gupta 43) in the Doctor. But the new *Doctor Who* (2005–), with Russell T. Davies as the initial head writer and producer, acknowledges a multiracial Britain and posits the Doctor as more of a radical and less of a paternalist. Both *Firefly* and the new *Doctor Who* thus emphasize individualism (especially in opposition to "evil" collectives like the Alliance and the Daleks) and espouse the rights of an underclass.

What remains telling is the fact that Mal Reynolds (Nathan Fillion) and the Tenth Doctor (David Tennant) are still formulaic television heroes who do little to upset hegemonic models of power. Fans are overeager to claim a feminist bent to these shows (particularly *Firefly*) and to read the male protagonists as liberal models of masculinity. But any trappings of freshness notwithstanding, these characters are hardly revolutionary. As a number of critics point out, Mal's roots can easily be traced back to characters ranging from the Ringo Kid (John Wayne) in *Stagecoach* (1939) and Josh Randall (Steve McQueen) in *Wanted: Dead or Alive* (1958–1961) to Han Solo (Harrison Ford) in *Star Wars* (1977). Michael Goodrum and Philip Smith conclude that Mal is "an anesthetizing rehearsal of a specifically American brand of masculinity" (xviii). And Piers Britton writes of the Doctor, "The ultimately solitary and nomadic Doctor does in fact adhere to a perfectly conventional model of masculinity in screen fiction—namely, the type identified in film scholarship as the 'narcissistic hero'" (88). Citing Laura Mulvey and Steve Neale, Britton extrapolates on this figure as an embodiment of phallic omnipotence and rebellious male heroism. Both Mal and the Doctor fit this mold, which hinges on a rejection of the Law and of such social institutions as marriage (although both men grudgingly welcome female companionship).

It is not Mal and the Doctor, then, who put a fresh spin on these space operas. Rather, it is Zoë and Martha, both of whom are counterparts to the protagonists and neither of whom is quite so predictable. Sidekicks though they appear to be, these female characters are implicitly qualified to do everything that the hero does (and sometimes more). Zoë is framed as Mal's double in clothing, demeanor, and expertise, while Martha is a doctor in training and thus an Other Doctor. Martha is as close as *Doctor Who* has ever come to casting a Doctor of color (although it takes a shift in perspective to see her that way). Doubles are a classic trope in speculative tales, as evinced by literary examples such as Mary Shelley's *Frankenstein; or, The Modern Prometheus* (1818) and Robert Louis Stevenson's *Strange Case of Dr. Jekyll and Mr. Hyde* (1886). A space opera like *Star Wars* frames epic Manichean battles between light and darkness but also includes doubles in the form of twin characters Luke Skywalker (Mark Hamill) and Princess Leia (Carrie Fisher). And SF often portrays clones, copies, doppelgängers, simulations, and so on. In *Firefly* and *Doctor Who*, the viewer gets to see a black woman who regularly matches and mirrors the feats of the white male protagonist. I argue that this unusual parallelism, which one does not see between Uhura and Kirk, affords a powerful symbolic agency to these black female characters. Although there are still questionable aspects to their characterization—Zoë sustains an almost mechanical loyalty to Mal and Martha falls in unrequited love with the Doctor—these women are not meant to be paragons. Rather, like the heroes with whom they travel, they are cast as imperfect but well worth following.

Lynne Joyrich discusses television as an exemplar of postmodern culture and a threat to "the great male story" ("All That Television" 135). If the medium is one that prioritizes fragments, serialization, ensemble casts, and nonlinearity, then television allows for more ambiguity regarding who is the hero at any given time or in any given episode. Of course, SF television also famously generated the first fan fiction (specifically in response to *Star Trek*) and thus motivated fans to read shows in subversive ways and place marginalized characters at the center of the narratives. In *Textual Poachers: Television Fans and Participatory Culture*, Henry Jenkins notes an elitist tendency among academics to ridicule fan fiction, the vast majority of which is written by women. But Jenkins argues that "[o]rganized fandom is, perhaps first and foremost, an institution of theory and criticism, a semistructured space where competing interpretations and evaluations of common texts are proposed, debated, and negotiated and where readers speculate about the nature of the mass media and their own relationship to it" (86). My training of an oppositional gaze on *Firefly* and *Doctor Who*, both of which have thriving fandoms, is not so very different from what fandoms themselves try to accomplish. If anything, the television medium and the SF genre lend themselves to fluid interpretations. And in the case of these two series, there is a remarkable and subversive parity between the black female "sidekick" and the white male hero, even if (as in fandoms) one has to do a little extra critical and creative work to see it.

Big Damn Heroes

In her biography of Joss Whedon, Amy Pascale describes Whedon's rationale for the space western *Firefly*: "For his next television series, he turned his attention toward something he found lacking in televised science fiction: 'a gritty realism that wasn't an "Alien" ripoff'" (199). Set in 2517, the show blends elements of a classic western with a deep-space setting where the United States and China are former superpowers. With Earth "used up," humans live on planets across the galaxy but under the control of a government called the Alliance. The narrative focuses on the adventures of a group of smugglers aboard a "firefly-class" ship named *Serenity*. But the show did not sustain high ratings and was canceled by Fox even before the entire first season had aired in 2002. The eighty-six-minute pilot and the thirteen forty-four-minute episodes were eventually collated in the intended viewing order on the 2003 DVD box set. An Internet campaign by fans, who have since become known as Browncoats—after the military side for which Zoë and Mal fought during the interplanetary war—also resulted in the production of a feature film, *Serenity* (2005), and a cult following for the series.

Afro-Cuban American actress Gina Torres was already associated with speculative fiction roles long before she was cast as Zoë Washburne on *Firefly*. She played small parts on *M.A.N.T.I.S.* (1994–1995), *Hercules: The Legendary Journey* (1995–1999), *Xena: Warrior Princess* (1995–2001), and *Angel* (1999–2004), and a main role on *Cleopatra 2525*. She also appeared in *The Matrix Reloaded* and *The Matrix Revolutions* in 2003. In response to the question of whether she gravitated to the genre, she answered, "In my 20's I was never anybody's ingénue. I'm damn near six feet tall so I couldn't start my career being the girlfriend or the wife because I hover. Sci-fi and action gave me a voice, a career, a world where I was not odd. I could fit. I could be a warrior" (Norton). Her comment indicates that SF remains a genre where underrepresented women can find representation and empowerment. Despite the brevity of *Firefly*, Torres's performance as Zoë, the rifle-wielding first officer on the *Serenity*, is central to the show's popularity, and her character lives on in everything from action figures to comic books.

Because *Firefly* was broadcast out of order, Zoë, like the rest of the cast, makes her first television appearance in "The Train Job" rather than the intended pilot, "Serenity." But her initial scene is still appropriate in terms of setting up her character, particularly in relation to Mal. Zoë sits with Mal and their fellow crewmate and gun for hire Jayne Cobb (Adam Baldwin) in a dimly lit bar playing a quiet game of the controversially named "Chinese Checkers." When Mal plays his turn, Zoë observes, "That's a bold move," to which Mal responds, "I live on the edge." Zoë then plays her turn, which involves leapfrogging the pieces of both her opponents and thus getting one step closer to winning. Irritated by Mal's poor decision, Jayne says to the captain, "Nice work, dumbass." When a drunken patron toasts the Alliance and insults the Browncoats, Mal leaves the board game to teach the drunk a lesson. But Mal's plan hinges on tacit teamwork with

Zoë—he distracts the man so that Zoë can knock him out from behind with her trademark Winchester rifle. Mal, Zoë, and a reluctant Jayne then brawl their way out of the bar and make it safely back to their ship. Everything that the viewer needs to know about Zoë is foregrounded in this short pre-credits opening scene.[1]

The close partnership between Zoë and Mal is evident in their camaraderie, banter, and tag-team fighting style. Their matching attire is already a semiotic clue that they are partners—fitted tan breeches, dark boots, holsters, and signature guns. By default, they are the Old West stars of the show in a way that the rest of the ensemble cast, including Zoë's husband, the "geeky" Hawaiian shirt–wearing pilot Hoban "Wash" Washburne (Alan Tudyk), are not. And unlike Jayne, who immediately declares his lack of allegiance to any side, Zoë and Mal are Browncoats, or Independents, who fought together in the Unification War. As Wash puts it in the later episode "War Stories," they are "old army buddies [who] have wacky stories that have ribcages in them." Indeed, an obvious template for the Zoë-Mal relationship is the "buddy" film. In *Working Girls: Gender and Sexuality in Popular Cinema*, Yvonne Tasker describes the subtle difference between a hero-sidekick pairing and a buddy pairing as follows: "The distinction, though difficult to draw precisely, lies with the extent to which the film emphasizes hierarchies of knowledge and skill: the relationship between two cop partners, however hierarchical is more equal than that of the professional and the amateur in need of protection" (74). By Tasker's definition, Zoë is not so much Mal's sidekick as his buddy (even though he outranks her) because they are both seasoned soldiers with a similar knowledge base and skill set.

An interracial and heterosexual buddy pairing involving a black woman and a white man remains incredibly rare in American cinema and television, not least because of the racist and sexist ways in which black women have been imagined on-screen in relation to white men. Although *Firefly* does not draw explicit attention to the gender and racial difference between Zoë and Mal, it dispenses with "the recurrent taboo on miscegenation" (Tasker 85) by having Zoë already married to another white man. This narrative backstory allows the buddy relationship to thrive on-screen even as it fosters periodic outbursts of resentment and jealousy from Zoë's husband. And while there is a familiar hierarchy in place—Mal is the (white/male) captain and Zoë is the (black/female) first mate—the buddy formula decenters the white male hero. As Tasker puts it, "The hero is treated as something of a joke, with films opting most often for a comic buddy partnership defined by an eroticized banter" (73).

"The Train Job" thus sets a precedent in which Mal is the butt of com-

Figure 5.1. Zoë (Gina Torres) and Mal (Nathan Fillion) in *Firefly* (2002).

edy and Zoë, a master of deadpan humor, is implicitly (and sometimes explicitly) laughing at his expense. During their board game, Zoë is the better player, deftly outwitting Mal despite his "bold move," which leads to Jayne calling Mal a "dumbass." Once the bar fight begins, Mal is comically thrown out the window while Zoë easily punches her way to the front door. And when Mal explains to Zoë that they lost the war for the same reason that they are losing the fight—"superior numbers"—Zoë drily responds, "Thanks for the reenactment, sir." In the opening episode, then, Mal is not the tactician, the fisticuffer, or even the quick wit that Zoë is. And while Zoë often generates humor with her biting sarcasm and clever wordplay, the humor is never at her own expense. The question of heroism, then, is more ambiguous than one might think. Undoubtedly, the camera foregrounds Mal, right up until the point where he nervously stands on a cliff edge flanked by Zoë and Jayne, waiting to be rescued by the *Serenity*. The very premise of a western suggests that Mal, the charismatic outlaw, *must* be the hero. But if Mal's heroism is partially defined by Zoë, then she does not quite perform the requisite "not-the-hero" function within their buddy relationship. Instead, she outshines him in just about every way possible.

As westerns go, Zoë automatically resists prescribed roles within that genre as well. Nonromantic pairings in the western invariably show men, whether as buddies, hero-sidekick duos, or rivals. The western buddy film—for example, *Butch Cassidy and the Sundance Kid* (1969)—typically involves two white men who both model the clichéd narcissistic hero. The Lone Ranger and Tonto on the ABC series *The Lone Ranger* (1949–1957) epitomize the racist hero-sidekick formula. The third variation of doubling in the western is what Mulvey—citing *The Man Who Shot Liberty Valance* (1962)—calls "a common splitting of the Western hero into two" ("Afterthoughts" 73). Here the two men are rivals, with one man as narcissistic hero and the other as an embodiment of social integration, particularly through marriage, family, and the Law. But again, as Mulvey explains, this oedipal narrative is always a male narrative in which female characters are little more than symbols of "marriage" for the hero(es). White women exist in these stories to be chosen (narrative resolution) or rejected (nostalgic and phallic narcissism). Black women rarely exist at all.

His partnership with Zoë notwithstanding, Mal is a classic narcissistic hero, and his resistance to social integration is one of the ongoing themes of the show. Although he accidentally marries a woman named Saffron (Christina Hendricks) in the episode "Our Mrs. Reynolds," the marriage proves to be a sham. And Mal's object of sexual desire for the duration of the series is the courtesan Inara Serra (Morena Baccarin), which cements his male role as heroic rebel and her female role as signifier of the erotic. Mal even callously introduces Inara to their resident preacher, Shepherd Book (Ron Glass), as a "whore." The other primary female characters on the show, the tomboyish mechanic Kaylee Frye (Jewel Staite) and the fragile but deadly teenager River Tam (Summer Glau), are precluded from being sexual prospects for Mal because they are framed as childlike and sisterly.[2] That leaves Zoë, the female lead in the series (Torres is the top-billed actress in the credits), as Mal's longest and closest female relationship. If the traditional western frames "woman" as one of three possible things to the male hero—his wife, his whore, or his sister—then Zoë simply does not fit. She is neither Mal's sexual prospect (through marriage or prostitution) nor his junior ward. In fact, she only exists in Mal's universe (or 'verse, to use the parlance of the series) as an independent and equal platonic partner and first officer. Because she is not easily reduced to secondariness, it makes more narrative sense to simply read her as a hero in her own right.

Mulvey concludes that placing a woman at the center of a western frames a powerful narrative shift that ostensibly appeals to female spectators. By way of example, Mulvey discusses the character Pearl Chavez (Jennifer Jones) in *Duel in the Sun* (1946). Unlike the traditional male hero, who may choose a wife or a prostitute (or both if the hero is split into two characters), the western heroine is faced with options that function differently: the dichotomy lies in choosing "feminine" wifehood (with a gentleman) at the expense of "masculine" agency (with an outlaw), or vice versa. Pearl's demise is cemented when she is unable to reconcile these two desires. Theorists such as Tania Modleski and Teresa de Lauretis describe a narrative like Pearl's as a female oedipal drama, namely, a conflict between an active masculinity (and repressed desire for the pre-oedipal mother) and a passive femininity (and desire for the father, which culminates in marriage to the Law). The point is that the heroine cannot have it both ways—she must choose between conflicting desires, neither of which guarantees her pleasure. But, as Tasker argues, "[t]he distinctiveness of at least some recent Western narratives involving female protagonists lies in their refusal of that Oedipal trajectory. Or, more precisely, a refusal of its implications: such as the renunciation of activity for passivity, masculinity for femininity, female friends for a man" (59).[3]

Zoë too is situated between two oppositional male characters who "represent different sides of her desire and aspiration" (Mulvey, "Afterthoughts" 76). Although Wash is hardly a stand-in for patriarchal Law, he is very much a symbol of marriage and family and thus a foil for Mal. But since Zoë is already married to Wash at the outset, the prospect of marriage is not a determining factor for her and marriage does not signify narrative closure.[4] She does not have to make a symbolic choice between a "good" man and a "bad" one. Instead, she comfortably balances her marriage to Wash with her equally strong partnership with Mal, whose name, as River points out, means "bad." And Zoë's identity as a wife (and potential mother since she fervently declares her desire for a child in "Heart of Gold") does not compromise her identity as an outlaw. She is thus able to diffuse the implicit contradictions of a female western hero in a way that an earlier cinematic character like Pearl is unable to do. Mulvey stresses that Pearl's suitors also signify a sexual dilemma for the heroine, who must choose either passive sexuality by way of marriage or active sexuality outside of marriage. But Zoë's sexually fulfilling marriage, which is made explicit in the episode "Shindig," again collapses these false dichotomies.

The episode that showcases Zoë's heroism is, appropriately, the one in which she must rescue "her men," as she puts it, from a sadistic villain named Niska (Michael Fairman). In "War Stories," a jealous Wash insists on accompanying Mal on a ground mission while Zoë stays "home" on the *Serenity*. The mission goes awry, the men are kidnapped, and it falls to Zoë to round up the posse. A plot like this one would be a stretch in the original *Star Trek*, not least because it involves a solitary black woman saving

Figure 5.2. Zoë prepares to storm a villain's stronghold.

two white men. Uhura might well be capable of attacking a stronghold to rescue Kirk and Spock, but the series never indulges such story lines (nor do the rebooted new millennial films, for that matter). That Zoë makes it seem natural speaks to her authority on the show and her categorical status as a western heroine. The episode portrays the female oedipal dilemma in very literal terms—Niska tortures Mal and Wash and then asks Zoë to pick one of them for release. Niska himself functions as a powerful symbol of patriarchy, a hyperbolic villain who finds pleasure in the fact that the heroine must choose only one symbolic side of herself, either the rebellion and independence that Mal represents or the wifehood and motherhood that Wash represents. But, in keeping with her entire narrative arc, Zoë resolves the conflict by choosing Wash in that moment (and quietly escorting him to safety) and then choosing Mal later (returning for him with backup support, explosions, and heavy weaponry). Given the onus on female characters to decide between so-called respectable and rebellious brands of femininity, this story line is a powerful deconstruction of that trope.

The conclusion of "War Stories" reassures the viewer that equilibrium between Zoë and "her men" has been reestablished. Mal jokes with Zoë about their "burning sexual tension" in front of Wash, which prompts Zoë to respond, "Take me, sir. Take me hard." The comic buddy formula thus remains intact. At the same time, Zoë flirts with Wash, tucking a napkin into his shirt so that she can feed him "wife soup." Their exchange ends with Wash mock-spanking Zoë and declaring to Mal, "We'll be in our bunk." This final tableau reiterates Zoë's multiple and not necessarily conflicting roles, which include the odd performance of domesticity. Mulvey extends the oedipal dilemma of a western heroine like Pearl to the female spectator, whose "phantasy of masculinization [is] at cross-purposes with itself, restless in its transvestite clothes" ("Afterthoughts" 79). In other words, the narrative indulges a female desire for active agency but then reminds the spectator that such an agency is untenable outside a phallic economy. This is not the case, however, with Zoë, who demonstrates to viewers across races and genders her ability to retain her "masculine" freedom and empowerment as a gunslinger without compromising her "feminine" identity as a woman.

Because of the show's abrupt cancellation, Zoë's story (like the stories of all the characters) is truncated, although her cinematic narrative continues in the feature film *Serenity*, as well as in the *Firefly* fandom. That Zoë is a unique and empowered black female SF character is a given. She transcends a number of the limits faced by Uhura—such as lack of screen time, exoticization, and sexual objectification—and affords viewers a nuanced and incredibly popular model of black womanhood in space. Despite one of the most predictable conditions for an intergalactic black female presence, namely, a white male lead, Zoë also resists secondariness and proves her visual and narrative necessity to the show time and again. In the episode "Safe," Zoë and Mal rescue two of their crewmates from a local mob by striding into town together with their rifles raised. "Appears we got here just in the nick of time," yells Mal to Zoë. "What does that make us?" Zoë's answer is an apt summation of their partnership but also, specifically, her character: "Big damn heroes, sir."

Martha Jones, You're a Star!

First broadcast by the BBC in 1963, *Doctor Who* ran for a remarkable twenty-six seasons before going off the air in 1989. The iconic show charts the adventures of the eponymous Doctor, the last surviving member of an ancient alien race known as the Time Lords. The Doctor travels the universe in his time machine, the TARDIS (Time And Relative Dimension In Space), which is permanently disguised as a blue police box. The show was rebooted in 2005 and has been a global hit ever since, with a massive following. Instead of attempting to examine this ongoing show comprehensively, I focus on the third season of the "new" series, which features the

Doctor's first black female companion, Martha Jones.[5] That season consists of thirteen forty-four-minute episodes written and directed by different people, although Russell T. Davies was head writer and executive producer for all of them.

Freema Agyeman, a British actress of Ghanaian and Iranian heritage, is arguably best known for the role of Martha. The character was lauded as a groundbreaking figure for the show because she was the first black woman to enter the TARDIS and team up with the Doctor. A medical student with a taste for adventure, Martha also quickly became a polarizing figure for Whovians (fans of the show) precisely because she was so different from her white female predecessors. Agyeman reprised her role as Martha for the *Doctor Who* spin-off *Torchwood* (2006–2011) and also played a main part on *Law and Order: UK* (2009–2014) and, most recently, the Netflix SF show *Sense8* (2015–). In a 2007 interview for the *Toronto Star*, Agyeman mentioned her influence on the next generation: "I get letters from black children, saying, 'I really want to be like you.' That is quite something. I mean, it's nice to have a role model that all children can look up to, that non-white children can also identify with" (Salem). Forty years after Nichelle Nichols inspired a young Whoopi Goldberg, there remains a need for black girls to see empowering versions of themselves on the big and small screens. And SF continues to be a genre where some of that creative work takes place.

The title of Martha's inaugural episode, "Smith and Jones," highlights the partnership between her and the Doctor, who temporarily adopts the generic name John Smith. And just as Zoë's first episode contextualizes her character, Martha's initial appearance similarly educates the viewer. Of course, Martha is a companion in a very long line of companions and thus inherits her secondary status. Britton writes of the new series that "female companions are placed at an emotional as well as an intellectual disadvantage to the Doctor, 'soft' vessels of feeling to his 'hard', thoughtful agent of social improvement and change" (117). If the hierarchy between the two characters determines whether they are a hero-sidekick duo or a buddy duo, then *Doctor Who* implements a hierarchy in which the companion can only ever be a sidekick. Regardless of the companion's skills, intelligence, and profession, she is always "only human" and he is always an omnipotent Time Lord. Given the original series' nostalgia for Empire and a British film and television history of marginalizing black women, Martha's juxtaposition with the white male Doctor takes on even greater psychic weight.

Most pernicious is the fact that Martha spends the entirety of her time on the series being explicitly and negatively compared to her immediate predecessor and the Doctor's love interest, Rose Tyler (Billie Piper). The Doctor himself and the *Doctor Who* fandom malign Martha for replacing Rose. This animosity, which is captured in quizzical article titles such as "Why Do Whovians Hate Martha Jones?" and blog posts like "Martha Jones and the Culture of Casual Racism," showcases the targeting of black female characters (and often the actresses behind the roles). Indeed, I will return to this trend in my coda, particularly because of the recent Twitter attack on Leslie Jones, the solitary black actress in the rebooted, all-female *Ghostbusters* (2016). When framing her theory of an oppositional gaze for black female spectators, bell hooks points out that, "[w]ith the possible exception of early race movies, black female spectators have had to develop looking relations within a cinematic context that constructs our presence as absence, that denies the 'body' of the black female so as to perpetuate white supremacy and with it a phallocentric spectatorship where the woman to be looked at and desired is 'white'" (*Black Looks* 118). Martha is a powerful example of the denied black female body whose presence is constantly questioned and overlooked because she is not the white, blond Rose. This pattern is often meant to be comic, as in "The Shakespeare Code" when the Doctor stares intently at Martha and says, "There's something missing, Martha. Something really close, staring me right in the face, and I can't see it. Rose would know." But of course, the joke is less funny in the context of a dominant cinematic tradition that willfully ignores black women.

And yet Martha remains one of the most subversive companions in the history of the series, even if she enables the Doctor's patriarchal identity as narcissistic male hero. The postcolonial feminist filmmaker and theorist Trinh Minh-ha interrogates those binaries that lock women of color into a default Otherness and uses the term "inappropriate/d other" as a means of decentering hegemonic models. Trinh describes this radical female subject as follows:

> She knows she is different while at the same time being Him. Not quite the Same, not quite the Other, she stands in that undetermined threshold place where she constantly drifts in and out. Undercutting the inside/outside opposition, her intervention is necessarily that of both a deceptive insider and a deceptive outsider. She is this Inappropriate Other/Same who moves about with always at least two/four gestures: that of affirming "I am like you" while persisting in her difference; and that of reminding "I am different" while unsettling every definition of otherness arrived at. (74)

Figure 5.3. Martha (Freema Agyeman) and the Doctor (David Tennant) in *Doctor Who: Series 3* (2007).

This description epitomizes Martha, whose difference is coded in the narrative—she is *not* Rose, she is *not* the Doctor, and so on. But Martha's sameness is clear in the fact that she too is British, she too is a doctor, and she too belongs in this series.

Although *Doctor Who* situates the Doctor as the obvious insider/outsider, a Time Lord in the guise of an Englishman, he is really only ever an insider, an ultimate Cartesian self. And his ability to test and traverse boundaries is a sign less of subversiveness than of privilege. The Doctor's "psychic paper," which affords him access to anything and anyone, can hardly be disassociated from his appropriation of a white male identity. Tellingly, the only two characters in the new series who prove immune to his psychic paper are other white men, William Shakespeare (Dean Lennox Kelly) in "The Shakespeare Code" and Fenton (Christopher Fairbank) in the *Series 8* episode "Flatline." The true Inappropriate Other/Same in the series is Martha, who consistently "affirm[s] 'I am like you' while persisting in her difference," and who "unsettle[s] every definition of otherness arrived at."

The fact that Martha is a medical student who dons a white coat three minutes into "Smith and Jones" is an important detail. On a symbolic level, she is *a* doctor, even as *the* Doctor first appears as a patient in the hospital where she works. When an alien species called the Judoon hijacks the hospital and transports it to the moon, Martha is the initial doctor-hero, comforting distraught patients, including the still incognito Doctor:

"I promise you, Mister Smith, we will find a way out. If we can travel to the moon, then we can travel back." Their formal introductions, during which the Doctor reveals his alien identity, frame Martha and the Doctor as the same (or the Same, as Trinh might put it) in a way that cannot be said for any of the previous companions on the show. "I'm the Doctor," he declares, to which she replies, "Me too, if I can pass my exams." This exchange becomes a pattern in the series, with Martha always maintaining her own claim to the title "doctor," which, she clarifies, "you've got to earn." When a man begins to choke to death in "The Shakespeare Code," the Doctor says, "Leave it to me. I'm a doctor," and Martha rebuts, "So am I, near enough." And in "Family of Blood," Martha explains to the Doctor's newfound, albeit fleeting, love interest, "I don't just follow him around. I'm training to be a doctor. Not an alien doctor, a proper doctor. A doctor of medicine."

Over the course of "Smith and Jones," Martha and the Doctor work together to catch the Plasmavore that the Judoon are hunting and return the hospital to Earth. Martha is more consultant than sidekick, with the Doctor periodically asking for her assessment of their situation. As a ruse to confuse the Judoon, the Doctor kisses Martha, thus transferring his genetic material so that she will register as nonhuman. Accordingly, the Judoon are unable to "catalog" Martha with their scanners and ask in frustration, "What are you?" This question, typically leveled at the Doctor, is instead presented to Martha, "a deceptive insider and a deceptive outsider." And much as Zoë saves Mal and Wash in "War Stories," Martha saves the Doctor in "Smith and Jones," a feat that she repeats in multiple episodes and that is often inextricable from her identity as a doctor. Martha performs CPR on the dead Doctor, administering chest compressions and mouth-to-mouth to revive him before herself falling unconscious from lack of oxygen.[6] At the end of the first episode, the Doctor's professed reason for inviting Martha to join him on his travels is that she "saved [his] life."

So *Doctor Who: Series 3* introduces a companion who is not merely an Other to the Doctor but an Inappropriate Other/Same who confounds binaries, a black female doctor who is "not quite the Same, not quite the Other" (Minh-ha 74). Martha allegedly does not belong (and is thus inappropriate), but neither does she fulfill expectations for Otherness (thus resisting appropriation). Negative fan reactions to Martha simply reiterate her ability to challenge viewers when it comes to hegemonic models. Her characterization is more provocative than, say, the transformation of her successor, Donna Noble (Catherine Tate), into the "DoctorDonna" in

Figure 5.4. Martha, in her role as medical doctor, examines the Doctor, in his role as patient.

Series 4. Martha does not take on her doctor identity by association with the Doctor but exists as one independently of him. Their partnership, like the Zoë-Mal relationship, merely highlights their sameness, despite gender and racial difference. That the Doctor begins to systematically demean Martha once she agrees to travel with him—he calls Rose irreplaceable and Martha a "novice" by comparison—speaks more to his perpetuation of the racist myopia that drove Whovians than any overt change in Martha's abilities. Martha's scientific knowledge and initiative are constant features from her first episode to her last, prompting the Doctor to exclaim in "The Lazarus Experiment," "Martha Jones, you're a star!"

Despite its tendency to avoid explicit references to social prejudices and the systems that underpin them, *Doctor Who* is not entirely oblivious to racism and sexism. Lindy Orthia applauds the "color-blind" casting of the new series but concludes that "*equal opportunity casting* is the beginning and the end of cosmopolitanism in *Doctor Who*" (216) because the series largely expunges histories like British colonialism. However, in casting Martha as a black female companion, the show is forced to at least acknowledge the prejudices that someone like Martha might face, even if that acknowledgment is sometimes trite. Martha's presence on the show is critical when it comes to interrogating the ideological racism and sexism that pervade cinema and television (something that Zoë, for all her agency, does not do on *Firefly*). It is through Martha, for example, that the show raises questions about the transatlantic slave trade in the context of Elizabethan England, even if the Doctor's flippant answer simply reiterates his own white male privilege: "Just walk about like you own the place. Works for me."

In the two-episode story arc "Human Nature" and "Family of Blood," Martha hides and guards an amnesiac Doctor (who thinks he is human) at a boys' boarding school in 1913. While the Doctor unconsciously becomes a naive history teacher and falls in love with the school nurse, Martha must consciously play the role of personal servant and scullery maid. Irony pervades this narrative, which plays on the fact that Martha is once again invisible to the Doctor, especially when juxtaposed with a white woman. The schoolboys' racist bullying and the nurse's skepticism that Martha, a dark-skinned "skivvy," could be a doctor are effective in affording a certain racial realism to this otherwise "color-blind" show. Certainly, Martha's transition from space-traveling doctor to domestic servant is an odd and yet poignant reversal of fortune in light of the fact that black women on television were once exclusively maids (hence Whoopi Goldberg's amazement at a character like Uhura).

The Doctor's narcissistic heroism is also a dominant theme in these episodes, which dwell on what Neale calls "the contradiction between narcissism and the law, between an image of *narcissistic* authority on the one hand and an image of *social* authority on the other" (14). Like Mulvey's split western hero, the Doctor becomes two men, the human John Smith (social authority) and the Time Lord (narcissistic authority). The former is a weak but honorable man who wishes to marry a woman and accept the Law and social responsibility. The latter, of course, is a lost but omnipotent masculine principle for which the world (and Martha) pines. In the end, the Time Lord awakens, reclaiming his phallic dominance and firmly rejecting social integration, especially in the form of marriage. Martha's role in the narrative is to sustain and promote nostalgia for the lost hero and to make sure that he returns. As a horrified John Smith says to her, "So your job was to execute me."

But even as Martha is reduced to the stereotypically female function of "the passive, the waiting" (Mulvey, "Afterthoughts" 72), she is not merely an erotic object to be chosen or rejected (like the nurse with whom Smith falls in love). Because she is not a love interest for the Doctor, Martha is again a kind of threshold figure, rejected as a potential lover yet chosen as a companion. If women are traditionally a threat to the narcissistic hero because they symbolize marriage, then Martha is a different kind of woman. Her obvious desire for the Doctor aside, Martha's enabling of narcissistic heroism rather than social integration has as much to do with her own identity as that of the Doctor. After all, Martha's first episode introduces her as a member of a loving but chaotic family, all of whom feature regularly in the series. So Martha too faces a symbolic conflict between social belonging and rebellious escapism.

If we return to the notion of a female oedipal trajectory, the heroine in question oscillates between opposing and frequently gendered desires, which she must eventually reconcile by making a choice. Zoë resolves this dilemma by sustaining her relationships with both Mal and Wash, who represent her conflicting desires. What is interesting about *Doctor Who* is that the titular character presents radical freedom and "not marriage" to his female companions, but always on terms that render him the ultimate patriarchal figure. In choosing the Doctor, a companion is completing the oedipal narrative trajectory (which guides her toward passive femininity and a husband/father figure) rather than subverting it. In this respect, Martha is unique, the one companion who, as Britton points out, "left him of her own volition, ostensibly to complete her medical training" (133). If Martha's enthrallment with the Doctor aligns her with Rose, her rejection of the Doctor sets her firmly apart. Martha's strongest challenge to the Doctor's narcissistic male heroism is her admission that he is *not* irresistible. As she puts it in her farewell speech, "This is me getting out."

In her final episode of the series, "Last of the Time Lords," Martha plays her most prominent role as a legendary hero, helping the Doctor to defeat another Time Lord, the Master. This finale sustains the theme of Martha's invisibility, albeit in a less comic and more critical way. With her family and the Doctor enslaved by the Master, Martha goes on the run and becomes a very literal rebel, traveling the world on a secret mission to save the world.[7] When one of her contacts remarks on her ability to evade detection, she explains that her TARDIS key "makes [her] sort of, not invisible, just unnoticeable." When he says, "I can see you," she responds, "That's because you wanted to." This loaded dialogue reiterates the ongoing predicament of black women on-screen, as well as the powerful need for a shift in perspective when it comes to their representation and spectatorship. Martha ultimately succeeds in her mission, even if that mission is to canonize the Doctor and thus rejuvenate his powers. But in their very last conversation, Martha brings the focus back to *her* identity as a doctor-hero: "Spent all these years training to be a doctor. Now I've got people to look after." And when the Doctor says, "Martha Jones, you saved the world," her answer is fitting: "Yes, I did. I spent a lot of time with you thinking I was second best, but you know what? I *am* good."

The Door Is Open

Television as a popular and accessible medium continues to thrive and evolve, especially in a global marketplace that now includes more options than ever before—network television, cable, and streaming platforms like Netflix and Hulu. But as Darnell Hunt points out, "Economically, culturally, and politically, popular television remains firmly in white control" (21). And though characters such as Zoë Washburne and Martha Jones are vital to shifting paradigms of white- and male-centered representation, they are also one-offs in the grand scheme of SF television and British and American television generally. Nor are they in starring roles along the lines of an Olivia Pope (Kerry Washington) in *Scandal* (2012–) or an Annalise Keating (Viola Davis) in *How to Get Away with Murder* (2014–). Of course, these two contemporary crime dramas on ABC are produced by Shonda Rhimes, herself one of the few black female presences behind the camera in the television industry. If anything, speculative television lags behind other genres in its ability to do or show anything fresh regarding black subjectivities (and speculative films lag further behind still), despite the fact that speculative material can often take the most poetic license.

Zoë and Martha are also increasingly dated characters. There are few new exciting black female figures, however, to whom one can turn in prime time. The CBS series *Star Trek: Discovery* premieres in May 2017 with a black female character, Rainsford (Sonequa Martin-Green), at the helm of the eponymous starship. And the new companion on *Doctor Who: Series 10*, which premiered in April 2017, is a black woman—the curiously named Bill Potts (Pearl Mackie). But these shows notwithstanding, space dramas in general have waned in television, a curious counterbalance to recent space blockbusters such as Alfonso Cuarón's *Gravity* (2013); Christopher Nolan's *Interstellar* (2014); Ridley Scott's *The Martian* (2015); Abrams's *Star Trek* (2009), *Star Trek into Darkness* (2013), and *Star Wars: The Force Awakens* (2015); and the latest installments of the last two franchises, Justin Lin's *Star Trek Beyond* (2016) and Gareth Edwards's *Rogue One: A Star Wars Story* (2016). Abrams's *Star Wars* broke numerous box-office records and is now one of the top three highest-grossing films of all time. And the critical and commercial hit *Hidden Figures* (2016) deserves mention here as well, although it is not speculative but rather the very opposite—a docudrama about three black women and their pivotal role in the 1960s space race. But space television has been outstripped by other speculative productions, particularly horror series such as *The Walking Dead* (2010–), epic fantasies such as *Game of Thrones* (2011–) and *Once Upon a Time* (2011–), and superhero shows such as *Jessica Jones* (2014–) and *Luke Cage* (2016–).

Notably, white female characters and (less frequently) black male characters continue to find more empowered lead roles in these speculative television shows, but black female characters rarely do. The popular show *Sleepy Hollow* (2013–) features a nuanced black female character in police officer Abigail "Abbie" Mills (Nicole Beharie), but like the majority of black women (and women of color generally) in speculative series, she is billed second to a white male lead; moreover, she becomes even less important when a white female counterpart enters the narrative. Vanessa Willoughby writes in her piece for *Bitch* magazine, "On television, viewers were delighted to see Black actress Nicole Beharie in an autonomous, intelligent, kick-ass leading role on FOX's *Sleepy Hollow*. Yet as the seasons went on, writers sidelined Beharie's leading lady in favor of Ichabod's wife, a white woman named Katrina. For sci-fi viewers, this sent the message that even when a Black woman is an integral part of a show, her white counterpart will always outrank her" (21). In terms of a pivotal and layered black female character, the most promising SF series currently on the air is HBO's *Westworld* (2016–), which showcases the shrewd bordello madam and "host" Maeve Millay (Thandie Newton).

That black women in SF television have found more empowering roles since Nichelle Nichols played Uhura is true—but not so true that one can point to a plethora of examples. Nichols quotes from memory something that Martin Luther King Jr. said to her and that made her reconsider her decision to leave *Star Trek*: "He said, 'Think about this, Nichelle. You have changed the face of television forever. They can never undo what they've done. The door is open!'" (Tyson). King's metaphor accurately captures the radical dimensions of Nichols's television role in the 1960s. But in the new millennium, the figurative door has yet to see any substantial change or movement. Instead, it remains slightly ajar, with characters like Zoë and Martha inching it open ever further but never throwing it wide. Such a shift can occur only if the entire system of production and distribution is radically altered. Only then will the door truly be open—or better yet, taken entirely off its hinges.

CODA

Final Frontiers

The heart of a woman falls back with the night,
And enters some alien cage in its plight,
And tries to forget it has dreamed of the stars
While it breaks, breaks, breaks on the sheltering bars.
GEORGIA DOUGLAS JOHNSON, "THE HEART OF A WOMAN" (1918)

The first time Uhura (Nichelle Nichols) ever appears on-screen is ten seconds into the *Star Trek* pilot, "The Man Trap" (1966). In this fleeting shot,
she sits at a console beside another (white male) officer; both of them wear
red uniforms and press buttons on their dashboards. A blue-clad Spock
(Leonard Nimoy) sits in the captain's chair behind Uhura and the unnamed officer, their configuration forming a triangle on the bridge of the
Enterprise. Although subsequent scenes reveal details like Uhura's notoriously short miniskirt (worn by all the female Starfleet officers) and her
frustration with the word "frequency," her introductory shot situates her
as a visual equal to her white male colleagues. Spock outranks both her
and her console counterpart, but she is framed as an integral member
of the bridge crew and as a peer of the officer sitting next to her. Fast-
forward roughly forty years to J. J. Abrams's *Star Trek* (2009), which functions as both homage to and reboot of the original series and maintains
the same ensemble characters from the starship *Enterprise.* In Abrams's
film, Uhura (Zoe Saldana) first appears after about twenty minutes—she
sashays into a crowded bar in the same red uniform, her long hair swish-
ing as she walks in time to the music. Theoretically, there is much promise
in this "new" Uhura, who now exists not only in the twenty-third-century
universe of *Star Trek* but also in our twenty-first-century "postfeminist"
and space-age world where a black man has been president of the United

Figure 6.1. Uhura (Zoe Saldana) on the bridge of the *Enterprise* in *Star Trek* (2009).

States. However, the new Uhura is not particularly radical; rather, she signals a kind of retrograde for the character, especially in her opening scene.

The camera stays close as Uhura sidles up to the bar to order a round of drinks. Via her ensuing conversation with a drunk James Kirk (Chris Pine), the viewer learns that she is a xenolinguist who can hold her own in a verbal sparring match and who comfortably rejects Kirk's advances. But her character is never developed much further. What her opening scene really does is set her up in one of the most clichéd cinematic roles for female characters, namely, object of heterosexual male desire. One can easily return here to Laura Mulvey's feminist analysis of classic Hollywood cinema, which posits the traditional female character as the passive object of the gaze and the traditional male character and spectator as the active bearer of the gaze. Mulvey argues that female characters are often reduced to fetishized icons while the male characters "make things happen and control events" ("Visual Pleasure" 63). Her description of the female characters in *Only Angels Have Wings* (1939) and *To Have and Have Not* (1944) perfectly captures Uhura in the rebooted *Star Trek*: "[T]he film opens with the woman as object of the combined gaze of spectator and all the male protagonists in the film. She is isolated, glamorous, on display, sexualized. But as the narrative progresses she falls in love with the main male protagonist and becomes his property" ("Visual Pleasure" 63–64). Although Uhura falls in love not with Kirk but with his co-lead, Spock (Zachary Quinto), Mulvey's point still stands.

Certainly, the camera functions as a proxy for a heterosexual male gaze of desire as it tracks Uhura into the bar, only to symbolically hand off to Kirk, who sustains the paradigm of voyeurism. The fact that she is first filmed from behind also recalls bell hooks's point that "[a]lthough contemporary thinking about black female bodies does not attempt to read the body as a sign of 'natural' racial inferiority, the fascination with black 'butts' continues" (*Black Looks* 63). Unlike her 1960s counterpart, the new Uhura is introduced as a faceless sexual object whose most distinguishing feature is her "sexy" walk. And once she rejects Kirk's advances, Uhura is visually and narratively marginalized and Kirk takes center stage by getting into a bar fight. Uhura becomes even more objectified when Kirk "accidentally" gropes her breasts during the fight. And her repeated orders to the men to stop fighting are entirely ignored—only when a senior white male Starfleet officer enters the room (looking for Kirk) does the fight stop.

Subsequent scenes featuring Uhura similarly eroticize and objectify her. For example, Uhura enters her Starfleet Academy bedroom at the end of the day, begins to undress in preparation for bed, and chats with her female roommate about picking up an emergency transmission from a Klingon prison planet. This transmission is significant to the plot and manifests later when Kirk raises it with his superiors. But in the bedroom scene, the words that Uhura speaks are meant to be innocuous, or "tuned out," to borrow a phrase from hooks. Hooks writes that "the voices of black women—giving orders, making threats, fussing—could be tuned out, could become a kind of background music, audible but not acknowledged as significant speech" (*Talking Back* 6). Although Uhura periodically has important things to say, her words carry less weight than those of her white male peers, a fact that is all the more ironic since she is a language specialist who, in Kirk's flirtatious words, "has a talented tongue." So while Uhura discusses her scientific discovery, Kirk, who was in the middle of a sexual tryst with Uhura's roommate, hides under the bed and enjoys the view of Uhura getting undressed.

From this point onward, Uhura, in greater alignment with her predecessor, has only a few minutes of screen time and always alongside one of her white male costars. She comforts Spock after the destruction of his home planet Vulcan and the death of his mother, gently asking him, "What do you need?" When Kirk and Spock leave together on a rescue mission, Uhura takes a few minutes to say farewell to Spock, kissing him tenderly, much to Kirk's smug amusement. Aside from these kinds of moments, she does little and is ultimately superfluous to the narrative, in keeping with Mulvey's observations on women in classic cinema. Uhura's final and dialogue-free scene takes place on the bridge of the *Enterprise*, which is now a recognizable tableau of the original. Spock walks past her, eliciting a girlish grin, and she then disappears from view. Abrams's sequel, *Star Trek into Darkness* (2013), and Justin Lin's third installment, *Star Trek Beyond* (2016), do little to improve on the precedent set in the 2009 film. Citing Mulvey's split western hero, Lynne Joyrich argues that "instead of a doubled or bifurcated hero, classic *Star Trek* provides a sort of triumvirate—McCoy, Spock, and Kirk (who are, in reverse order, the starship's captain, first officer, and chief medical officer, the three constantly intertwined men who figure centrally in almost every episode)" ("Feminist" 73). The new millennial films extend this formula, which charts the oedipal struggles of multiple white male heroes over and over again but never tells the story of the solitary black female crew member.

If one looks to other current examples, they are similarly disheartening. For all that Abrams's *Star Wars: The Force Awakens* (2015) shattered box-office records, it did little to change the status quo for black women in SF. Vanessa Willoughby expresses disappointment in the part assigned to Academy Award winner Lupita Nyong'o: "Instead of an elegant, otherworldly humanoid or lightsaber-wielding Jedi, Nyong'o's character was a CGI, bandana-wearing, green-skinned alien. Nyong'o's *Star Wars* role exemplifies how Hollywood superficially honors diversity without having to actually show it onscreen" (21). Jack Thorne's 2016 stage play *Harry Potter and the Cursed Child* debuted with black British actress Noma Dumezweni as the adult Hermione Granger, a casting decision that immediately caused controversy. J. K. Rowling, who cowrote the original story with Thorne, fiercely defended the possibility of a black Hermione. And sold-out tickets indicate that the play is having a robust first run. But Dumezweni continues to be the target of racist vitriol on social media, which she commented on in an interview with the *Sunday Times*: "I am a black woman who has been given this character called Hermione to play on the stage. But actually, we've all grown up with the books, with Emma Watson playing her in the films. Imagery is so strong" (Wise).

Most recently, the African American actress Leslie Jones made global headlines because of the vicious Twitter campaign launched against her in the opening week of the rebooted SF comedy *Ghostbusters* (2016). Directed by Paul Feig, the film casts the titular "ghostbusters" as four women. Although this casting incited backlash from fans of the original *Ghostbusters* (1984), Jones became the primary target of a blatantly racist online assault that resulted in her temporary leave from Twitter and the suspension of multiple accounts for their use of hate speech. In an interview with

Seth Meyers, Jones explained that she was "used to the insults" but that "what scared [her] was the injustice of a gang of people jumping against [her] for such a sick cause" (Meyers). Jones's choice of words eerily recalls the kind of racism that once motivated lynch mobs. Of course, cyberspace attacks take the form of blogs, posts, and tweets, but if online trolls seem harmless, they nonetheless practice a familiar mob mentality: they don masks of anonymity in order to collectively and maliciously deride an individual because of their race, gender, class, sexuality, and so on.

One is tempted to ask a simple question: where do "we" go from here? But the last impression from this book, its case studies, and the future directions to which it points should not be one of mere victimization where black women are concerned. On the contrary, I have tried to argue that each of the films and series discussed here is unusual and that these black female characters (and the actresses who portray them) afford radical versions of black femininity, often despite the clear limitations of the roles. Naomie Harris's Selena remains one of the most nuanced horror heroines in the history of British cinema. Sanaa Lathan's Lex may well be the only black woman in *any* Western horror film to be the last one standing. Clare-Hope Ashitey's Kee challenges viewers with her very excess as a signifier, transcending the obvious boundaries set for her character. And Quvenzhané Wallis's Hushpuppy is revolutionary, a black girl child who demands centrality for the duration of a Hollywood film. Gina Torres's Zoë continues to be a hit over a decade after the cancellation of *Firefly*, a fact that speaks to a rare mainstream appeal for a black female character. And Freema Agyeman's Martha, though a divisive figure for fans, is the companion who ultimately, and perhaps surprisingly, chose herself over the Doctor.

Given my focus on black women in speculative fiction, a concluding reference to the #BlackGirlMagic meme is appropriate. CaShawn Thompson created the hashtag in 2013 as a means of sharing encouraging (rather than hateful) messages about black femininity. In an interview with the *Los Angeles Times*, Thompson explained her logic for creating and naming the hashtag: "I say 'magic' because it's something that people don't always understand. Sometimes our accomplishments might seem to come out of thin air, because a lot of times, the only people supporting us are other black women" (Thomas). A movement like this one reminds us that magic is not limited to the worlds of science fiction and fantasy and that superheroes also exist in our own "real" world. In July 2016, Marvel Comics writer Brian Michael Bendis revealed to *Time* magazine that the new Iron Man would be a black female teenager named Riri Williams (Dockterman). While this new character is (once again) controversial and (pre-dictably) originates with a white male writer, she models incremental change and hints at a major protagonist role in future film productions. More importantly, she points to the "real" superheroes that Bendis drew on for inspiration, namely, the everyday black women who regularly defy odds, challenge limits, break molds, and make magic.

Notes

Introduction

1. By sheer coincidence, *Star Trek* premiered on Canada's CTV on the same day that the prime minister of South Africa and champion of apartheid Hendrik Verwoerd was assassinated in Cape Town's House of Assembly.

2. The Canadian writer Margaret Atwood makes the following distinction between SF and speculative fiction: "What I mean by 'science fiction' is those books that descend from H. G. Wells's *The War of the Worlds* . . . things that could not possibly happen—whereas, for me, 'speculative fiction' means plots that descend from Jules Verne's books . . . things that really could happen but just hadn't completely happened when the authors wrote the books" (6). Atwood acknowledges that her definition does not necessarily align with the definitions of other writers and critics. And she distinguishes the "could not possibly happen" from the "really could happen."

3. The Oracle (Gloria Foster and Mary Alice), Niobe (Jada Pinkett Smith), Storm (Halle Berry), and the "new" Uhura (Zoe Saldana) are largely peripheral in these respective franchises.

4. Examples include Anastasia "Dee" Dualla (Kandyse McClure) in *Battlestar Galactica*, Michonne (Danai Gurira) in *The Walking Dead*, Abigail "Abbie" Mills (Nicole Beharie) in *Sleepy Hollow*, Roberta Warren (Kellita Smith) in *Z Nation*, Amanita (Freema Agyeman) in *Sense8*, and Maeve Millay (Thandie Newton) in *Westworld*.

5. Incidentally, Saldana's blackness is virtually erased in the first two titles by way of computer-generated imagery (CGI) and body makeup.

6. Monica White Ndounou's *Shaping the Future of African American Film: Color-Coded Economics and the Story Behind the Numbers* (2014) provides an excellent discussion of the Ulmer Scale, a list of Hollywood stars and their so-called bankability as compiled by the journalist James Ulmer. Ndounou argues that the scale perpetuates the commodification of black bodies and falls short when it comes to fairly representing people of color. According to the official website, the Ulmer Scale assigns an overall "bankability rating" between zero and 300 by combining scores out of 100 in three film categories—art house, midrange, and big-

budget studio. The total score determines a star's status as A-list, B-list, and so on. As Ndounou also points out, "the scale itself is difficult to access" (179) and available only by special order for $199. But Ndounou's own reproduction of the scale's 2009–2010 data provides some sense of the rankings for black actors in Hollywood. There are no black women in the A-list range and only two black men, Will Smith and Denzel Washington. Halle Berry is the highest-ranked black female celebrity, with a B+ rating. By comparison, Zoe Saldana is rated a D-list star, alongside actresses such as Taraji P. Henson, Viola Davis, and Kerry Washington. None of the black actresses whom I focus on in this book—Naomie Harris, Sanaa Lathan, Clare-Hope Ashitey, Quvenzhané Wallis, Gina Torres, and Freema Agyeman—appears in Ndounou's appendix of selected actors on the Ulmer Scale. Based on the rankings themselves and the fact that the data are over five years old, it is possible that these actresses do not feature on the scale at all.

7. James Snead's *White Screens/Black Images: Hollywood from the Dark Side* (1994) and Donald Bogle's *Toms, Coons, Mulattoes, Mammies, and Bucks: An Interpretive History of Blacks in American Films* (2001) provide comprehensive examinations of codes and stereotypes of blackness in American cinema.

8. This is not to say that black female filmmakers do not exist. A number of websites are dedicated to showcasing black women directors from around the world; Sisters in Cinema (www.sistersincinema.com) and the Centre for the Study and Research of African Women in Cinema (www.africanwomenincinema.org) are two such examples. And some of these filmmakers have directed SF or more broadly speculative cinema. The British director Ngozi Onwurah released *Welcome II the Terrordome* in 1995. In a non-Western context, a number of African female directors have been spotlighted for their recent forays into speculative cinema. Zimbabwean writer and director Tsitsi Dangarembga's short film *Kare Kare Zvako: Mother's Day* (2004), a feminist folk tale with fantastical elements, was featured at the 2005 Sundance Film Festival. Similarly, Kenyan director Wanuri Kahiu's short Afrofuturist film *Pumzi* (2009) was featured at Sundance in 2010. But black female directors are largely absent in the mainstream British and American speculative film and television industries, and almost as rare in leading on-screen roles.

9. Interdisciplinary exchange and conversation have been essential to the formation of film and television studies, as well as to critical race and feminist approaches within these fields. This range of theoretical frameworks allows me a richer engagement with my case studies than would be possible relying only on film and television theories, not least because black femininity and spectatorship have been so overlooked within these disciplines.

10. Afrofuturism, a black cultural ethos formulated in the late twentieth century, has become a twenty-first-century phenomenon (thanks to contemporary black female artists such as Janelle Monáe) and yielded at least one book-length study, Ytasha Womack's *Afrofuturism: The World of Black Sci-Fi and Fantasy Culture* (2013). Comparable works, which again prioritize literary case studies rather than cinematic ones, are De Witt Kilgore's *Astrofuturism: Science, Race, and Visions in Space* (2003) and *Race in American Science Fiction* (2011) by Isiah Lavender III.

11. There are also more comprehensive studies of blacks in Western cinema, such as Manthia Diawara's *Black American Cinema* (1993), Ed Guerrero's *Framing Blackness: The African American Image in Film* (1993), Snead's *White Screens/Black*

Images, Bogle's *Toms, Coons, Mulattoes, Mammies, and Bucks*, and Bourne's *Black in the British Frame*.

12. Yvonne Sims's *Women of Blaxploitation: How the Black Action Film Heroine Changed American Popular Culture* (2006) and Stephane Dunn's *"Baad Bitches" and Sassy Supermamas: Black Power Action Films* (2008) are genre-based studies. There are also works that examine black women as consumers and producers of cinema, such as Jacqueline Bobo's *Black Women as Cultural Readers* (1995) and Kwakiutl Dreher's *Dancing on the White Page: Black Women Entertainers Writing Autobiography* (2008).

13. See examples such as J. Fred MacDonald's *Blacks and White TV: African Americans in Television since 1948* (1992), Herman Gray's *Watching Race: Television and the Struggle for Blackness* (1995) and *Cultural Moves: African Americans and the Politics of Representation* (2005), Bogle's *Prime Time Blues: African Americans on Network Television* (2001), Darnell Hunt's *Channeling Blackness: Studies on Television and Race in America* (2005), Smith-Shomade's *Watching While Black: Centering the Television of Black Audiences* (2012), and Timothy Havens's *Black Television Travels: African American Media around the Globe* (2013).

14. There are also related studies such as Robin R. Means Coleman's *Horror Noire: Blacks in American Horror Films from the 1890s to Present* (2011) and Sandra Jackson and Julie Moody-Freeman's edited collection *The Black Imagination: Science Fiction, Futurism, and the Speculative* (2011).

15. Selena is relegated to one of the "girls" that the white male protagonist saves (Nama 65). Granted, Nama clarifies in his introduction that "where others have chosen to privilege the social relations of class or gender in their textual reading of SF cinema, I have purposefully privileged black racial formation" (5). So gender is not Nama's priority, and he does not address black female characters in any depth.

16. André Carrington's *Speculative Blackness: The Future of Race in Science Fiction* (2016) merits attention because it includes a chapter on Nichols's Uhura (though she is once again the sole focus in a discussion of black women in SF).

17. Kinitra Brooks promotes hooks's oppositional gaze as a useful methodology for horror cinema and undertakes her own critical reading of Selena in "The Importance of Neglected Intersections: Race and Gender in Contemporary Zombie Texts and Theories." I affirm Brooks's point and add simply that Wallace's and hooks's related theories of black female spectatorship are powerful tools for engaging with speculative cinema more broadly.

18. Gary Westfahl defines postmodern space opera as follows: "Stories aspire to the epic scope of classic space opera but may be tempered by a hard-edged cynicism, deeper than the self-serving pragmatism of Ruritanian space opera, or even grave pessimism about humanity's future" (206).

Chapter 1

1. The opening scene is reminiscent of Stanley Kubrick's *A Clockwork Orange* (1971), in which the protagonist Alex DeLarge (Malcolm McDowell) is forced to watch violent images as a form of therapy.

2. In *The Omega Man*, blood holds an inverted meaning, as Adilifu Nama dis-

cusses: "Red is virtually a character, a presence that is reinforced at every visual opportunity to signal a connection between the color, blood, and white male virility" (51). Along with its title, which points to white masculinity as a "last" or "ultimate" masculinity, *The Omega Man* uses the color red as a symbol for its white male hero. Thus, *28 Days Later* complicates this particular cinematic predecessor by reframing blood as a symbol of female power.

3. As Kinitra Brooks argues, "Selena complicates Clover's paradigm of the final girl not simply because of her race, but also by being placed within a zombie context" (472). Indeed, Selena challenges or evades expectations for a range of cinematic horror tropes, including the Final Girl, the monstrous-feminine, and the *femme castratrice*.

4. It may be more accurate to say that Selena is the only *adult* black female lead in British horror cinema, since the 2016 zombie film *The Girl with All the Gifts* stars a black female child protagonist, Melanie (Sennia Nanua). This very recent but largely unavailable movie, which had a limited theatrical release, would certainly be worth reading alongside *28 Days Later*.

5. Turner plays a similar figure as Aunty Entity in the 1985 Australian post-apocalyptic film *Mad Max Beyond Thunderdome*.

6. Jones starred in the fantasy film *Conan the Destroyer* (1984) the previous year. The Bond films, of course, have recruited a number of black female singers, most notably Shirley Bassey, to sing the title songs.

7. In Hollywood, this particular trope dates back to early films such as *Drums o' Voodoo* (1933), *Chloe, Love Is Calling You* (1934), *The Devil's Daughter* (1939), and *King of the Zombies* (1941). And it has remained a popular trope, as evinced by films such as *Sugar Hill* (1974), *The House on Skull Mountain* (1974), *Angel Heart* (1987), *Eve's Bayou* (1997), *Midnight in the Garden of Good and Evil* (1997), *Queen of the Damned* (2002), *The Skeleton Key* (2005), and *Venom* (2005), as well as television shows such as *Once Upon a Time* (2011–) and *American Horror Story: Coven* (2013–2014).

8. It *is* possible that the very end of the film, which shows the trio as a renewed oedipal family living in an idyllic cottage (while the Infected die off from starvation), undermines its whole feminist project. But, as I discuss, the conclusion of *28 Days Later* still evades the patriarchal conventions of horror cinema.

9. A massive replica of the sculpture *Laöcoon and His Sons* (also known as *The Laöcoon Group*) occupies the foyer of the mansion and serves as a backdrop in a number of scenes. The sculpture is arguably a foreboding sign of what is in store for this particular patriarchy and those who ascribe to it.

10. This line, which does not appear in Garland's screenplay, speaks to a Western history of violent curiosity where black female sexuality is concerned and a specific tradition of rape in the context of slavery. As Norma Manatu writes, "The literature on the black woman's sexual history in U.S. culture suggests that both her blackness and female form have evoked and embodied all the hidden sexual fantasies and desires that have captured white men's imagination since the beginning of slavery" (27). This sexual objectification of black women, which also took place in British colonies, is recalled in *28 Days Later*.

11. Consider the epithet "scarlet woman," which ostensibly originates in the red-clad "whore of Babylon" in the Book of Revelation.

12. Nama stresses the fact that Mailer is a black man and argues that this racialized portrayal of an Infected is damaging: "Like the victims of the Tuskegee 'experiment,' the ailing black man in *28 Days Later* is an object of pathological spectacle and voyeuristic subjugation" (66). Similarly, G. Williams reads the blackness of Mailer and Selena as inextricable from their roles as Others: "He and, interestingly, Selena—our other and initial outcast in the film—are the only black characters in the film. This echoing of Rochester's imprisonment of Bertha in the attic of his manor as a creature too savage to civilize may be unintentional on Boyle's part, but its colonial traditionalism rings loudly in the hinterlands of the British empire" (41). Without discounting these points, which have merit but need further explication, I would point out that the film includes at least one other black character, a soldier named Private Bell (Junior Laniyan), who is very much aligned with West and his patriarchy. Bell is the character who runs out of bullets and then begs Jim not to leave him.

13. The NATO phonetic alphabet corresponds to the twenty-six letters of the English alphabet and runs from "Alfa" and "Bravo" to "Yankee" and "Zulu."

14. There is also a more tongue-in-cheek alternative ending that is identical to the official one except that Jim is absent from the Lake District scenes. In this version, only Selena and Hannah make it to the farmhouse, with Jim presumably dead from his gunshot wound. While sitting at the sewing machine, Selena has a brief and initially strange conversation with an unseen listener: "We're going to have to fertilize you. We need offspring. Or in the long term, this isn't going to work." Any vague possibility of the listener being Jim is dispelled when the camera shows a chicken perched on the table. Hannah enters on cue to declare the arrival of the jet, the two female characters signal the plane from their giant sign, and the credits role after Selena speaks the last line.

Chapter 2

1. A major award or nomination does not guarantee stardom for actors, and black women are no exception. Black women have been sporadically nominated for Best Actress and Best Supporting Actress Academy Awards over the last century, and the majority of these actresses remain D-list celebrities, according to the Ulmer Scale. The most recent Best Actress nominees (since Berry's historic 2001 win) are Gabourey Sidibe, Viola Davis, Quvenzhané Wallis, and Ruth Negga. The new millennium has been more rewarding, quite literally, for black women in the Best Supporting Actress category. Queen Latifah, Sophie Okonedo, Ruby Dee, Taraji P. Henson, and Naomie Harris have each received a nomination, and Jennifer Hudson, Mo'Nique, Octavia Spencer (nominated twice), Lupita Nyong'o, and Viola Davis (nominated twice) have each won an Oscar in the category.

2. The lack of diversity in Oscar nominations has long been a point of contention but was highlighted in the nominations for 2015 and 2016, consecutive years in which no black actors were nominated. The controversy led to boycotts of the ceremony and promises of change from the Academy, currently led by its only African American board officer, Cheryl Boone Isaacs.

3. In showing a black woman climbing Mount Everest—instead of the dare-

devil exploits of a white male hero or, less frequently, a white female hero—*AVP* breaks new ground in Lex's opening scene and shows audiences something unexpected.

4. The fact that the container for the guns is a sarcophagus seems significant from a feminist perspective—the guns are symbolic phalli within a symbol of death. One could certainly undertake a Freudian analysis of this tableau.

5. The debate recently resurfaced around the fact that the World Fantasy Awards presents trophies in the form of a Lovecraft bust. Nnedi Okorafor, who made history in 2011 as the first black person to win the Best Novel prize (for *Who Fears Death*), subsequently wrote a blog post on the contradictions of the statuette. Protests that originated with Donald Wandrei in 1984 and culminated in a petition started by Daniel José Older in 2014 resulted in the Lovecraft statuette being "retired" in 2015.

Chapter 3

1. Framestore, "Children of Men," https://www.framestore.com/childrenof men.

2. *Village of the Damned* (1960), *Rosemary's Baby* (1968), *Enemy Mine* (1985), *The Fly* (1986), *Star Trek: The Next Generation* (1987–1994), *The X-Files* (1993–2002), *The Invader* (1997), *The Astronaut's Wife* (1999), and the *Alien* and *Terminator* franchises are just a few examples of twentieth-century SF films with memorable pregnancy and/or birth scenes. New millennial films and television have also produced a range of pregnant characters and depictions of childbirth in the genre, including the following: *Kill Bill: Volumes 1* and *2* (2003 and 2004), *Battlestar Galactica* (2003–2009), *Star Wars Episode III: Revenge of the Sith* (2005), *The Curious Case of Benjamin Button* (2008), *The Walking Dead* (2010–), *The Twilight Saga: Breaking Dawn—Part 1* (2011), *Game of Thrones* (2011–), *Midnight's Children* (2012), *Mad Max: Fury Road* (2015), and *Sense8* (2015–).

3. For *Mandela: Long Walk to Freedom* (2013), Harris had to master a Xhosa accent, and her performances in *Miami Vice* (2006) and *Moonlight* (2016) called for an American accent.

4. In light of recent events such as Brexit and the proposed US travel bans on specific Muslim countries, *Children of Men* is pertinent, if not prophetic.

5. The names of all the cities featured on the screen are as follows: Paris, Moscow, Washington, Kuala Lumpur, Tokyo, Brussels, Hong Kong, Berlin, Jakarta, New York, Stockholm, Rome, Shanghai, Caracas, Copenhagen, Mexico City, Amsterdam, Atlanta, Geneva, Marseilles, Lisbon, Seoul, Singapore, San Diego, Naples, Boston, and Antwerp.

6. Janice, a former photojournalist, was tortured by the British government, a detail that is conveyed through the collage of newspaper clippings and photographs that cover one wall of their home.

7. Amago discusses this mantra particularly in relation to T. S. Eliot's *The Waste Land*: "While Eliot and Cuarón envision a blighted urban space peopled by unknowing drones, both *The Waste Land* and *Children of Men* not only conclude at

the water's edge but also with the repetition of the ancient Sanskrit words 'Shantih, Shantih, Shantih,' which come from a formal ending to the Upanishads, defined by Eliot as 'The Peace which passeth understanding'" (219).

8. This scene is another moment that can be read alongside Morrison's *Beloved*, which also features a pregnant black woman whose body is objectified by white men in a barn.

Chapter 4

1. *Doctor Who Magazine* ranked this particular episode the worst of the new series in both a 2009 and a 2014 poll. Without making overly grand deductions from this detail, it is telling that the least popular episode of the rebooted series is the one with a young black girl as its focal character.

2. The film was adapted from the 2014 M. R. Carey novel of the same name. But in the novel, Melanie is a white child, and her beloved teacher and the main adult female character, Helen Justineau, is an attractive, dark-skinned black woman. The film generated some controversy by reframing the respective female leads as a black child and a white teacher, a change that may have stemmed from nontraditional or "color-blind" casting.

3. I disagree with hooks's take on the film, but my purpose in this chapter is not to provide a point-by-point rebuttal to her review. A number of critics have already done that, including the blogger Travis Bean, who posted "A Response to bell hooks's Critique of *Beasts of the Southern Wild*" on *Cinema Beans*, and Patricia Yaeger, who argues in "*Beasts of the Southern Wild* and Dirty Ecology" that hooks is "off the mark."

4. The clothesline functions as a symbolic umbilical cord between Wink and Hushpuppy and connotes food in the sense that Wink pulls on the clothesline, which is attached to a bell, to signal "feed-up time."

5. Most of the music for the film was composed by the director, Zeitlin, and Dan Romer.

6. Wink's performance of "fighting" the storm, which is intended to reassure Hushpuppy, is not so different from when the soldiers in *28 Days Later* display their firepower in front of Selena or when the mercenaries in *AVP* proudly model their guns for Lex.

7. A number of things about *Beasts of the Southern Wild*, including its portrayal of a black female protagonist caught in a climactic storm, make it a compelling comparative text for Zora Neale Hurston's *Their Eyes Were Watching God* (1937). Zeitlin's imagery of the Bathtub evokes Hurston's portrayal of life in "the muck." And Hushpuppy's first-person voice-over narrations and the film's use of folklore also resonate with Hurston's novel, which was adapted to the screen in 2005 with Halle Berry starring as Janie Crawford.

8. In *Children of Men*, the Ark of the Arts symbolizes a final and futile refuge for white, Western, and patriarchal "civilization." By contrast, the Ark in *Beasts of the Southern Wild* is a matriarchal refuge for disenfranchised Others who already exist outside so-called modernity.

9. Zeitlin was resistant to computer-generated imagery (CGI) and wanted to make the aurochs look as real as possible. The film uses five Vietnamese potbellied pigs in costume to play the small herd of aurochs.

10. Although Hathaway is not credited as "Mama," the DVD special feature "The Making of *Beasts of the Southern Wild*" includes behind-the-scenes footage of Hathaway shooting the alligator scene.

Chapter 5

1. One can compare the bar fight in *Firefly* to the bar fight in J. J. Abrams's *Star Trek* (2009). The latter also features witty dialogue between a black female character, Uhura (Zoe Saldana), and a white male hero, James Kirk (Chris Pine), followed by a brawl. But where Zoë is a participant in the action, Uhura is immediately reduced to a spectator and sexual object for Kirk, who even gropes her breasts during the fight.

2. In addition, their agency and independence are frequently undercut by their naïveté and infantilization.

3. One of the most compelling SF westerns on television is the HBO series *Westworld* (2016–), which features the nuanced and primary black female character Maeve Millay (Thandie Newton).

4. The marriage of Zoë and Wash is an important story line in *Firefly*, albeit one that Whedon had to fight for when Fox executives tellingly suggested that the marriage "be stricken from the show entirely, and the angst of early romance slotted into its place instead" (West 99). As a black woman married to a white man, Zoë also collapses and complicates those boundaries that *Star Trek* could only test thirty-four years earlier in the 1968 kiss between Uhura and Kirk.

5. The Doctor's companion in *Doctor Who: Series 10*, which premiered in April 2017, is a black woman named Bill Potts (Pearl Mackie).

6. Her actions mirror those of Selena in *28 Days Later*, who revives Jim with an adrenaline shot and CPR.

7. In this episode, Martha's mother Francis (Adjoa Andoh) and sister Tish (Gugu Mbatha-Raw) are forced to be maids, complete with uniforms, on the Master's airship, thus reenacting Martha's maid status in "Human Nature" and "Family of Blood." Mbatha-Raw has since become something of a breakout star after acting opposite Will Smith in *Concussion* (2016) and featuring in "San Junipero," one of the most highly acclaimed episodes of the series *Black Mirror* (2011–).

Works Cited

Alibar, Lucy. *Juicy and Delicious*. New York: Diversion Books, 2012.

Alibar, Lucy, and Benh Zeitlin. *Beasts of the Southern Wild*. Screenplay. 5 July 2012, www.alexcassun.files.wordpress.com/2012/12/botsw_final_draft_2.pdf.

Amago, Samuel. "Ethics, Aesthetics, and the Future in Alfonso Cuarón's *Children of Men*." *Discourse: Journal for Theoretical Studies in Media and Culture*, vol. 32, no. 2, 2010, pp. 212–235.

Anderson, Paul W. S. *AVP: Alien vs. Predator*. Shooting Script, www.dailyscript.com/scripts/AVP-FinalProduction.RTF.

———. "The Making of *Alien vs. Predator*." Audio Commentary. DVD Bonus Feature. *AVP: Alien vs. Predator*, directed by Paul W. S. Anderson, 20th Century Fox, 2004.

Atwood, Margaret. *In Other Worlds: SF and the Human Imagination*. New York: Random House, 2011.

Bacon, Terryl, and Govinda Dickman. "'Who's the Daddy?' The Aesthetics and Politics of Representation in Alfonso Cuarón's Adaptation of P. D. James's *Children of Men*." *Adaptation in Contemporary Culture: Textual Infidelities*, edited by Rachel Carroll, London: Continuum, 2009, pp. 147–159.

Barr, Marleen, editor. *Afro-Future Females: Black Writers Chart Science Fiction's Newest New-Wave Trajectory*. Columbus: Ohio State University Press, 2008.

Barzilai, Shuli. *Lacan and the Matter of Origins*. Stanford, CA: Stanford University Press, 1999.

Baxter, Charles. "The Hideous Unknown of H. P. Lovecraft." Review of *The New Annotated H. P. Lovecraft*, edited by Leslie S. Klinger, *New York Review of Books*, 18 Dec. 2014, www.nybooks.com/articles/2014/12/18/hideous-unknown-hp-lovecraft/.

Bean, Travis. "A Response to bell hooks's Critique of *Beasts of the Southern Wild*." *Cinema Beans*, 17 Sept. 2012, www.cinemabeans.blogspot.com/2012/09/beasts-of-the-southern-wild.html.

Bellin, Joshua David. *Framing Monsters: Fantasy Film and Social Alienation*. Carbondale: Southern Illinois University Press, 2005.

Bobo, Jacqueline. *Black Women as Cultural Readers*. New York: Columbia University Press, 1995.

Bogle, Donald. *Brown Sugar: Over One Hundred Years of America's Black Female Su-perstars.* London: Continuum, 2007.

———. *Prime Time Blues: African Americans on Network Television.* New York: Far-rar, Straus and Giroux, 2001.

———. *Toms, Coons, Mulattoes, Mammies, and Bucks: An Interpretive History of Blacks in American Films.* London: Continuum, 2001.

Booker, M. Keith. "The Politics of *Star Trek.*" *The Essential Science Fiction Television Reader,* edited by J. P. Telotte, Lexington: University Press of Kentucky, 2008, pp. 195–208.

Bourne, Stephen. *Black in the British Frame: The Black Experience in British Film and Television.* London: Continuum, 2001.

Boyle, Danny, and Alex Garland. "Alternate Theatrical Ending." Audio Commen-tary. DVD Bonus Feature. *28 Days Later,* directed by Danny Boyle, 20th Cen-tury Fox, 2002.

———. "The Diseased World." Interview. *Filmmaker,* Summer 2003, www.film makermagazine.com/archives/issues/summer2003/features/diseased_world .php#.V6j7yoVBBu4.

Britton, Piers. *TARDISbound: Navigating the Universes of Doctor Who.* London: I. B. Tauris, 2011.

Brooks, Kinitra. "The Importance of Neglected Intersections: Race and Gender in Contemporary Zombie Texts and Theories." *African American Review,* vol. 47, no. 4, 2014, pp. 461–475.

Brown, Jeffrey. *Dangerous Curves: Action Heroines, Gender, Fetishism, and Popular Culture.* Jackson: University Press of Mississippi, 2011.

Butman, Jeremy. "'Beasts of the Southern Wild' Direction: Louisiana Is a Danger-ous Utopia." *The Atlantic,* 27 June 2012, www.theatlantic.com/entertainment /archive/2012/06/beasts-of-the-southern-wild-director-louisiana-is-a-dan gerous-utopia/259009/.

Carrington, André. *Speculative Blackness: The Future of Race in Science Fiction.* Min-neapolis: University of Minnesota Press, 2016.

Chaudhary, Zahid. "Humanity Adrift: Race, Materiality, and Allegory in Alfonso Cuarón's *Children of Men.*" *Camera Obscura: A Journal of Feminism, Culture, and Media Studies,* vol. 24, no. 72, 2009, pp. 73–109.

Citizen, Robyn. "Are Black Women the Future of Man? The Role of Black Women in Political and Cultural Transformation in Science Fiction from the US, UK, and Cameroon." *The Liverpool Companion to World Science Fiction Film,* ed-ited by Sonja Fritzsche, Liverpool: Liverpool University Press, 2014, pp. 191–207.

Clover, Carol. "Her Body, Himself: Gender in the Slasher Film." *The Dread of Differ-ence: Gender and the Horror Film,* edited by Barry Keith Grant, 2nd ed., Austin: University of Texas Press, 2015, pp. 68–115.

———. *Men, Women, and Chain Saws: Gender in the Modern Horror Film.* Princeton, NJ: Princeton University Press, 1992.

Coleman, Robin R. Means. *Horror Noire: Blacks in American Horror Films from the 1890s to Present.* New York: Routledge, 2011.

Cornea, Christine. *Science Fiction Cinema: Between Fantasy and Reality.* New Bruns-wick, NJ: Rutgers University Press, 2007.

Creed, Barbara. "Horror and the Monstrous-Feminine: An Imaginary Abjection." *The Dread of Difference: Gender and the Horror Film*, edited by Barry Keith Grant, 2nd ed., Austin: University of Texas Press, 2015, pp. 37–67.

———. *The Monstrous-Feminine: Film, Feminism, Psychoanalysis*. London: Routledge, 1993.

Cuarón, Alfonso. "Interview: *Children of Men* Director Alfonso Cuarón." *Cinematical*, 25 Dec. 2006, www.moviefone.com/2006/12/25/interview-children-ofmen -director-alfonso-cuaron/.

———. "Theo and Julian." Audio Commentary. DVD Bonus Feature. *Children of Men*, directed by Alfonso Cuarón, Universal, 2007.

DasGupta, Sayantani. "(Re)Conceiving the Surrogate: Maternity, Race, and Reproductive Technologies in Alfonso Cuarón's *Children of Men*." *Gender Scripts in Medicine and Narrative*, edited by Marcelline Block and Angela Laflen, Newcastle, UK: Cambridge Scholars Publishing, 2010, pp. 178–211.

De Lauretis, Teresa. *The Practice of Love: Lesbian Sexuality and Perverse Desire*. Bloomington: Indiana University Press, 1994.

Diawara, Manthia, editor. *Black American Cinema*. New York: Routledge, 1993.

Doane, Mary Ann. *The Desire to Desire: The Woman's Film of the 1940s*. Bloomington: Indiana University Press, 1987.

———. *Femmes Fatales: Feminism, Film Theory, Psychoanalysis*. New York: Routledge, 1991.

Dockterman, Eliana. "Exclusive: Marvel's New Iron Man Is a Black Woman." *Time*, 6 July 2016, www.time.com/4394478/iron-man-riri-williams-tony-stark/.

Doherty, Thomas. "Genre, Gender, and the *Aliens* Trilogy." *The Dread of Difference: Gender and the Horror Film*, edited by Barry Keith Grant, 2nd ed., Austin: University of Texas Press, 2015, pp. 209–227.

Douglas, Mary. *Purity and Danger: An Analysis of the Concepts of Pollution and Taboo*. London: Routledge, 1966.

Dreher, Kwakiutl. *Dancing on the White Page: Black Women Entertainers Writing Autobiography*. Albany: State University of New York Press, 2008.

Dunn, Stephane. *"Baad Bitches" and Sassy Supermamas: Black Power Action Films*. Urbana: University of Illinois Press, 2008.

Dyer, Richard. *White*. London: Routledge, 1997.

Ebert, Roger. "Quvenzhané: A Small Force of Nature." *Roger Ebert's Journal*, 22 June 2012, www.rogerebert.com/rogers-journal/quvenzhan%C3%A9-a -small-force-of-nature.

Fanon, Frantz. *The Wretched of the Earth*, translated by Richard Philcox, New York: Grove, 2004.

Gallardo-C, Ximena, and Jason Smith. *Alien Woman: The Making of Lt. Ellen Ripley*. New York: Continuum, 2004.

Gilman, Sander L. "Black Bodies, White Bodies: Toward an Iconography of Female Sexuality in Late Nineteenth-Century Art, Medicine, and Literature." *Critical Inquiry*, vol. 12, Autumn 1985, pp. 204–242.

Goodrum, Michael, and Philip Smith. "Introduction." *Firefly Revisited: Essays on Joss Whedon's Classic Series*, edited by Michael Goodrum and Philip Smith, Lanham, MD: Rowman and Littlefield, 2015, pp. ix–xxiii.

Grant, Barry Keith. "Introduction." *The Dread of Difference: Gender and the Horror*

Film, edited by Barry Keith Grant, 2nd ed., Austin: University of Texas Press, 2015, pp. 1–13.

———. "Taking Back the *Night of the Living Dead*: George Romero, Feminism, and the Horror Film." *The Dread of Difference: Gender and the Horror Film*, edited by Barry Keith Grant, 2nd ed., Austin: University of Texas Press, 2015, pp. 228–240.

Gray, Herman. *Cultural Moves: African Americans and the Politics of Representation*. Berkeley: University of California Press, 2005.

———. *Watching Race: Television and the Struggle for Blackness*. Minneapolis: University of Minnesota Press, 1995.

Grimshaw, Patricia, and Peter Sherlock. "Women and Cultural Exchanges." *Missions and Empire*, edited by Norman Etherington, Oxford: Oxford University Press, 2005, pp. 173–193.

Guerrero, Ed. *Framing Blackness: The African American Image in Film*. Philadelphia: Temple University Press, 1993.

Gupta, Amit. "*Doctor Who* and Race: Reflections on the Change of Britain's Status in the International System." *The Round Table*, vol. 102, no. 1, 2013, pp. 41–50.

Hall, Stuart. *Race, the Floating Signifier*, produced by Sut Jhally, Northampton, MA: Media Education Foundation, 1997.

Handler, Rachel. "Love and Hollywood: Sanaa Lathan Prepares for Her Comeback in 'The Perfect Guy.'" Interview. *Grantland*, 11 Sept. 2015, www.grantland.com /hollywood-prospectus/love-and-hollywood-sanaa-lathan-prepares-for-her -comeback-in-the-perfect-guy/.

Havens, Timothy. *Black Television Travels: African American Media around the Globe*. New York: New York University Press, 2013.

Hegel, George. *Lectures on the Philosophy of History*, translated by J. Sibree, London: George Bell and Sons, 1894.

Hochscherf, Tobias, and James Leggott, editors. *British Science Fiction Film and Television: Critical Essays*. Jefferson, NC: McFarland, 2011.

hooks, bell. *Black Looks: Race and Representation*. Boston: South End, 1992.

———. *Killing Rage: Ending Racism*. New York: Henry Holt, 1995.

———. "No Love in the Wild." Review of *Beasts of the Southern Wild*, directed by Benh Zeitlin, *New Black Man (in Exile)*, 5 Sept. 2012, www.newblackmaninexile .net/2012/09/bell-hooks-no-love-in-wild.html.

———. *Talking Back: Thinking Feminist, Thinking Black*. New York: Routledge, 2015.

Hunt, Darnell. *Channeling Blackness: Studies on Television and Race in America*. Oxford: Oxford University Press, 2005.

Hunter, Sandy. "*28 Days Later*: An Interview with Danny Boyle." *Danny Boyle Interviews*, edited by Brent Dunham, Jackson: University Press of Mississippi, 2011, pp. 78–82.

Hurston, Zora Neale. *Their Eyes Were Watching God*. Philadelphia: J. B. Lippincott, 1937.

Jackson, Sandra. "Terrans, Extraterrestrials, Warriors and the Last (Wo)Man Standing." *African Identities*, vol. 7, no. 2, May 2009, pp. 237–253.

Jackson, Sandra, and Julie Moody-Freeman, editors. *The Black Imagination: Science Fiction, Futurism and the Speculative*. New York: Peter Lang, 2011.

James, P. D. *The Children of Men*. London: Faber and Faber, 1992.

Jenkins, Henry. *Textual Poachers: Television Fans and Participatory Culture*. New York: Routledge, 2013.

Joyrich, Lynne. "All That Television Allows: TV Melodrama, Postmodernism and Consumer Culture." *Camera Obscura: A Journal of Feminism, Culture, and Media Studies*, vol. 6, no. 1, Jan. 1988, pp. 128–153.

——. "Feminist Enterprise? 'Star Trek: The Next Generation' and the Occupation of Femininity." *Cinema Journal*, vol. 35, no. 2, Winter 1996, pp. 61–84.

Kaplan, E. Ann. *Looking for the Other: Feminism, Film, and the Imperial Gaze*. New York: Routledge, 1997.

——. *Women and Film: Both Sides of the Camera*. London: Routledge, 1991.

Kilgore, De Witt Douglas. *Astrofuturism: Science, Race, and Visions of Utopia in Space*. Philadelphia: University of Pennsylvania Press, 2003.

Kuhn, Annette. "Introduction." *Alien Zones II: The Spaces of Science Fiction Cinema*, edited by Annette Kuhn, London: Verso, 1999, pp. 1–8.

Lacan, Jacques. "Family Complexes in the Formation of the Individual," translated and abridged by Carolyn Asp, *Critical Text*, vol. 5, 1988, pp. 12–29.

Lavender, Isiah, III. *Race in American Science Fiction*. Bloomington: Indiana University Press, 2011.

MacDonald, J. Fred. *Blacks and White TV: African Americans in Television since 1948*. Chicago: Nelson-Hall, 1992.

Mama, Amina. "Sheroes and Villains: Conceptualizing Colonial and Contemporary Violence against Women in Africa." *Feminist Genealogies, Colonial Legacies, Democratic Futures*, edited by M. Jacqui Alexander and Chandra Talpade Mohanty, New York: Routledge, 2012, pp. 46–62.

Manatu, Norma. *African American Women and Sexuality in the Cinema*. Jefferson, NC: McFarland, 2003.

Mandel, Geoffrey. *U.S.S. Enterprise Officer's Manual*. New York: Interstellar Associates, 1980.

Martin, Michel. "Star Trek's Uhura Reflects on MLK Encounter." Interview with Nichelle Nichols. *Tell Me More*, NPR, 17 Jan. 2011.

Mask, Mia. *Divas on Screen: Black Women in American Film*. Urbana: University of Illinois Press, 2009.

McClintock, Anne. *Imperial Leather: Race, Gender and Sexuality in the Colonial Contest*. New York: Routledge, 1995.

Meyers, Seth. "Interview with Leslie Jones." *Late Night with Seth Meyers*, NBC, 22 July 2016.

Minh-ha, Trinh T. *When the Moon Waxes Red: Representation, Gender and Cultural Politics*. London: Routledge, 1991.

Modleski, Tania. *Feminism without Women: Culture and Criticism in a "Postfeminist" Age*. New York: Routledge, 1991.

Morales, Wilson. "An Interview with Clare-Hope Ashitey." *Black Film*, 26 Dec. 2006, www.blackfilm.com/20061222/features/clarehopeashitey.shtml.

Morgan, Jennifer. "'Some Could Suckle over Their Shoulder': Male Travelers, Female Bodies, and the Gendering of Racial Ideology, 1500–1770." *William and Mary Quarterly*, vol. 54, no. 1, Jan. 1997, pp. 167–192.

Morrison, Toni. *Beloved*. New York: Vintage Books, 1987.

Mudimbe, V. Y. *The Idea of Africa*. Bloomington: Indiana University Press, 1994.

Mulvey, Laura. "Afterthoughts on 'Visual Pleasure and Narrative Cinema' Inspired by *Duel in the Sun*." *Feminism and Film Theory*, edited by Constance Penley, New York: Routledge; London: BFI, 1988, pp. 69–79.

———. "Visual Pleasure and Narrative Cinema." *Feminism and Film Theory*, edited by Constance Penley, New York: Routledge; London, BFI, 1988, pp. 57–68.

Nama, Adilifu. *Black Space: Imagining Race in Science Fiction Film*. Austin: University of Texas Press, 2008.

Ndounou, Monica White. *Shaping the Future of African American Film: Color-Coded Economics and the Story behind the Numbers*. New Brunswick, NJ: Rutgers University Press, 2014.

Neale, Steve. "Masculinity as Spectacle: Reflections on Men and Mainstream Cinema." *Screening the Male: Exploring Masculinities in Hollywood Cinema*, edited by Steve Cohan and Ina Rae Hark, London: Routledge, 1993, pp. 9–20.

Nichols, Nichelle. *Beyond Uhura: Star Trek and Other Memories*. New York: G. P. Putnam's, 1994.

Norton, Al. "Another Gina Torres Interview!" *Live Journal*, 18 Aug. 2012, www.ohnotheydidnt.livejournal.com/71254442.html.

O'Connell, Dee. "Naomie That Girl . . ." *The Guardian*, 20 Oct. 2002, www.theguardian.com/film/2002/oct/20/features.magazine.

Orthia, Lindy. "'Sociopathetic Abscess' or 'Yawning Chasm'? The Absent Postcolonial Transition in *Doctor Who*." *Journal of Commonwealth Literature*, vol. 45, no. 2, 2010, pp. 207–225.

Pascale, Amy. *Joss Whedon: The Biography*. Chicago: Chicago Review Press, 2014.

Petro, Patrice. "Mass Culture and the Feminine: The 'Place' of Television in Film Studies." *Cinema Journal*, vol. 25, no. 3, Spring 1986, pp. 5–21.

Regester, Charlene. *African American Actresses: The Struggle for Visibility, 1900–1960*. Bloomington: Indiana University Press, 2010.

Richardson, Ben. "Behind the Cinematography of *Beasts of the Southern Wild*." *The Creators Project*, 2 Jan. 2013, www.beastsofthesouthernwild.com/news/behind-the-cinematography-of-beasts-of-the-southern-wild.

Roberts, Adam. *Science Fiction*. 2nd ed. London: Routledge, 2006.

Rony, Fatimah Tobing. *The Third Eye: Race, Cinema, and Ethnographic Spectacle*. Durham, NC: Duke University Press, 1996.

Said, Edward. *Orientalism*. New York: Random House, 1978.

Salem, Rob. "Who's That Girl? The Doctor Does Not Tend to Travel Alone." Interview with Freema Agyeman. *Toronto Star*, 7 July 2007, www.thestar.com/news/2007/07/07/whos_that_girl.html.

Sharrett, Christopher. "The Horror Film in Neoconservative Culture." *The Dread of Difference: Gender and the Horror Film*, edited by Barry Keith Grant, 2nd ed., Austin: University of Texas Press, 2015, pp. 281–304.

Shelley, Mary. *Frankenstein; or, The Modern Prometheus*. London: Lackington, Hughes, Harding, Mavor & Jones, 1818.

Siegel, Deborah. *Sisterhood, Interrupted: From Radical Women to Grrls Gone Wild*. New York: Palgrave Macmillan, 2007.

Silverman, Kaja. *The Acoustic Mirror: The Female Voice in Psychoanalysis and Cinema*. Bloomington: Indiana University Press, 1988.

Sims, Yvonne. *Women of Blaxploitation: How the Black Action Film Heroine Changed American Popular Culture*. Jefferson, NC: McFarland, 2006.

Smith-Shomade, Beretta. *Shaded Lives: African-American Women and Television*. New Brunswick, NJ: Rutgers University Press, 2002.

———, editor. *Watching While Black: Centering the Television of Black Audiences*. New Brunswick, NJ: Rutgers University Press, 2012.

Snead, James. *White Screens/Black Images: Hollywood from the Dark Side*, edited by Colin MacCabe and Cornel West. London: Routledge, 1994.

Spillers, Hortense. "Mama's Baby, Papa's Maybe: An American Grammar Book." *Diacritics*, vol. 17, no. 2, Summer 1987, pp. 64–81.

Spurr, David. *The Rhetoric of Empire: Colonial Discourse in Journalism, Travel Writing, and Imperial Administration*. Durham, NC: Duke University Press, 1993.

Stevenson, Robert Louis. *Strange Case of Dr. Jekyll and Mr. Hyde*. London: Longmans, Green & Co., 1886.

Tasker, Yvonne. *Working Girls: Gender and Sexuality in Popular Cinema*. London: Routledge, 1998.

Taubin, Amy. "The 'Alien' Trilogy: From Feminism to AIDS." *Women and Film: A Sight and Sound Reader*, edited by Pam Cook and Philip Dodd, Philadelphia: Temple University Press, 1993, pp. 93–100.

Thomas, Dexter. "Why Everyone's Saying 'Black Girls Are Magic.'" *Los Angeles Times*, 9 Sept. 2015, www.latimes.com/nation/nationnow/la-na-nn-everyones-saying-black-girls-are-magic-20150909-htmlstory.html.

Trimble, Sarah. "Maternal Back/Grounds in *Children of Men*: Notes Toward an Arendtian Biopolitics." *Science Fiction Film and Television*, vol. 4, no. 2, 2011, pp. 249–270.

Tyson, Neil Degrasse. "A Conversation with Nichelle Nichols." *Star Talk Radio*, 11 July 2011.

Wagner, Annie. "Politics, Bible Stories, and Hope." Interview with Alfonso Cuarón. *The Stranger*, 28 Dec. 2006, www.thestranger.com/seattle/politics-bible-stories-and-hope/Content?oid=128363.

Walker, Alice. "In Search of Our Mothers' Gardens: The Creativity of Black Women in the South (1974)." *Ms.*, Spring 2002, www.msmagazine.com/spring2002/walker.asp.

Wallace, Michele. "Race, Gender and Psychoanalysis in Forties Film: Lost Boundaries, Home of the Brave and The Quiet One." *Black American Cinema*, edited by Manthia Diawara, New York: Routledge, 1993, pp. 257–271.

West, Michelle Sagara. "More Than a Marriage of Convenience." *Finding Serenity: Anti-Heroes, Lost Shepherds, and Space Hookers in Joss Whedon's Firefly*, edited by Jane Espenson, Dallas: BenBella Books, 2004, pp. 97–104.

Westfahl, Gary. "Space Opera." *The Cambridge Companion to Science Fiction*, edited by Edward James and Farah Mendlesohn, Cambridge: Cambridge University Press, 2003, pp. 197–208.

Williams, G. Christopher. "Birthing an Undead Family: Reification of the Mother's Role in the Gothic Landscape of *28 Days Later*." *Gothic Studies*, vol. 9, no. 2, 2007, pp. 33–44.

Williams, Linda. "'Something Else Besides a Mother': 'Stella Dallas' and the Maternal Melodrama." *Cinema Journal*, vol. 24, no. 1, Autumn 1984, pp. 2–27.

————. "When the Woman Looks." *The Dread of Difference: Gender and the Horror Film*, edited by Barry Keith Grant, 2nd ed., Austin: University of Texas Press, 2015, pp. 17–36.

Willoughby, Vanessa. "Geeking Out: Four Writers on Nerding while Black—The Fan." *Bitch*, Winter 2016, pp. 20–21.

Wise, Louis. "Noma Dumezweni Has Her Magic Moment." *Sunday Times*, 19 June 2016, www.thetimes.co.uk/article/noma-dumezweni-has-her-magic-moment -zrqg9nooh.

Womack, Ytasha. *Afrofuturism: The World of Black Sci-Fi and Fantasy Culture*. Chicago: Lawrence Hill Books, 2013.

Wood, Robin. *Hollywood from Vietnam to Reagan . . . and Beyond*. New York: Columbia University Press, 2003.

Yaeger, Patricia. "*Beasts of the Southern Wild* and Dirty Ecology." Review of *Beasts of the Southern Wild*, directed by Benh Zeitlin, *Southern Spaces*, 13 Feb. 2013, www.southernspaces.org/2013/beasts-southern-wild-and-dirty-ecology.

Žižek, Slavoj. "The Possibility of Hope." Audio Commentary. DVD Bonus Feature. *Children of Men*, directed by Alfonso Cuarón, Universal, 2007.

Index

Film stills are denoted by the letter f following the page number; for actresses and actors discussed in this work, the first named film is the most central.

science fiction (SF). *See* speculative fiction

Scott, Ridley, 46, 140

Selena (character), 4, 14, 15, 21–25, 27–32, 28f, 29f, 33, 36f, 38f, 43f, 34–44, 45, 58–59, 62, 65, 68, 70, 71, 87, 93, 94, 99, 146, 151n15, 151n17, 152nn4, 153n12, 153n14, 155n6, 156n6

Sense8, 4, 133, 149n4, 154n2

Serenity (2005 film), 126, 132

sexuality, female, 14, 66, 146; as deviant, 37, 48, 61, 68, 152n10; repression of, 20, 46, 130. *See also* black female characters

Shatner, William, 2, 122

Shawl, Nisi, 11

Shelley, Mary, 7, 124

Sidibe, Gabourey, 153n1

Silverman, Kaja, 102–103

Simon, Josette, 122

Skeleton Key, The, 152n7

Skyfall, 25

slavery, 113, 152n10

Sleepy Hollow, 4, 141, 149n4

Sliders, 122

Smith, Jada Pinkett, 149n3

Smith, Kellita, 149n4

Smith, Will, 67, 149–150n6, 156n7

Smith, Zadie, 25

Snipes, Wesley, 67

Something New, 49

Space: Above and Beyond, 122

space opera, 17, 124, 151n18

Spectre, 25

speculative fiction, 2, 16, 49, 66, 97, 108, 114, 124, 126, 140; black femininity in, 7–9, 11–13, 17, 24, 44, 69–71, 93–94, 105, 120, 141, 146, 150n8, 151n17; definition of, 3; 4, 5, 149n2; and psychoanalysis, 10

Spencer, Octavia, 153n1

Spillers, Hortense, 97, 116

Stagecoach, 124

Stark Love, 100

Star Trek (1966–1969 series), 1, 2, 2f, 3, 6, 17–18, 120, 122, 123, 125, 130, 141, 142, 145, 149n1, 156n4

Star Trek (2009 film), 4, 5, 17, 140, 142–145, 143f, 156n1

Star Trek Beyond, 4, 5, 17, 140, 145

Star Trek: Discovery, 140

Star Trek: First Contact, 3

Star Trek into Darkness, 4, 5, 17, 140, 145

Star Trek: The Next Generation, 3, 93, 120, 122, 123, 154n2

Star Wars franchise, 124, 140, 145, 154n2

Stenberg, Amandla, 94

Stevenson, Robert Louis, 124

Staite, Jewel, 129

Strange Days, 3, 13, 24, 67, 70

Streep, Meryl, 50

Sugar Hill, 152n7

Super 8mm film, 31

Supernova, 24, 70

Super 16mm film, 94

Super 35mm film, 73, 94

TARDIS (Time And Relative Dimension In Space), 132, 133, 139

Tasker, Yvonne, 127, 130

Tate, Catherine, 136

Tavener, John, 84

Tennant, David, 17, 124, 135f

Terminator franchise, The, 13, 66, 154n2

Terrible Place, 22, 27, 32, 39, 40

Texas Chainsaw Massacre, The, 47

"third eye" perception, 96–97, 103, 118. *See also* returned gaze

Thomas, Gay, 122

Thompson, CaShawn, 146

Thurman, Uma, 66

Time Runner, 24

To Have and Have Not, 143

Tommy, 24

Torchwood, 133

Torres, Gina: in *Firefly*, 4, 16, 123, 126, 128f, 129, 146, 149–150n6; other roles, 122, 126. *See also* Washburne, Zoë

tragic mulatto, 6

Trinh Minh-ha, 134, 136

Trip to the Moon, A, 7

Tudyk, Alan, 127